T0032013

ALSO BY NEELI CHERKOVSKI

POETRY

Don't Make a Move
The Waters Reborn
Public Notice
Love Proof
Juggler Within
Clear Wind
Animal
Elegy for Bob Kaufman
Leaning Against Time
Naming the Nameless
From the Canyon Outward
From the Middle Woods
Manila Poems
The Crow and I
Elegy for My Beat Generation
Hang On to the Yangtze River
ABCs

NONFICTION

Ferlinghetti: A Biography
Whitman's Wild Children
Hank: The Life of Charles Bukowski
Coolidge and Cherkovski in Conversation
Bukowski, A Life: The Centennial Edition

FERLINGHETTI: A LIFE

FERLINGHETTI
FERLINGHETTI
FERLINGHETTI
FERLINGHETTI
FERLINGHETTI
FERLINGHETTI
FERLINGHETTI
FERLINGHETTI
FERLINGHETTI
FERLINGHETTI

A LIFE: EXPANDED EDITION

NEELI CHERKOVSKI

BOSTON

BLACK SPARROW PRESS

2022

Published in 2022 by BLACK SPARROW PRESS

GODINE
Boston, Massachusetts
www.godine.com

Copyright © 1979 and 2022 by Neeli Cherkovski

ALL RIGHTS RESERVED
No part of this book may be used or reproduced in any manner whatsoever without written
permission from the publisher, except in the case of brief quotations embodied in critical
articles and reviews. For more information, please visit www.godine.com

Excerpts by Lawrence Ferlinghetti, from *A Coney Island of the Mind*, copyright ©1958
by Lawrence Ferlinghetti; from *Her*, copyright ©1960 by Lawrence Ferlinghetti; from
Open Eye, Open Heart, copyright ©1973 by Lawrence Ferlinghetti; from *These Are My
Rivers*, copyright ©1979 by Lawrence Ferlinghetti; from *Wild Dreams of a New Beginning*,
copyright ©1979 by Lawrence Ferlinghetti. All reprinted by permission of New Directions
Publishing Corporation.

"Thou Shalt Not Kill" By Kenneth Rexroth, from *Selected Poems*, copyright ©1956 by
Kenneth Rexroth. Reprinted by permission of New Directions Publishing Corp.

LIBRARY OF CONGRESS CATALOGING-IN-PUBLICATION DATA
Names: Cherkovski, Neeli, author.
Title: Ferlinghetti : a life / Neeli Cherkovski.
Description: Expanded edition. | Boston : Black Sparrow Press, 2022.
  Includes bibliographical references and index.
Identifiers: LCCN 2021052620 (print) | LCCN 2021052621 (ebook)
ISBN 9781574232592 (paperback) | ISBN 9781574232608 (ebook)
Subjects: LCSH: Ferlinghetti, Lawrence. | Authors, American--20th
  century--Biography. | Beats (Persons)--Biography.
Classification: LCC PS3511.E557 Z6 2022 (print) | LCC PS3511.E557 (ebook)
  DDC 811/.54 [B]--dc23/eng/20211105
LC record available at https://lccn.loc.gov/2021052620
LC ebook record available at https://lccn.loc.gov/2021052621

Frontispiece Cherkovski and Ferlinghetti at the Savoy Tivoli in San Francisco. Copyright ©
1978 by Ira Nowinski.
Cover Illustration Joe McKendry

First Printing, 2022
Printed in the United States of America

Dedicated to Sam and Clare Cherry

EDITOR'S NOTE

This book originally appeared in 1979 as *Ferlinghetti: A Biography*. It was the first biography of Lawrence Ferlinghetti ever written. The poet, publisher, bookseller, and activist was sixty years old at the time and worked closely with Neeli Cherkovski as he researched and wrote the book.

This expanded edition, *Ferlinghetti: A Life*, is the result of the now-septuagenarian Cherkovski working diligently through the summer and fall of 2021. It contains a new foreword, a new afterword, and an epilogue that endeavors to touch on, in broad strokes, some of the high points of Ferlinghetti's busy life between the original book's publication and his death forty-two years later, in 2021. The text of the original 1979 biography—tics, hiccups, opinions, warts, mistakes courtesy of LSD, and all, with the exception of the occasional addition of a comma and a few *which*es that become *thats*—has been retained to honor the historical artifact. Please file any complaints about the decision to take this approach with Mr. Walt Whitman in Heaven.

P.S. Books not bombs.

CONTENTS

FROM THE CITY OF ANGELS
TO THE CITY OF POETS

T WO TABS OF acid illustrated with underground comic artist R. Crumb's white-bearded imp Mr. Natural took me by the hand, plunked me down in front of an old Underwood typewriter with broken keys, and helped me to write my proposal for the first biography of Lawrence Ferlinghetti. In no time at all, I conjured up a ten-page document that made the case for my project and promised big sales. *Ferlinghetti: A Biography* was the title.

"Not bad," I assured myself. "It's as clear as can be."

I owed it to the acid.

THREE YEARS BEFORE that drug-inspired evening, I arrived in San Francisco from my native Los Angeles. It was 1974 and I was twenty-nine years old. I drove across the Bay Bridge entranced by the lights.

I was moving to the city to work on the mayoral campaign of George Moscone. A longtime state senator, Moscone was a native San Franciscan and had set his sights on City Hall. He was a clear favorite among the liberal-minded voters. The city, with its large Asian population and vigorous Latino community, had a strong labor tradition, especially along the busy docks. Back then, progressive politics of inclusivity like Moscone's were appealing to working-class people.

The City of Poets is how I thought of my new home-to-be. I believed San Francisco was the epicenter of contemporary literature. Frank Norris's disturbing 1899 novel, *McTeague*, brought the city to life, as did Djuna Barnes's 1937 cult classic, *Nightwood*. Kenneth Rexroth arrived in the 1930s, followed in droves by writers who came to make up the San Francisco Renaissance and the Beat Generation of the 1950s. The scene was far-reaching, evolving to encompass a wide range of styles and ideas, from esoteric gay poets such as Robert Duncan to Richard Brautigan, the naive king of counterculture hippie writers in the 1960s.

At the center of all these writers was City Lights Booksellers & Publishers. Opened in 1953 in the North Beach neighborhood at a nexus of the city's Asian and Italian communities, City Lights stood as a shrine to avant-garde and outsider writing traditions, to dissident political and social thinking.

Crossing the Bay Bridge, I triumphantly recited the opening lines of Allen Ginsberg's "Howl," a bardic shout inspired by Walt Whitman and famously first read in public by Ginsberg at the Six Gallery, in the city's Marina District, on October 7, 1955. Lawrence Ferlinghetti, the founder of City Lights Booksellers & Publishers, was in the audience. He wrote Ginsberg a telegram that night: "I greet you at the beginning of a great career. When do I get the manuscript?" Then he asked for more poems, enough to make a full collection. In 1956, *Howl and Other Poems* was published—complete with an introduction by William Carlos Williams—by City Lights as number four in its Pocket Poets Series.

Thinking about what came immediately after the book's publication, I almost bounced my car off the bridge's railing: The San Francisco Police Department arrested Ferlinghetti and Shigeyoshi Murao, the bookstore's manager, and charged them with disseminating obscene literature. City Lights—and modern poetry itself—was on trial! With the help of the American Civil Liberties Union, Ferlinghetti prevailed. "We were lucky," he said after the verdict. "I mean, it really put us on the map in a way that nothing else would have." I gripped the steering wheel and smiled at Ferlinghetti's puckish response. The lights of the City of Poets' downtown skyscrapers twinkled and set me right. I pulled off the bridge at the first exit.

It was 9:30 at night. I drove around with no sense of where I was going. The backseat and the trunk were filled with books and clothing, and as I went up and down the steep hills in Chinatown, everything slid around into disarray. I found myself in North Beach just in time to see the clerk locking up City Lights Booksellers. The Moscone campaign had advised me to get a rental before I arrived but in my excitement I had forgotten, and it suddenly occurred to me that I had to find a place to sleep.

I stopped at an all-night doughnut shop on the edge of North Beach, closer to the Financial District, and ordered glazed doughnuts and what turned out to be an absolutely horrific cup of coffee. Two young guys in paint-splattered clothes were sitting at the next table. We began talking. They were working as house painters and had an apartment just a few blocks away. I told them my predicament and they invited me to spend the night on their couch, which after two or three hours of conversation and a great many beers I gladly accepted.

I slept well and woke early. It was my first morning in San Francisco. I left a note of thanks on the kitchen table and went out to try and get my bearings in the city and stake my claim, such as it was. Sadly, I never saw those guys again. They were handsome, and I'd have been happy to snuggle in with either—or both—if I had been asked.

WHEN I FOUND the Moscone for Mayor campaign headquarters and reported for duty, they told me to take a week and get to know San Francisco. Now, that sounded good! I told myself that this was just the kind of job I needed: no supervision and lots of free time. I began exploring the city's neighborhoods and found a room to rent downtown in one of the most decrepit buildings I'd ever seen.

Back at campaign headquarters, I was given a desk and I sat there for a week or so doing basically nothing. I attended some strategy meetings, but I wasn't given any assignments. Again I thought: *This is the job for me!* Moscone came into town from Sacramento, where he was still serving as a state senator, and I found him entertaining.

Eventually, I was asked to drive around the city and drop off press releases to various media outlets. This did not make me happy, as I was not asked to write the press releases, which had been one of my jobs in previous political work. On top of that, I got two or three traffic tickets and the campaign expressed no interest in paying them.

The strategy meetings I attended left my head in a whirl. I began to realize that the campaign wasn't going to be the exciting adventure I hoped it might be. I simply wouldn't be able to focus enough to study the issues as much as I should in order to write press releases, much less any position papers—my inborn hyperactivity just wasn't going to allow me to grasp the important political details, whether or not I put my mind to it. I was a writer, sure, but it was my natural inclination to spontaneity that had led me to poetry. What could be simpler than an empty white page that you fill up with whatever words that appear in your mind?

At our meetings in the campaign office, I knew my coworkers could see my eyes wandering to the windows, just as they had when I was trapped in school. I would watch the trees, the branches swaying in the breeze or in a heavy wind, and I would count the birds as they came and went. This was good for a poet, but it was not going to help Moscone land in City Hall. I knew my days in politics were numbered. The bohemian life loomed. That would be okay, I decided. I'd write poetry and literary criticism and short stories, probably tackle a novel or two, and then write my memoir—all in a day's work. While I waited for the ax to fall, I sat at my desk and looked busy as I typed up a pile of poems.

One afternoon, the campaign manager—an old coot who had directed the presidential campaign of Lyndon Johnson, in the late 1960s—called me into his office. He sat me down and said I seemed more interested in my poetry than in Moscone's campaign. I had to confess: He had good instincts.

I left the office that day and never looked back. I secured good unemployment benefits that seemed to go on and on—they kept me supplied in all the comforts a bohemian poet could hope for. Moscone, of course, went on to win the mayorship without me.

FOR A TIME, I lived at the Italian-American Hotel, on Sansome and Broadway, a place filled with dockworkers and immigrants from Spain and Italy. There was a communal kitchen, as well as communal toilets and showers. I had a room that looked out onto a street that led down to what looked to me like canyons of the dead in the Financial District.

I became a regular at the Caffè Trieste, about two blocks from City Lights, and one by one I met the city's poets. The Greek poet Nanos Valaoritis, who taught at San Francisco State University and owned an island in Greece, approached me one day while I was sitting in the café.

"I know you," he said. "Neeli Cherry, Bukowski's secretary."

I got a kick out of that: it's just the sort of thing a European literary figure would say.

I got reacquainted with the poet Harold Norse, whom I had known in Los Angeles, but always with our mutual friend Charles Bukowski present. His book *Hotel Nirvana* had just been published by City Lights in the Pocket Poet Series and he was riding high. Norse and I became close friends after I told him I was just as gay as he was.

One day, Lawrence Ferlinghetti walked in and sat down with me and Norse. He teased me about being from Los Angeles, but I came to the defense of my beloved hometown. Then Ferlinghetti asked what it was like hanging out with Bukowski.

"It could be a blast," I said, "but not enough to keep me in L.A."

When I told Ferlinghetti I had recently left the Moscone campaign, he approved.

"Now you can be a leisure-class poet here on the beach," he said, referring to Jack Hirschman and other left-wing poet-activists.

He asked if I'd ever been to Paris.

"Sure, and I made it my business to look up Paul Verlaine," I said. Norse chuckled and Lawrence grinned.

"You should have gone down to Aden to find Rimbaud," he said.

A few days after meeting him, Ferlinghetti invited me to have dinner with him at the U.S. Restaurant, which served enormous plates of Italian working-class cuisine. The two cooks and the waitress, Marie, doted on Ferlinghetti, who was forever aware of his weight; that night, I gorged on lamb chops.

We began going to the movies together, including Chaplin's *City Lights* at the Times Theater, the ornate little neighborhood nickelodeon. Ferlinghetti invited me on some of his reading trips out of town, usually just the two of us driving somewhere in his 1960s Volkswagen van. Eventually, Ferlinghetti helped find me a three-room apartment in North Beach, just across from where he was living. The landlord was an old Italian wary of poets but happy to rent me the space for $135 a month. My apartment would quickly become the gathering spot for an ongoing neighborhood salon. Ferlinghetti often participated, along with Bob Kaufman, Gregory Corso, and Philip Lamantia.

On our drives or over dinners, Ferlinghetti and I often talked about the state of literature. He confessed that he wished he'd published Jack Kerouac, but said he felt back in the day that so much of the writing was derivative of Thomas Wolfe.

"I loved all those great American epiphanies," he said. "And wolves riding. They stuck with me through the years."

I asked him about William Burroughs. He said that in the late 1950s, Ginsberg had tried to interest him in Burroughs's novel, but he couldn't make sense of it and felt it was unfinished.

During the course of our many conversations, I began to see that Ferlinghetti was committed to clarity, not just in prose but in poetry as well. His thinking led to "The Populist Manifesto," a poem decrying what he considered to be the insular sensibility of contemporary poetry. He felt that many writers were being deliberately obscure, a stance Bukowski took as well. He didn't talk about it much, but Ferlinghetti had been influenced early in his life by the popular American poets Carl Sandburg and Edger Lee Masters. At the same time, he praised Philip Lamantia, a great latter-day surrealist.

"Philip can push the language in new directions, and yet still write a poem you can follow," he said to me. That was one of same the reasons Ferlinghetti always loved Corso's poetry.

One day he confided that being a publisher meant that he had to reject too many poets, which he disliked. But City Lights received many submissions from hopeful writers. "It's hard to imagine publishing *everybody*," he said with a sigh. "You'd have to be a billionaire just to afford the paper."

When Ferlinghetti asked me about my own writing, I wouldn't tell him much. I preferred to turn the conversation toward politics, an area in which we agreed. As we were both on the far left side of the spectrum, there was rarely an argument. I marked him up as a sentimental anarchist. I, on the other hand, liked being invited to one or another of the many local campaign events because it meant free food and plenty of alcohol. At these events, I was often plied with questions about the writing community huddled around North Beach, and when it got around that I was hanging out with Ferlinghetti, they asked about him, too. When it was suggested that I approach him to publicly support Moscone, I declined. The politics we discussed weren't usually local. He rarely expressed anger to me but when he did, it was often about politics; it's no surprise to me that he wrote so many political poems and poems of protest. Ferlinghetti and I usually talked about overseas events, because I didn't want to get into potentially tense local matters with him. But I did detect in our conversations that Ferlinghetti thought San Francisco would soon take a turn to the mainstream, and that would mean more business on top of business, something the city had, at that time, to an extent avoided.

Ferlinghetti had dismissed the idea of expanding City Lights to other cities, and that was important to him. He had staked his claim in the most European-style city he could find in America and he was satisfied: No matter where he traveled, he loved his adopted city of San Francisco the most of all.

Not long after I first met Ferlinghetti, he handed me the keys to his cabin in Big Sur. Getting to escape to the rustic hideaway in isolated Bixby Canyon was a gift without measure. I would drive down Highway 101, take the Monterey exit, swing down Pacific Coast Highway 1 past Carmel, and come to the great, arching Bixby Canyon Bridge. From there, a rough narrow road led to the canyon floor. Ferlinghetti's cabin was hidden behind tall, thick bushes and one had to walk a couple of hundred yards to a clearing with the small cabin and a beautiful meditation hut—I'd sit in that Japanese-style shelter for entire days writing in my notebook. In the evening, I cooked on the open-air pit and watched the flames shoot into the air.

It was easy to feel as if I had fallen into something quite wonderful, and it was all because of Ferlinghetti's generous nature. But I certainly wasn't the only one who had been given the keys. A quarter of a mile down the road sat Ferlinghetti's original cabin, where Jack Kerouac wrote *Big Sur*, catching the many moods of the land, the shadows and sea breezes, the sun being swallowed by the walls of the coast early in the afternoon, and the sound of the creek running down to the sea. Focusing on the canyon's smallest details on one of his many visits, Allen Ginsberg wrote "Tiny orange-wing-tipped butterfly / fluttering sunlit / from violet / blossom to violet / blossom," in his poem "Bixby Canyon Ocean Path Word Breeze."

Ferlinghetti himself wrote several poems catching all of this, of course, and it didn't take much to understand why he savored this counterbalance to his sometimes hectic and obligation-filled North Beach life, where there was a bookshop to help run, piles of manuscripts to read, and no shortage of people who wanted his attention for one thing or another. But no matter how busy things got, the City of Poets held his heart: "I've got Big Sur and Paris, just like Henry Miller," he told me. "When you add San Francisco, you really have something that you want to hold on to."

IN THE FIRST months of my friendship with Lawrence Ferlinghetti, I learned that despite his incredible ability to get things done and stay on top of his many obligations, he had an insecure side. He was vulnerable, which isn't particularly surprising for a poet, I suppose. I learned that he had a good feeling for younger writers and made it a point to find himself among them as often as possible, being present and participating as much as he could as simply one of the poets. He was never one of the old guard who'd mutter, "My God, what's wrong with this new generation . . ." He was open-minded and respectful.

Somewhere along the line, during one of our dinners or over a coffee, I mentioned to Lawrence that I'd like to do a biography of him. His response was that nobody would want to read it.

"Somebody should do Allen's biography," he said. "He's really the one. What have I done that people are going to be interested in?"

I reminded him that he was a best-selling poet and that this was a very rare thing to be. He smiled and shook his head. We let it go with that, but the idea stayed in my mind as a possibility.

I was enjoying my lollygagging, bohemian days but I knew my unemployment was going to run out. Sooner or later, I'd have to stop making trips to the unemployment office down beyond Market Street, in a shadowy part of town. I loved my unemployment benefits, which I wrongly considered free money. I was thrifty and managed to save some of it, as well as some of my salary from working on the Moscone campaign. But my meager savings wouldn't hold me for long and I needed a plan. Remarkably, I stumbled into a way to earn some decent bread one afternoon while sitting in the crowded Caffè Trieste. Puccini was on the jukebox and Yolanda was behind the espresso bar summoning frothy cappuccinos for the multitudes. I was at one of the front tables with my usual gang. A short, inquisitive-looking fellow was sitting next to me in what looked like a rumpled suit, although it might've just been the style of the clothing he wore. When I glanced at him, he smiled.

"Are you from New York City?" he asked.

I laughed and told him I came from Southern California, that I'd been born in Santa Monica, a small seaside community right up against the L.A. city limits.

"Are you sure?" he asked, amused.

"Okay," I replied. "There was a secret subway that went directly to Times Square while I was growing up, and I took it every day."

He laughed and said it was my hand gestures and loud voice that made him think I was a born and bred New Yorker. He asked what I did for a living. I told him that I was living on unemployment, but it was soon to run out. I gave him my usual line: "It's kept me in caffeine and good food and a lot of Merlot."

"What are you going to do?" he asked.

I said I wanted to write a biography of Lawrence Ferlinghetti. He nodded and said he thought that was a good idea. Then he said, "Oh, by the way, my name is Jerry Rubin."

Yes, sitting in Caffè Trieste that day was the very Jerry Rubin whose 1968 protest at the Democratic National Convention led to his being tried as one of the Chicago Seven, among them his fellow Yippie Abbie Hoffman. This was just the sort of thing you could almost expect to happen in San Francisco in the 1970s.

Jerry said he would call his literary agent and tell him about my project. "You'll like John Brockman," he said, and rushed to the payphone in the corner of the café.

A few minutes later, Jerry motioned me over to the phone and I found myself talking to an affable-sounding, real-life New York agent who loved the idea of the biography. Brockman asked me to talk to Ferlinghetti and get the go-ahead for his cooperation and then get back to him.

I talked to Ferlinghetti that evening. When I told him the biography would probably happen because I'd landed an agent, he seemed at first a bit unnerved. He was worried about the privacy of his son and daughter, and of exposing too much of his private life. It took him a few days before he decided that it would be just fine and he would give his full cooperation.

I phoned Brockman back. He asked me to write a proposal for the biography and get it to him as quickly as possible. That was precisely when two tabs of Mr. Natural acid seemed necessary. Instinctively, I knew it was the way to go. Back then, I sometimes referred to myself as Old Uncle Acid because I handled a trip fairly well. To this day, I believe one trip enabled me to take my car and fly on a sort of Mr. Toad's Wild Ride over the rooftops of San Francisco with my friend the poet Ken Wainio. The only problem was that afterwards, Ken had no memory of the experience—he just thought I'd been driving rather erratically.

At any rate, the acid did the job: Brockman took my smashingly well-written proposal and immediately sold it to Doubleday for a handsome advance.

I wish I had seen Rubin again after that encounter in the café and after what he had so spontaneously and thoughtfully done for me. But that would not be the case. As with so many others in my life, he simply went one way and I went the other.

BY THE TIME I began working on the biography, I was fairly clearheaded. I conducted hours of interviews with Ferlinghetti, his friends, and his associates. I didn't know how to write a biography—I'd never written anything so long, much less something that required so much research and careful stitching together—but I figured it out as I went.

Sometimes when I interviewed Ferlinghetti, I found that his natural shyness meant I had to really coax information from him. I'd ask, "What did you think when you first read Ginsberg?"

Silence. Silence. Silence.

Then he'd say enthusiastically, his voice rising, "Oh, I *loved* Allen's work."

Silence. Silence. Silence.

I'd ask, "But what did you *think* of it?"

Silence. Silence. Silence.

And so it went.

It's not that Ferlinghetti was ever hiding anything; it was simply his natural inclination—likely because of his troubled childhood—to hold back and put up a kind of protective cloak against the outside world. But I had a whole book to write, so I kept cajoling him.

At times I would procrastinate. On one occasion I dropped some more Mr. Natural acid at a party and as I munched on some potato chips, I heard a voice from the big plastic bowl of chips: "Ferlinghetti is the word you eat." It freaked me out so much that I ducked out of my friend's house and walked to a nearby park that had a sweeping view of the city. I believe the scenery saved me. Still, it was a week or more before I could get back to the book.

I worked on the biography for a long time, which was difficult for a poet with a wandering mind and hyperactivity. I remember Ferlinghetti saying to me, "You can't sit still. Sometimes I don't know how you could even finish a haiku . . . and that's only three lines." But I worked hard. I read portions of the work in progress to my boyfriend at the time as Vivaldi or Bach floated through my apartment.

When I was almost finished with the biography, Mayor Moscone was assassinated. Sitting in North Beach, I heard over the television that he'd been killed by Dan White, a disgruntled city supervisor. I was devastated and tried to get through to City Hall to reach old friends in Moscone's office but was unsuccessful. The next day, I wandered across the city and tried to reach City Hall, but the police turned people back.

As the book's publication drew near, Ferlinghetti began to worry that I might reveal too much, but I assured him that I didn't like biographies that probed too deeply. I didn't want either a book of gossip or a book of academic-style criticism—I was a poet, after all, writing on another poet, not some stuffy, erudite soul on a year's sabbatical. I also decided I didn't want the book to be a massive tome, nor authoritative. I wanted to gather and put down on paper the practical details of his life and what he'd accomplished because I believed there was historical value in his story.

The saving grace of the seemingly never-ending project was that the more I learned and wrote about Lawrence Ferlinghetti, the more I appreciated him.

And this is the book I wrote to celebrate him.

— Neeli Cherkovski
San Francisco, 2021

FERLINGHETTI: A LIFE

CHAPTER ONE

L AWRENCE FERLINGHETTI WAS born in a small white clapboard house in Yonkers, New York, on March 24, 1919. He was the last of the five sons of Charles and Clemence Ferlinghetti. His father died of a heart attack several months before Lawrence's birth. His mother's grief left her so physically and emotionally shattered that she was unable to care for her newborn child. It was a long time before Lawrence was able to write about the first years of his life. In 1971, after years of self-searching, he finally got to the heart of his lost childhood in a Brechtian poem called "True Confessional," which is included in *Open Eye, Open Heart*:

> I lawrence ferlinghetti
> wrought from the dark in my mother long ago
> born in a small back bedroom—
> in the next room my brother heard
> The first cry,
> many years later wrote me—
> "Poor Mom—No husband—No money—Pop dead—
> How she went through it all—"
> Someone squeezed my heart
> to make it go
> I cried and sprang up
> Open eye Open heart where
> do I wander
> I cried and ran off
> into the heart of the world
> Carried away
> by another I knew not

And which of me shall know my brother
"I am my son, my mother, my father."

It is his brother Harry, the third oldest, whom Ferlinghetti refers
to in the poem. Harry, who took care of their mother during her
later years, recalls, "She would often ask about Lawrence, but that
whole early period was difficult for her to remember. It was such a
dark time for her. So much was lost. I didn't know much either and
couldn't help Lawrence like I wanted to."

Their father had been an auctioneer in an Italian neighborhood of
Brooklyn. It was the first job he got after emigrating from the northern
Italian area of Lombardy in the late 1890s. It is probable that he did
the same kind of work there. By the time Lawrence was conceived his
father had a real estate office on Forty-second Street in Manhattan.
He had moved his family to Yonkers in an effort to get them away from
the ethnic community and into the mainstream of American life. Harry
remembers the family talking about the future, about the great oppor-
tunities in real estate, and about the big "deals" his father was always
just on the verge of making.

Clemence Ferlinghetti was the daughter of a Frenchwoman,
Clemence Carrin, and a Sephardic Jew, Herman Mendes-Monsanto. Herman's family settled in the Netherlands Antilles and in the
Virgin Islands in the early 1800s. They first lived in Curaçao. Eventually some of the family moved to the island of St. Thomas. The
tombstone of Abraham Mendes-Monsanto, one of Herman's fore-
bears, can be seen today in the Jewish Cemetery of St. Thomas. It
announces that he died in 1819 at the age of thirty-nine and that he
had been "a good father and husband."

Ferlinghetti's maternal grandfather grew up in a house filled with
books of all sorts and plenty of servants to tend to his needs. He was
educated in a private school and in a European university. During
the late nineteenth century he moved to the United States, where
he met and married Lawrence's grandmother, who had come to this
country with her daughter by a previous marriage.

Herman Mendes-Monsanto taught at the Naval Academy at Annapolis and later took a position at a small New York City college. He was the author of several textbooks, the most successful of which, a Spanish grammar, brought royalties to Clemence Ferlinghetti until her death. During the Depression she once received a thousand-dollar royalty check, which helped the family out immensely.

Lawrence's maternal grandmother wanted to retain her French heritage. As a result, Clemence Ferlinghetti was able to speak French as fluently as English. It was through this talent that she developed a friendship with Charles Ferlinghetti after the two had been introduced to each other. He, too, was well educated and spoke several languages, including French. Clemence was fascinated by the fact that he was multilingual.

Soon after Charles's death and Lawrence's birth, the family moved from the new house on Saratoga Avenue and its promise for a bright future. They went on to a succession of ever cheaper quarters as Clemence struggled in vain to keep them together. There was never enough money, and little outside help. Her emotional condition became increasingly tenuous, and it soon became quite clear that she would have to be institutionalized.

Clemence was placed in the State Hospital in Poughkeepsie, New York, where she remained for five years. The older boys were sent to a boarding home in Ossining. Charles, the oldest, found a job, later marrying the daughter of the boardinghouse owner. Clement, the second oldest, lied about his age and was hired as a guard at Sing Sing Penitentiary, working his way up after several years to the post of assistant warden.

The family decided that the baby should be cared for by a relative. So Lawrence, who was about a year old, went to live with Clemence's uncle Ludwig Mendes-Monsanto and his wife, Emily, in their home on Manhattan's Riverside Drive. Emily looked forward to taking care of Lawrence, since she had no children of her own.

Soon after they adopted Lawrence, Ludwig and Emily began to have marital difficulties. Emily left her husband, took the baby, and went to live in France, her homeland. Once again Lawrence was deprived of a father. Emily, whom Lawrence always referred to as his "French mother," is remembered today by the Monsanto family as a woman of mystery. She was tall, slender, and slightly regal in appearance. She had a kind of "cloche" look, Lawrence remembers. Her hair was always worn in the latest style and she was interested in clothes and fashion trends. She was passionately devoted to France and had originally come to the United States only because she felt she might find the fortune she was seeking.

She and Lawrence lived in the Alsatian capital of Strasbourg in a traditional French home. Lawrence's earliest memory is of being held in his aunt's arms on a balcony of the house in Strasbourg as a parade passed by. He must have been about three years old. He remembers his aunt helping him wave at the troops on the streets below. In the distance were the mountains of Alsace, capped in snow, with the sun beating down on them. In 1961, Lawrence wrote:

> When I was born the world was still ringing with marching feet. My French mother held me on a balcony in Alsace and waved my hand at the passing parade. A touching gesture, all things considered. Today it's still happening. I'm still waving, only the expression on my face has changed . . .

Lawrence was well taken care of in Strasbourg but can remember little about the years he spent there. For the first five years of his life he spoke French and formed a lifelong attachment to France and its language. In fact, throughout much of his early childhood he thought of himself as French.

Emily frequently took him through the streets of Strasbourg, a kind of mini-Paris, with exquisite centuries-old buildings. At night before putting him to bed she read him stories and told him some that she created in which both she and Lawrence played a part. She continually emphasized to him that he came from a well-educated, cultivated family. Emily had learned to play the piano as a child and she introduced Lawrence to music during their time in Strasbourg.

In the meantime Emily and Ludwig had been corresponding and he convinced her to return home. Four years after going to France,

Lawrence was back in New York, where he began to learn English from his uncle.

But things were not as ideal as Emily had hoped. Ludwig, who had been working as an instructor in languages at City College, lost his job and financial difficulties began to press in on him. There were constant arguments about money, and finally there wasn't even enough to buy milk for the child. Lawrence developed a case of rickets. Ever the enterprising person, Emily kept trying one financial scheme after another, but nothing worked. She realized she had to go out and find a job. That meant placing her nephew in an orphanage. She found one in Chappaqua, a town not far from Ossining, where, unknown to him, his brothers lived. Farther up the Hudson, his mother was still hospitalized. Ironically the entire family was within fifty miles of one another but Lawrence had no idea such a family even existed. As far as he knew, his name was Lawrence Ferling Monsanto and Emily was his mother.

Lawrence was in the orphanage only seven or eight months, although to the lonely little boy it seemed like years. He was terribly unhappy and felt totally deserted. He can recall only one trivial incident from the entire period. On his first day at the home he was served sticky tapioca pudding for dessert. The other kids called it "cat's-eyes." To this day he is unable to eat tapioca. Even looking at it makes him feel ill. The memory of those lonely days is preserved in his novel *Her*:

> . . . he finds himself in his own body in an orphanage to end all orphanages, where in swaddled clothes he eats the undercooked tapioca cat's-eyes of baby reality and pukes his way into someone's heart who takes him away and away he goes and the next thing he knows he is walking . . .

It was Emily who took him away. She had left Ludwig again and found a job in the home of wealthy people. Emily was excited about her new position; if she couldn't be rich herself at least she could be surrounded by wealth.

Lawrence was six years old when he and his aunt went to live in Lawrence Park West, an exclusive section of Bronxville, New York, a fifteen-minute walk from the center of town. Emily had been hired as a French tutor for the daughter of Presley and Anna Lawrence Bisland. Their mansion was called Plashbourne, and it looked like something out of *Wuthering Heights*, with its impressive gables, huge stone walls, and the rich greenery surrounding it. The house was guarded by sprawling formal gardens and a series of stone walls to which time and ivy had added the warmth of nature.

If Emily was impressed, Lawrence was overawed. It took him some time to get used to the size of the house, and he spent endless hours wandering from room to room, touching, staring, absorbing, and wondering. Why was he here? Where did he really come from? How long would he stay in this place? How often would he find a new home and then, just as the warmth and comfort began to seep through, be snatched away to again be a stranger? Where was reality? What did a dream mean? How could God do this to him? Why was he at the mercy of these grown-ups who told him where to live, how to dress, how to behave, how to talk, how to think—but who told him nothing of who he really was?

He tightened the door on his own privacy, closing off unhappiness and creating mind poems and images of his own. What he could not face in reality he rearranged in his imagination. He drew pictures, imagined fathers, planned futures, and behind the wall of his growing isolation he emotionally withstood his fate.

Lawrence's active, developing imagination took the place of playthings. However, as he moved through the rooms of his new home, the one thing he could not create in his mind was other children. The orphanage had been a dreary place, but there had at least been kids his own age with whom he could play. Now there were only grown-ups, the family and the household staff. He envied the children he saw playing on the sidewalks whenever he was driven somewhere in the Bislands' chauffeured car. Out of his loneliness he made Gerhard Rulof, the chauffeur, and other members of the staff at Plashbourne his surrogate playmates. Lawrence spent hours in the garage talking to Gerhard. To the impressionable seven-year-old, the garage was an exciting, masculine place with its elaborate tools and the shining automobiles. The companionship of the chauffeur became the most important friendship of his young life. When the family went on trips, he rode up front with Gerhard, imagining that he was driving the car. The memories of those days are still vivid.

The Bisland cook was an Irish lady with bright rosy cheeks who never tired of spending time with Lawrence. Her improbable name was Delia Devine, and she gave him the hugging and warmth that he craved. She was a happy, open kind of person, easy to be with and genuinely interested in Lawrence's activities. Her attention and affection nourished him as much as the food she prepared in her warm kitchen, where Lawrence spent happy hours.

Emily and Lawrence lived in a small room in the third-floor servants' area. On the same floor Lawrence discovered a large dark attic crammed full of souvenirs of the Bislands' past and their travels. Presley Bisland had participated in the last big cattle drive on the old Chisholm Trail, a fact of which he remained proud all his life. His old dusty saddles, trail blankets, and other paraphernalia were a reminder of those days of the old West, and Bisland treasured them long after the last frontier had closed and his own personal wealth had grown. Sitting alone on the saddles in the dark attic, Lawrence imagined himself out on the prairie spurring on an illusionary horse.

Sometime in his early years Lawrence had been to Coney Island, and in his imagination it became a place of escape. In this carnival land he journeyed to a world where people were happy, where there was a constant interplay of shifting colors and noise. Coney Island was a carnival he entered simply by imagining himself there amidst laughter and lights and shining excitement.

While Lawrence led a lonely life at the Bislands', Emily seemed to enjoy her job. She made lengthy preparations for her weekly Sunday off, always grooming herself carefully and completing the job with one of many fancy hats with fruits and flowers on them. She kept up the practice of reading to Lawrence at night and soon began to give him books of his own and encourage him to read them himself.

One day she returned from her time off with a copy of *Little Lord Fauntleroy*, the story of a poor American boy who inherits a great English fortune and goes to live in style in England. This was the first book Lawrence read completely on his own. He was enthralled, especially since he could identify with a little boy who went to live across the ocean in a foreign country. He was proud of having been overseas himself and often asked Emily questions about their time together in France.

One week after she gave Lawrence the book, Emily disappeared. No one ever explained to Lawrence what happened to her. She simply failed to reappear after a Sunday off. Lawrence has often wondered whether the Bislands might have asked her to leave. There was no question about his going, however. They wanted him to stay. At the abrupt disappearance of his "mother," Lawrence once again experienced a wrenching feeling of loss. He sensed that he would never see her again.

Years later, when he was in the Navy, he received a communication from Central Islip State Hospital in Long Island saying that Emily Monsanto had died there at the age of fifty-six and had listed him as her only living relative. She apparently had kept track of his where-abouts. He never discovered what had happened to her after she left the Bislands'. Emily's life was another closed door, and Lawrence is still searching for the key.

The Bislands were kind people and they genuinely wanted Lawrence to remain with them, but they were undemonstrative and re-served. After Emily's departure, Lawrence rarely experienced any physical expression of affection.

Mrs. Bisland and her husband had had a son who died in early childhood. His name—and Mrs. Bisland's maiden name—was Lawrence. Ferlinghetti now wonders how often Mrs. Bisland might have looked at him, remembering, longing for her own lost child, wanting to touch him but prevented by her reserve from doing so. There is no question that Mrs. Bisland felt some kind act of fate had caused this boy named Lawrence to be left in her care. From time to time she wistfully spoke of Lawrence in connection with her lost son.

As for Lawrence, he was obviously starved for affection. Mrs. Bisland often found him crouched next to her bedroom door, sitting on his knees in the hall, his head bent forward, waiting for some attention from the woman who had now become his "mother." But instead of hugging him, she would say in a firm but gentle voice, "Lawrence, why don't you get up and come downstairs with me," or would suggest that he go out and play.

It is easy to imagine even today how awesome a figure she was to that small child left in her home. She was awesome even to others. Very cultivated, authentic New York aristocracy. The only time she expressed her pleasure openly with Lawrence was when he did well in school. That seemed to be a subject on which it was safe to be enthusiastic.

Mrs. Bisland was active in the community affairs of Bronxville, carrying on a tradition started by her father, William Van Duzer Lawrence, who founded Sarah Lawrence College, near Bronxville. The college was named after Mrs. Bisland's mother, and the college's administration building, still in use today, was originally the Lawrence family home. Mrs. Bisland was devoted to her father's concept of a self-contained community thriving economically with the college as one of its chief assets. She was pleasurably involved in looking after the Lawrence family business affairs and in the business world in general. In her later life she wrote a history of the Lawrence family. Her writing is lucid and concise, and contains none of the flowery prose often associated with such histories.

Her brother, Dudley Lawrence, also wrote a family history, seen from his viewpoint as the "'patriarch" of the family businesses. In his writings he refers to Presley Bisland's unique brand of humor. Presley Bisland was a Southern gentleman. His humor, reminiscent of Mark Twain, who was one of his heroes, frequently echoed through the house and softened much of its formality. He had been raised in Natchez, Mississippi, the son of an old aristocratic family that had originally come to the South from Scotland near the end of the eighteenth century, and had settled in both Louisiana and Mississippi.

Bisland was schooled in the Greek and Latin classics, and never lost interest in them. He was profoundly interested in the literature of the nineteenth-century American and English writers. Books by Sir Walter Scott, volumes of Longfellow, William Cullen Bryant, James Russell Lowell, and Whittier lined his library walls. The huge leatherbound volumes, many etched in gold, fascinated Lawrence. Bisland encouraged him to read through them, and the boy spent long hours doing so.

Bisland was fond of recounting stories about his years in the West, when, at the age of sixteen, he left home to ride on the Chisholm Trail. On the last cattle drive he and his companions were responsible for more than 2,500 head of cattle, and at one point they had to guide them through hostile Indian territory.

After the cattle drive he worked in a variety of jobs, including some time in the oil fields of the South, followed by railroad work with the Kansas City, Fort Scott, and Memphis Railroad. In 1889 he worked for the New York Central Railway. He was also involved in mining and power company work. He finally became president of Abbot Coin Counting Company, in 1912, although he disliked having to be involved in a business. As a public relations measure for customers and employees, he put out a small newsletter that included poetry and short creative prose sketches. His rejection slips were often biting when he felt the submitter to be somewhat pompous about his or her work. Despite his aristocratic background, he was a plain-spoken man and he had an abhorrence of anyone who was not straightforward. Much of this philosophy seemed to have become part of Lawrence's personal development.

Bisland wanted to write the story of his experiences in the West but never found the time. But he did compose a number of short stories after settling in Lawrence Park West. He was spurred on by his Lawrence relatives, since they shared a deep interest in literature and creative writing. Among the titles of Presley Bisland's works that still survive are "'Er Good Ole Religion"; "Runt: A Biography of a Pig"; "The Old Sugar Kettle"; "Joshua's Rival," and "Uncle Pumblechook." The stories, like the titles themselves, are in the Mark Twain tradition, and they display Bisland's unique style: a combination of his Southern upbringing, an adventuresome spirit, and the restraining influence of New York gentility.

When Lawrence was eight years old, the Bislands sent him to the Riverdale Country School, a boarding school not far from Bronxville. There he had other children to play with and he was well cared for. Although his schoolwork was not particularly outstanding, he began to come out of his shell. During the summer he was sent to a camp run by the school, and he learned to swim and developed an interest in sports, though he never became more than an average athlete.

Back home at Plashbourne, he had a new room on a sort of mezzanine that was reached by a narrow separate staircase. There were still no playmates at Plashbourne, and in contrast to the companionship he had at Riverdale, Lawrence felt lonely and isolated in the formal gardens behind the mansion's stone walls.

Lawrence was never allowed to put pictures on the walls of his room and he was afraid of making marks on the floors. Everything was extremely clean. There was a huge, comfortable bed with four posters rising to the ceiling. It stood far off the ground and had fancy bed coverings on it, not the kind of bed a young boy could just throw himself onto, facedown, and relax. The most beautiful things about his room were the windows. From these he could look out on a row of huge oak trees, the branches of which climbed up the side of the house, almost as if they were ivy. The image of the trees and their ever-changing moods remained forever fixed in Lawrence's mind. They were dark green in the spring and summer, turning interesting shades of yellow and brown in the colder months. Just below his room was a music room with a fancy grand piano. The room was lined with white statuary and had inlaid marble floors. Big French doors opened onto a patio where Lawrence used to like to stand and look out at "his" stream. It was a poetic scene, especially in the early evening when a breeze played through the oak trees and the sound mingled with that of the stream rushing on its downhill course. During the winter he would slide down the icy stream on a small sled.

As Lawrence grew older, Bisland introduced him to the Greek and Roman classic writers. By the time he went away to college, he knew the classics, and the poets who created them, better than most students of his age. He was often questioned about some fact concerning one of the ancient poets. Bisland would say, "Young man, you've been to school. Who was Horatius?" Then he would wait good-naturedly for an answer. Mr. Bisland enjoyed displaying his own knowledge of even the most obscure poets of antiquity.

During his years with Emily, she had often told Lawrence about her own desire to be a writer. She never found the time. She was too busy working to gain the basic necessities of life to write. Still, her ambitions, as well as Presley Bisland's writing, gave Lawrence the idea that being an author was a dignified profession. As he became more and more familiar with the Bisland library, he grew interested in how books are printed and put together. In his mind he saw them bearing the same secrets that he kept inside himself: books unread for years and sitting neglected on the shelves seemed to him like his own hidden doors waiting to be opened.

One Sunday when Lawrence was about ten and a half years old, he had an unusual and traumatic experience. Without any advance warning his real mother and brothers came to Plashbourne. Mrs. Bisland had told him that he had a real family, but he never really believed that they existed or that he would ever meet them. To this day he doesn't know how the visit came about But it was a day he will never forget. An old car drove up to the front of the big mansion and his mother, Clemence, and his two brothers Clement and Harry appeared. His mother went directly to another room to talk to Mrs. Bisland. The brothers, who were already grown men, stayed with Lawrence, making uncomfortable attempts at conversation. Then his mother and Mrs. Bisland returned. Next to the great lady of Plashbourne, Clemence seemed small and unassuming. And according to Harry, his mother was overwhelmed by the size and splendor of the place, especially in contrast to the small house in Ossining where she now lived with her sons. After several hours of stilted talk, Lawrence was given a preposterous decision to make. He was asked to decide whether to go to live with his mother and brothers or to remain with the Bislands. He had never, to his knowledge, seen his family before. He was incapable of making any decision but the one he came to. He chose to stay with the Bislands. "It was a hell of a choice to leave up to a kid," he now says. "Perhaps if I had gone with my family things would have been much better for me. Maybe I wouldn't feel so bad about my childhood. But my real family was really like a bunch of strangers." Over the years Lawrence has often relived that painful episode. He has approached it from various angles, but he always comes to the same conclusion. There had been so many moves during the first six years of his life. The Bislands were the only real "family" he knew. There was no choice but to stay with them.

After his mother and brothers left Plashbourne late that afternoon, Lawrence walked off by himself through the walled gardens. He circled three stone fountains, stopping by the one with the birdbath in the center and the statue rising out of it, watching the goldfish in their pond and then standing on the bridge over the creek. He imagined a happier place, where ten-year-old boys didn't have to make the kind of choice he had just been forced to make. He dreamed about a place where families stayed together always. Then he went up to his room, closed the door, and sat by the window looking out at the familiar trees. The noise of the stream grew louder.

A few weeks later it was decided that Lawrence was to make a move of another kind. Unknown to him, the Bislands had arranged for him to live with a family in Bronxville and attend the public school. They had lost considerable money in the stock market crash of 1929 and could no longer afford the high cost of Riverdale. Since Bronxville had one of the most progressive public school systems in the country, they decided to send Lawrence there.

Lawrence went to live with Zilla Larned Wilson, a widow who had come to New York from Ohio with her son, Bill, who was five years older than Ferlinghetti. Bill soon became Lawrence's hero. He took the younger boy to local football and baseball games, spent a lot of time with him in vacant lots playing baseball, and became the older brother Lawrence so desperately needed at that time.

The Wilsons lived on Parkway Road, literally on "the other side of the tracks" from the main part of town and Plashbourne. Lawrence stayed with them during his last two years of grammar school and through three years of junior high school. Mrs. Wilson was paid a certain amount each month for his room and board. There were many neighborhood children for Lawrence to play with and he joined the local Boy Scout troop. He was less lonely than he had been at Plashbourne.

Every morning Lawrence would get up early to deliver newspapers on his bicycle. He soon became as fascinated with newsprint as he had been with the books at Plashbourne, and he often dreamed of seeing the inside of a newspaper office. The entire process of putting out a paper intrigued him as he learned more about it. He read some of the stories in the paper several times and marveled at the reporters who could say so much in so few words. He wanted to learn to set type and to lay out the stories on the page. But most of all he dreamed of becoming a journalist.

Thanks to Bill Wilson's coaching, Lawrence got to be rather good at basketball, and he was a member of a team that was so successful that they stayed together all during junior high school. The coach doubled as the instructor in the school print shop. As a result, Lawrence finally got the opportunity to work with print. Print shop was almost the only subject that interested him. It was one of the few in which he excelled.

In "Autobiography," in *A Coney Island of the Mind*, he makes reference to "an unhappy childhood" and writes, "I am looking for my old man, who I never knew." Generally he describes a kid growing up in the suburbs of America—a normal life. One passage focuses on the Wilson period of his childhood.

> I was an American boy
> I read the American Boy magazine
> and became a boy scout
> in the suburbs . . .
> I had a baseball mitt

and an American Flyer bike
I delivered the Woman's Home Companion
at five in the afternoon
or the Herald Trib
at five in the morning.
I still can hear the paper thump
at five in the morning.

It's a description of the boy in the Norman Rockwell painting, surrounded by the symbols of American boyhood: baseball bat, *American Boy* magazine, newspaper route. At the Wilsons', Lawrence did gradually become outgoing, though he retained more than a normal share of shyness and inwardness. He was happier than he had ever been. He had a real home, an older brother, and he had the freedom of the streets. He could play with kids his own age, identify with them, laugh with them. It was the closest thing to a normal childhood he had ever known.

Years later, when he read *Black Spring*, by Henry Miller, Lawrence recognized Miller's feelings about the streets of his childhood, the Fourteenth Ward of Brooklyn. Miller was a child of lively, animated streets. Unlike Lawrence, he had been free his entire life and wrote freely, openly, and joyously of his youth.

Lawrence had been uprooted as a child, and the abiding symbol of his early years continued to be the fantasy carnival—the Coney Island of his imagination—far off in the distance, unreachable but always calling. To this day he has trouble recalling the realities of his childhood.

Much of it is still buried. When he writes about his youth he uses death imagery instead of the mundane symbols of his everyday life.

During the last year in Bronxville, Lawrence began to write poetry. On his sixteenth birthday Sally, the daughter of Presley and Anna Bisland, gave him a copy of Baudelaire in French and English. It was the first collection of poems he ever read from cover to cover, and he was particularly pleased that the book was printed in the two languages he knew. He began composing poems, and soon realized that they helped him to define his own "being." In his poetry he felt that he was in direct communication with himself and that he controlled the confusing world around him. When he wrote a poem he was his own boss; there was no one telling him what to do. There were no rules. He tried to put down on paper, through the medium of his poetry, the sadness he felt, his buried emotions, his longing for the father he never knew, his confusion about his family, his questions about his brothers. The closed doors began to open as he explored the images he had, up until now, kept half formed in his mind.

He rose through the ranks of the Boy Scouts and was made an Eagle Scout, an achievement of which he was very proud. He then began running around with a neighborhood gang called the Parkway Road Pirates. In *Her* he puts himself in another gang:

> I saw a girl with dirndl hoop and her communion dress all white when we ran round the corner with our baseball hats to play the Parkway Road Pirates and all of them still alive someplace now but still all pushed into the crypts of time to sleep so soundly with the dead that one same shadow blankets both confusing both. . . .

The Parkway Road Pirates began running through the downtown area of Bronxville, at first playing games, and then, when they became bored, they began to commit various petty thefts. They stashed the things they stole in an old abandoned storefront. Nothing they took was of much use to them, but the act of stealing was itself exciting, and Lawrence became one of the leaders of their illegal expeditions.

"I got caught stealing pencils from the five and dime the same month I made Eagle Scout," he writes. He was bailed out of jail by his scoutmaster, who contacted Mrs. Wilson. For some time Lawrence's restlessness and his involvement with the Parkway Road Pirates was more than Mrs. Wilson could handle, and after his arrest she decided she could no longer take care of him. The Bislands agreed, and under the impression that he would develop greater independence in a boarding school, they enrolled him in a private high school, Mount Hermon, near Greenfield, Massachusetts, on the Connecticut River.

Lawrence felt sad about leaving his Bronxville friends behind. At the same time he looked forward to the new experience. Being uprooted had become a way of life for him. At least this time he was old enough to know what was happening to him.

Mount Hermon School, founded by Dwight L. Moody, of the Moody Bible Institute in Chicago, was primarily a work school for the sons of missionaries. Students were required to attend chapel every day and take courses in the Bible. The school had high academic standards and an excellent record of success with students. It was just what Lawrence needed at this restless time of his life.

Part of each day was spent working on the school farm. Classes were long and the evenings were spent studying for the next day's assignments. At Bronxville, Lawrence had regularly cut classes. That was impossible at Mount Hermon, and although he didn't always do well, Lawrence gained the discipline of regular attendance. The teaching was rigorous, the faculty were strict, and the student body was more intellectually oriented than his classmates at Bronxville had been.

His first roommate, Jim Alter (later a valedictorian at Yale), a large athletic boy, was interested in philosophy, and he introduced Lawrence to the subject in a unique way. Wrestling him to the floor, he announced he wouldn't let Lawrence up until he could prove that he existed. This was a new concept to Lawrence, who managed to come up with some kind of an answer. The incident opened up a whole new train of thought for him, one that he puzzled over and discussed for some time.

Another student, Alden Monroe, nicknamed "Rube," a tall, gaunt boy from Peabody, Massachusetts, became Lawrence's best friend at Mount Hermon. Rube had an authentic Peabody accent and carried a tattered copy of Thomas Wolfe's *Look Homeward, Angel* in one hand and Hemingway's *The Sun Also Rises* in the other. They were his personal portable library. Later, when Rube and Lawrence became roommates, Rube gave him both books to read and *Look Homeward, Angel* quickly became one of Lawrence's favorites. The subtitle, "A Study of a Buried Life," struck a chord in him. He understood the loneliness that seemed to pour out of the pages. He identified with the long, dark soliloquies and such lines as "Which of us has known his brother?" And "Ye have been an exile in another land and a stranger in our own" seemed to apply directly to his own life. Wolfe helped bring him further out of himself than he had ever been before. Lawrence began to realize the universality of many of his heretofore hidden feelings.

Wolfe imparted to Lawrence a notion of the possibilities that existed in this vast country: "Only the earth endures—the gigantic American earth—this broad terrific earth that had no ghosts in it." In particular Wolfe presented a vision of the South as a broad and open land. Eugene Gant (hero of *Look Homeward, Angel*) had gone to college at Pulpit Hill (Chapel Hill), South Carolina, the school Wolfe had attended. Lawrence decided that was where he would go upon graduation from high school.

Another book Lawrence first encountered at Mount Hermon was *Walden*, by Henry David Thoreau. It was a revelation to him, and reinforced the lessons about self-reliance that Presley Bisland had taught him at Plashbourne.

Intellectual pursuits, however, were hardly Lawrence's only concern at Mount Hermon. He was still a young, restless boy, and he and Rube shared mischievous adventures. They regularly used a rope that was designed as an emergency fire escape to make nighttime forays on Northfield Academy, a nearby girls school. Although they never even caught sight of any girls, the thrill of running through the fields in the dark of night in what they called their "rat racing" clothes was enough excitement. Before sunrise they were back in their beds, and they were never punished for their adventures.

However, Lawrence was caught smoking tobacco, a major offense in those days, and he was temporarily expelled. As punishment he was sent off to a nearby farm in Colrain, Massachusetts, where, under the tutelage of the owner, Calvin Call, he learned to milk cows and plow fields and for excitement was allowed to drive the hay wagon into town on weekends.

Back at Mount Hermon, Lawrence worked hard. He continued to expand his reading with such books as *The House of the Seven Gables* and *The Scarlet Letter*, and he even managed to read *Don Quixote* from beginning to end.

In his senior year Mrs. Bisland took him for a visit to his family in Ossining. The big chauffeured Cadillac drove up to a small house on a quiet side street, and in the first of many such visits, he spent several warm and memorable hours with his mother and brothers. The void caused by the long separation was obvious. He tried to bridge the gap by changing his name in later years. All through his youth he was Lawrence Ferling Monsanto. His family had taken the abbreviated name many years earlier. Now, approaching college age, he changed his name to Lawrence Monsanto Ferling.

Lawrence graduated from Mount Hermon in June of 1937 and made preparations to go to the University of North Carolina at Chapel Hill. Besides its connection to Thomas Wolfe, the university had an excellent journalism school, and Lawrence still hoped for a career in the newspaper field. Chapel Hill had about nine thousand residents when Lawrence first came there. Largely due to the influence of the campus, it was one of the most liberal communities in the South. Until World War II the business section of the town consisted of one street and the majority of the buildings were of Georgian Colonial style. Chapel Hill had no industries and no commercial center of any size. It was a typical sleepy southern college town.

Lawrence joined a fraternity, Sigma Kappa, and he became the circulation manager of the college newspaper, *The Daily Tar Heel*, which gave him just enough money to live on through the school year. He was also on the sports staff of *Carolina* magazine, a campus publication for which Thomas Wolfe had once written while at the university.

Lawrence found the first two years of college relatively easy after the strenuous, rigid academic life of Mount Hermon. He wrote short stories, none of which survives, and he read *Studs Lonigan*, by James T. Farrell, the works of John Dos Passos and Hemingway, and the novels of William Faulkner. Wolfe remained his favorite, and he made three or four starts on novels of his own in the tradition of *Look Homeward, Angel* and *You Can't Go Home Again.*

During the summer following his second year at Chapel Hill, Lawrence and two friends traveled to Mexico. One of the boys was the nephew of Josephus Daniels, who was our ambassador to Mexico at the time. Under the mistaken impression that the ambassador would put them up when they got to Mexico City, the three rode freight trains and hitchhiked their way into Mexico. The ambassador did not open his doors to the three travelers from Chapel Hill, and so they searched the city for a place to stay, settling on an inexpensive pension. Lawrence, imagining himself a foreign correspondent, wrote news stories about the politics of Mexico and naively sent them off to such outlets as *Time* magazine. Of course, nothing came of his dispatches, which Lawrence felt were an accurate commentary on what was happening on Mexico's political front.

Back at Chapel Hill, Lawrence immersed himself in classwork. Perhaps the most rewarding were those classes conducted by Professor Phillips Russell, the creative writing instructor. "He held classes outside on the lawn near this stand of trees and didn't lay down any rigid rules," Lawrence remembers. "I dedicated one of my books to him and really feel he was a major influence on me. I read Carl Sandburg, Edgar Lee Masters, Vachel Lindsay, and other Populist writers. This early Populist influence is reflected in the 'Populist Manifesto' I wrote in 1975. I liked the way these writers communicated directly. None of them was obscure."

Professor Russell didn't restrict himself to the Populists. He covered a wide range of poets. He often stressed the humorous element in poetry, cautioning his students not to take themselves or their work too seriously.

Lawrence wrote quite a lot of poetry in those days, but none of it survives. He didn't start keeping notebooks of his work until 1940, and although he feels it is important for a poet to keep his early work, he remembers his first attempts at poetry as "pretty derivative stuff."

When Lawrence graduated from Chapel Hill, in 1941, Carl Sandburg was the commencement speaker. Lawrence's description of the
event is one of the earliest examples of his writing.

> Carl Sandburg, as commencement speaker, was slight in physical
> stature, straight-white-haired, out of place, but impressive. His de-
> livery, excellent, almost too dramatic. He cast a spell. He spoke of
> ours as the "bridged generation," one foot in one war, the other in
> the second one.

Immediately after college and before the war touched him and
his classmates, Lawrence spent three months in Maine on an island
some friends named "Little Whaleboat Island," after a small boat
they had. The island was north of Portland and in a small brown
spiral notebook Lawrence wrote a piece that "centered" himself the
same way Stephen Dedalus had in Joyce's *A Portrait of the Artist as
a Young Man*.

> Lawrence Ferling
> Little Whaleboat Island
> South Harpswell
> Casco Bay
> Maine
> New England
> The USA
> The Western Hemisphere
> The World
> The Universe
> The Cosmos
> In the year of our Lord
> Nineteen Hundred
> And
> Forty-one
> The eighth day
> of the eight month
> today . . . at Noon.

The same sort of notebooks contain a series of poems, which were scratched out with heavy pencil marks. Lawrence was beginning to work toward his own poetic voice—but was very much aware that he had a long way to go.

The rent was thirty-five dollars for the entire summer on Little Whaleboat Island. This included use of the entire island (a few hundred yards long), a small cabin, and a boat. The three friends spent much of their time lazing around. Eventually they found that they could make money selling the Irish moss that grew in abundance there. They used long rakes to harvest it, then dried it on the beach. When it was properly dried, they put it in their small boat and took it to Portland, down Casco Bay. The moss was sold to a chemical company, to be used for making explosives. Lawrence and his friends made twenty-five dollars a week from their harvest.

"Little Whaleboat Island was like a resting place before World War II," Lawrence recalls. "We worked hard with the moss, a necessary ingredient for some explosives, but gorged ourselves on Maine lobster. They grew large there and we had many feasts."

Soon the summer was over for Lawrence and his friends. The war began.

CHAPTER TWO

I n "Autobiography," Ferlinghetti writes:

> I landed in Normandy
> in a rowboat that turned over.
> I have seen the educated armies
> on the beach at Dover.

It is one of the few references in his body of work that goes back to his experiences in World War II. By the time he became an experienced poet, the "educated armies" were all too destructive. Back in 1941, however, he was caught up in patriotic fervor. He enlisted in the Navy before Pearl Harbor. Many of the poets he came in contact with later had spent World War II in conscientious objector camps. In 1941 the sheltered young man from Bronxville didn't know what a conscientious objector was. As one by one his friends enlisted in the Navy, he grew more and more eager to join in the battle.

He was sent to midshipmen's school in Chicago. In a "memory notation" preserved in one of his growing number of thin brown writing tablets he wrote:

> Me—
> in the Navy, here,
> At
> 111 E. Pearson St.
> Room Seven Hundred
> And Eleven
> (the eleventh room
> on the Seventh deck)

In Chicago
In the part that was never burned.
Old Chicago by the Lake
before Mrs. O'Leary's
Cow
the lantern kicked:
there
In the Fall of the Year
Nineteen Hundred and Four-one
The Sixteenth day
It is,
Of October,
The day of days that
We are sworn in
As midshipmen.

In discussing his World War II experiences, Ferlinghetti recalls, "Joining the Navy was the thing to do then. Everyone my age was getting ready for war. I found myself in Chicago . . . looking around town, waiting for my orders and spending a lot of energy thinking about the waitress I was trying to date. Then my orders came for the Third Naval District in New York City. I thought this would be a great chance to see the Bislands, so I called them up and told them that I'd be down to spend some time with them. They were both very old by then. Mr. Bisland had been slowing down in his work, but Mrs. Bisland was going as strong as ever. The old man still had a great sense of humor. He kept it up all through the war. The letters he wrote me were always full of his sharp wit. They really cheered me up. I came down to New York City in a Navy patrol boat."

The first boat Ferlinghetti served on was a wooden fishing vessel that had been converted to become part of the United States fleet. It had stood the test of the Atlantic winters, and Ferlinghetti heard that it had also been used in World War I. He now held the rank of Ensign and became the Third Officer, serving under First

Lieutenant J. Pierpont Morgan III, the grandson of the great financier. Morgan was an easygoing commander, about thirty years old, and although he tended to use some very formal-sounding rhetoric he was, in fact, a relaxed and unflappable sort of person. Ferlinghetti and he got on quite well. Once on leave in Manhattan they shared a taxi. When they arrived at the Morgan mansion on Fifth Avenue, opposite Central Park, they stood awkwardly on the sidewalk until Morgan said, in his typically gentlemanly voice, "May I offer you the conveniences of my home," but Ensign Ferling only felt more uncomfortable. He told Morgan that he had another pressing engagement and thus missed the opportunity of seeing the inside of the mansion.

Throughout the winter of 1942 they patrolled off New York Harbor and in New England. They were based on Staten Island, but took off for Manhattan every chance they could. The trip over on the ferry took about fifteen minutes. Usually the ship would patrol for four ors five days and then be in port for three. Ferlinghetti often got a chance to go out to Bronxville to visit the Bislands. Whenever he could, he stayed overnight in his old room on the mezzanine, suspended between the two floors of the great mansion.

On his trips into Manhattan, Ferlinghetti wandered around Greenwich Village, attracted by what he had read about the writers and artists who had made the area their home. There was still a deeply ingrained authentic bohemian spirit in the Village of the early forties. Ferlinghetti found the narrow streets and quaint architecture appealing, and they were a welcome change from the cold concrete of the city.

As shy as ever, he made few friends on his trips to New York. On one visit, however, he met Laura Lou Lyons, a Swarthmore student. She and her friends were part of a group of college intellectuals who hung around the Village passionately discussing political issues from a radical perspective. Some of the people in her crowd were aspiring writers and artists. Unlike the quiet and naive young sailor who shared their desire to write, these were high-powered New Yorkers, eager to express their opinions. As a willing listener Ferlinghetti was a rarity in this group of radical young thinkers. For the first time he was exposed to the idea of pacifism and to pro-communist or leftist ideology. America's involvement in the war, which had given rise to patriotism in Ferlinghetti, had evoked a negative response from the radicals he met in Greenwich Village.

On one occasion Laura took Ferlinghetti to her home in the Village to meet her brother. Ferlinghetti had the impression he was not well received. Years later he realized that it must have been his formal Navy whites that disturbed the brother. 'I looked like something out of Gilbert and Sullivan," he remembers.

The war didn't interrupt Ferlinghetti's reading. Never a fast reader, he was meticulous and often marked down interesting passages or key phrases. He began reading E. E. Cummings and Kenneth Patchen, and he was impressed by T. S. Eliot and Ezra Pound, both of whom he began to imitate in his writing.

When he wasn't reading poetry he was studying Navy training manuals, and he soon became an expert at Navy procedures. By the end of the day's work he was often so tired that he found relaxation only in reading. Writing was too taxing an occupation after a day spent working on the ship.

His tour on the patrol boat was followed by assignment to the *Ambrose Lightship*, which sailed in Ambrose Channel. Ships entering New York's port relied on the *Lightship* to help them into port. On the *Ambrose*, Ferlinghetti became an expert at signaling. He was a walking storehouse of the codes. "We signaled all ships coming in with secret codes twenty-four hours a day," he recalls. "I became a fast signalman. I was an officer but often did my own signaling. You'd go up in freezing cold with parka and hood and gloves. If a convoy came in you'd have twenty or thirty ships to handle. At the end of each word from the signalman on another ship you would turn your light down to let him know that you got his word. Sometimes I'd feel real cocky and hold it up all the time and the other guy would try to burn me—to make me miss a word. Later, on other ships, the crew was always astonished that I knew signaling as well as I did. They were used to officers who didn't even know the Morse code. I was on this assignment for six months. We would stay out for a few weeks at a time and then get a week off in town. I'd still go down to the Village, where I continued to see Laura Lyons and her friends."

His next assignment toward the middle of 1943 was on a subchaser on coastal patrols out into the Atlantic. He was on several convoys into the North Atlantic. "There was hardly anyone on board over thirty. It was rough out there and the food wasn't much. Hardtack and things like that," Ferlinghetti recalls. "Most of the crew had beards and wore earrings in their ears. When a new recruit came on board the crew would throw him down on deck and pierce his ear— then put an earring in. There would be an earring in the right ear for deck rate and in the left ear for below-deck rate. It was a carry-over from old English Navy days. It was really a rough-looking crew. It was good to be on a ship that didn't have a lot of regulations. I really loved it. And I really loved the sea."

On its first Atlantic crossing the subchaser was put on the deck of a large vessel. In Liverpool it was taken off the larger ship and sailed for Belfast. It stayed there a couple of months waiting for a Norwegian crew. After the crew was assembled, late in 1943, Ferlinghetti was assigned as a special messenger in England. He traveled in first-class compartments on the English trains in a triangle between London, Liverpool, and Glasgow, accompanied by two armed sailors. Often he would be carrying nothing more essential than some expensive scotch whisky. The assignment gave him free time and the chance to cycle all over Devonshire, attend dances in various small towns, and observe firsthand what really amounted to the American occupation of Great Britain. Finally he was transferred back to the United States and assigned to another subchaser.

On his new assignment Ferlinghetti was made skipper and was sent to Norfolk, Virginia, to pick up his ship. When he reported to the commanding officer at the naval yards—a grizzled veteran of many years of service—the commander looked at him as if he had just left home. Ferlinghetti describes himself as "a skinny kid. I'd been on all those convoys and had quite a bit of experience, but I did look quite young." In a gruff voice the veteran sailor asked the new skipper, "What qualifications do you have to take over command of this ship?" Ferlinghetti gave him a rundown of his experience. The commander listened, looked over Ferlinghetti's papers, and finally told him to go down and get the ship. "I don't think he believed I could get the ship out of the harbor. The last guy wasn't able to— he had run it into shore." Ferlinghetti fared better and successfully took the ship into the open sea, out beyond Cape Hatteras. He had thirty sailors and two officers serving under him. "We didn't have any time for saluting. It was another rough crew—but there was a certain amount of discipline. I would climb up the mast to the crow's nest when it was real foggy and shout out orders to the helmsman down below. It was a great experience for people who loved ships." This ship was also sent across the Atlantic on the decks of another freighter in June 1944, not long before the Normandy invasion.

During the war Ferlinghetti had regularly been receiving mail from Plashbourne. Increasingly as the war went on Ferlinghetti noticed that Presley Bisland's handwriting grew more and more shaky. Although most of the letters were typewritten, Presley always signed them by hand and usually added a handwritten personal note. In a letter received in January 1944, Bisland writes on Kensington Plaza Garages, Inc., stationery:

Dear Admiral:

Just a scratch of the pen, my boy, to enclose the two obviously very important letters to you. One from Uncle Sam asking to share your large income with him and the other a V-Mail letter the Madame wrote to you under the date of November 5, 1943, which returned here unsealed, as you will note.

Our hearts were rejoiced and exceedingly glad by your letter of January 13, for we had begun to worry about you, fearing you were out sinking subs, sub-rosa. As it has been a long time since we had received anything informative from you to cheer the old home and fireside . . .

We have everything well in hand at Plashbourne, as since you

left nothing got out of hand that I know of . . .

Cheerio, I'll B'cing you before long I hope with lotions of best wishes from us both, I remain your true friend and well wisher,

General Bisland

Later, in April 1945, Bisland writes:

Admiral,

Sir, the top of the morning to you and the rest of the day to myself . . .

All is serene at Plashbourne, we are enjoying our fair modicum of health and happiness. I assume you are off on a long Cruise and it may be quite awhile before we hear from you again. Let us hear, however, whenever you can, as we are always interested in your welfare . . .

Hoping old Father Neptune will keep a watchful eye on you.

With a Cheerio from us all, I remain, yours for bigger and Better Wars,

General Bisland

The subchaser that Ferlinghetti commanded was let off in Liverpool. "We were given orders for the invasion of Normandy after some preparation. But the weather was so bad, Eisenhower called the fleet back. I remember this small port we were in. It was like in Shakespeare, with soldiers around their campfires waiting silently for orders to be given. There were miles and miles of lorries. Like a whole army piled up. Munition trains—landing craft—all kinds of equipment, and it was all dark because of the blackouts. All these men sitting around. They had this plan so that everybody left at different hours, so they could converge on the beachhead at different hours. Everywhere on the horizon I saw nothing but the ships on the water."

Ferlinghetti's boat was one of the screening vessels for the Normandy invasion, watching for submarines. When the actual invasion came, the subchaser was never really close to the beach. "We saw the last of the Luftwaffe on the beach. We never fired at anyone. We did see one dead soldier close up, floating in the channel. I performed a burial at sea. I took out the Navy manual and read how to do it."

Near the beach a breakwater had been made out of sunken Liberty ships to facilitate landing onshore and the disbursement of equipment. "We were tied up behind this breakwater, things breaking loose all over the place. I got under way, but couldn't get out from the breakwater. I tried to put an anchor down, but first lost one and then another. There was all kinds of debris floating around the water. Loose lumber cables, too. Some kind of cable got wound around one of our screws and then around the other, so the propellers wouldn't work. So two men went over the side and got one free. We started up. We were only a few feet from the beach, and kept getting swept up on it. It was hard to work on the cable because it was the middle of the night. Finally we got the cable off the one screw just at the last minute. The Liberty ships had an island in the back, then a low part, and then the bridge, and then an indentation and then the bow comes up. It was high tide. There was water between the bridge and the stern island. I figured if we were lucky I could go over the ship instead of going all the way around. It was two miles around the breakwater. We could never have made that. So I took the chance and went right over the Liberty ship between the bridge and stern, where water was running over the whole thing, right out to open sea. We were all wrecked up. One engine was fouled up bad. At that time we were under command of the British Admiralty. We sent them a message: 'Both engines broken down, proceeding under sail.' We went on until we came to Plymouth. The sailors jumped off the ship and hit the ground. Actually, they kissed the ground. They really had thought they were goners. Then we were in a shipyard in Cowels, a famous shipyard where a lot of yachts were kept. While the ship was being repaired, I spent most of my time in a hotel in London. London was really something then."

After the invasion got under way, Ferlinghetti's ship was repaired and sent to patrol the coastal waters of France. "We went back to the Normandy beachhead several weeks after we had first been there," he remembers. "We signaled over to a big warship and asked them for some ice cream. They signaled back and asked us what flavor we wanted." It was a real contrast to the life of the foot soldiers who were crawling all across France.

On V-E Day, Ferlinghetti's boat was in Cherbourg. His men had liberty and he and his junior officer, Davy Crane, drove a jeep they had found abandoned down the coast. They were headed for Paris, but along the way the jeep broke down and they had to change their plans.

In the town of Saint-Brieuc in Brittany, Ferlinghetti found a paper tablecloth on which was scrawled a poem. Ferlinghetti took the tablecloth with him. This was his strange introduction to the poet he would later translate and, in turn, introduce to the English-speaking public in 1954 in *City Lights* magazine and later in a City Lights Pocket Poets book *Paroles*. In the introduction to the book Ferlinghetti writes:

"I first came across the poetry of Jacques Prévert written on a paper tablecloth in Saint-Brieuc in 1944. This, so romantic, sentimental circumstance is no doubt at the root of my effort to perpetuate Prévert . . ."

After V-E Day, Ferlinghetti went back on patrol and then to Plymouth. He returned to the States in December 1944 and was assigned as navigator on a large freighter, his first duty on a bigger vessel and one that he didn't particularly enjoy since he was by now accustomed to being in command of his own ship.

The duty itself was taxing since the skipper was inexperienced and kept getting Ferlinghetti up at all hours to take sightings. However, the ship traveled to many interesting ports. It went through the Panama Canal, stopping off in Panama City, and then to several Pacific islands. During the winter of 1945 they brought supplies to American bases at Midway, the Philippines, and other islands. They landed in Japan on the first day of United States occupation of that country. The port was deserted.

Ferlinghetti and several shipmates took a train to Nagasaki, where they saw the aftermath of the atomic bomb, which had been dropped six weeks earlier. The whole town was flat and covered with a mulch. It looked as if the entire area had been run through a blender. The sight was shocking and unforgettable. "You'd see hands sticking out of the mud . . . all kinds of broken teacups . . . hair sticking out of the road—a quagmire—people don't realize how total the destruction was," Ferlinghetti says. What he saw at Nagasaki was indelibly imprinted on his memory.

A few days later the freighter sailed for Portland, Oregon, where Ferlinghetti received his discharge from the Navy.

CHAPTER THREE

AFTER HIS DISCHARGE Ferlinghetti returned to Bronxville. It was good to be home, although part of him continued to probe and question his relationship to his foster parents. He stayed in his old room in Plashbourne. The sprawling stone mansion provided him with the "refuge" he needed while he began looking for a job in Manhattan.

In New York he was caught up by the energy he felt on the streets, and he fantasized working in the newsroom of one of the big papers or magazines. As he went from place to place for interviews, he found that a degree in journalism from outside New York City didn't mean much in Manhattan. In addition, in those postwar years there was plenty of competition for the available jobs both from seasoned journalists who had been serving overseas and from those who had taken their places while they were gone.

Discouraged, Ferlinghetti began to make the rounds of the advertising agencies. He soon decided that he would not fit into the agency world. Finally he was offered a job in the mail room of *Time* magazine. He had hoped to be assigned to the copy reading section but there were no openings, so he took the job he was offered and found himself buried in the basement of the Time-Life Building doing tedious, routine work.

He had found a small apartment in Greenwich Village and every night he pounded out stories he thought the magazine might accept. In fact he gave one of his pieces—a feature about a wino crash pad on the Bowery—to a friend in *Time's* editorial department. That was the last he ever saw of his manuscript.

Chafing from this rejection and worn out after eight months in the mail room job, Ferlinghetti quit. He decided to take advantage of the G.I. Bill of Rights and enrolled at Columbia University Graduate School. During his year and a half at Columbia, he lived in the Village and spent some time in Bronxville.

Presley Bisland died in the summer of 1947. The funeral services were held at the Dutch Reformed Church in Bronxville. After her husband's death Mrs. Bisland grew closer to Ferlinghetti. She was impressed by his decision to continue his education and approved of the methodical way he approached the things he did. Perhaps she recognized some of her husband's wit and humor in her foster son.

Plashbourne continued to be a shelter from the rigors of the city, and although it was still associated for Ferlinghetti with a great many unhappy memories, he now saw it with new, more mature eyes. Occasionally he visited his real mother and his brothers, but never for more than a few hours at a time.

Ferlinghetti was reading the poetry of Marianne Moore and William Carlos Williams, and he continued to buy any new work by E. E. Cummings and Kenneth Patchen, both of whom were living in the Village in the forties. In acknowledging their early influence on him Ferlinghetti says, "They were . . . like a political education for me. Cummings has been passed over by the Beat poets. William Carlos Williams is always mentioned for his American language. Well, Cummings' American language is more colloquial than Williams' was . . . His speech was more American lingo, street talk sometimes. So was Patchen's."

During his first year at Columbia, Ferlinghetti heard about the avant-garde publishing company New Directions, which had been founded by James Laughlin and was publishing much of the new poetry. Friends in the Village pointed out the New Directions Building. "This was the tower of gold as far as I was concerned," he recalls. "New Directions was publishing Ezra Pound and Dylan Thomas. I was reading Thomas then. He was an enormous influence on me. These were the great early days of New Directions. Laughlin published things no one else would touch in his New Classics series."

War novels, such as Norman Mailer's *The Naked and the Dead*, were popular in those days, but Ferlinghetti preferred to read books by Henry Miller, and he continued reading James Joyce, whom he had first come across at Chapel Hill. Miller's reminiscences of his days in Paris and Gertrude Stein's *The Autobiography of Alice B. Toklas*, along with Eliot Paul's novel *The Last Time I Saw Paris*, kindled in Ferlinghetti the increasingly attractive idea of living in Paris. During the time he spent working in the Columbia Library on his thesis, he thought seriously about spending some time there after he got his degree.

By now he had begun reading the poetry of William Butler Yeats. Ferlinghetti had found a copy of Yeats's poems on a seat in the Third Avenue El, and he writes about the experience in "Poem 26" of *Pictures of the Gone World*:

> Reading Yeats I do not think
> of Ireland
> but of midsummer New York
> and of myself back then
> reading that copy I found
> on the Thirdavenue El
> the El
> with its flyhung fans
> and its signs reading
> SPITTING IS FORBIDDEN
> the El
> careening thru its thirdstory world
> with its thirdstory people
> in their thirdstory doors
> looking as if they had never heard
> of the ground
> an old dame
> watering her plant
> or a joker in a straw
> putting a stickpin in his peppermint tie
> and looking just like he had nowhere to go
> but coneyisland

or an undershirted guy

rocking in his rocker

watching the El pass by

as if he expected it to be different

each time

Reading Yeats I do not think

of Arcady

and of its woods which Yeats thought dead

I think instead

of all the gone faces

getting off at midtown places

with their hats and their jobs

and of that lost book I had

with its blue cover and its white inside

where a pencilhand had written

HORSEMAN, PASS BY!

Ferlinghetti had a love/hate relationship with New York City. He wanted to work and live there, but at the same time he was alienated by the traffic and the huge blocks of glass and steel. Though the city drew him by virtue of its great energy, it also drained him. In *A Coney Island of the Mind* he wrote: "that bridge was too much for me," referring to the Brooklyn Bridge. He could never get close to that bridge across the East River the way Henry Miller, Hart Crane, or Federico García Lorca had.

The faculty at Columbia at that time was very distinguished, and Ferlinghetti attended classes in which he was not enrolled just for the chance of listening to and learning from these famous men and women. With their guidance he began expanding his library, still reading slowly, marking passages he particularly liked, and even recording some phrases in his notebooks. Lionel Trilling introduced him to Alfred Kazin's *On Native Grounds*, which includes a detailed section on Thomas Wolfe. Ferlinghetti attended as many of Trilling's classes as he could, as often as five days a week.

Another memorable course—for which Ferlinghetti was not officially enrolled—was Mark Van Doren's class on tragedy and comedy. Van Doren, who had been literary editor of *The Nation* in the twenties, edited several anthologies of verse and won the Pulitzer Prize for poetry in 1939.

Ferlinghetti took William York Tyndall's course on James Joyce and took an extension course from Babette Deutsch, the poet and critic. He attended lectures by Joseph Wood Krutch and by Marjorie Nicholson, who spoke so wittily about seventeenth-century literature that she made it as alive as the contemporary writing in which Ferlinghetti was more passionately interested.

Ferlinghetti's own poetry began to change. New York images appeared in his notebooks. But he was not yet free of the influence of Eliot and Pound. Like many young writers, he was still too self-conscious in his own work to allow himself to break loose from his preconceptions about poetry. It was not until he was in his thirties, with New York and Paris behind him, that he would loosen himself from his past, take himself out of time, and confront whatever it was that made him write in the first place. When that happened, he began to break new ground of his own.

For his thesis topic Ferlinghetti had chosen to explore the relationship between the critic John Ruskin and the painter J. M. W. Turner. "I practically lived in the Columbia Library. It is one of the greatest in the world, and had the Kelmscott editions of John Ruskin. They were enormous volumes, with full color reproductions of Turner's works. Ruskin wrote precise descriptions of the painting and through them described the art world of his time and painting from the early Renaissance on to build Turner's reputation. He showed how light burst off the canvas in Turner's work. As his work progressed, Turner became more obsessed with light until some of his canvases are almost all light. They are similar to some of the abstract expressionist canvases of today."

As his time at Columbia drew to a close, Ferlinghetti made plans to go to Paris, where he wanted to work on a doctorate. His G.I. Bill payments had three more years to run, and so, late in 1947, after receiving his master's degree, he left for France.

CHAPTER FOUR

ERLINGHETTI WENT TO Paris in 1948, eager to understand the city he had yearned to see and searching, even more avidly, for himself. As he later wrote in the novel *Her*, "looking for the main character of my life, blundering along, stopping for an absinthe here, a coffee there, following the daylight ghosts of myself through the continuous landscape, death and resurrection in a tongue alack. Perhaps I was merely a dumb member of the audience strayed onto the stage by mistake." Could he wander into some café in Montparnasse and find his true self there, shorn of all insecurities and ready to forge ahead independently?

Away from the things that were familiar to him, he hoped to decipher his environment. He had to leave his own country in order to be able to see it from a new perspective. He needed to look at himself in a strange land with a different language. Bronxville and Manhattan had long ago yielded themselves up to him, although there still remained in him the remnants of that child who felt constrained by Plashbourne's formality and the stone walls of its gardens.

In Paris what emerged more strongly than ever before was a young man who lived inside himself and continually questioned who and what he was:

> I grew and did not renew myself but grew sad and wrinkled as I was
> my son and I was my Father not known and not forgotten, and then
> I was grown out of school at last in a Brooklyn spring in which the
> odor of patchouli, garlic and stale beer permeated the premises of
> a groaning wooden boarding house . . . I see myself bummed back
> to France and her lost poppy countryside riding the wooden trains,
> back and forth over the autumn country, toothbrush and sketchbook

45

in sack. And ended that year where all the trains end, fell out into
the Gare Montparnasse, and into a pension de famille on the far
side of the Bastille . . .

On his first day in Paris it snowed. He stood near the Tuileries
gardens waiting for the bus to take him out to a part of town near
the Père Lachaise Cemetery, where he had the address of a family
who rented out rooms. Their house was on the Place Voltaire, not
far from Place Bastille. Satchel in hand, he got on the open back of a
bus and soon found himself before the apartment of Edgar Letellier.
His first impression of Letellier was that he looked something like
Ludwig van Beethoven, which was perhaps a cultivated appearance
since Letellier was a teacher of classical music who instructed pupils
in his home. Mme. Letellier, a warmhearted motherly woman, immediately made him feel welcome. There were two daughters not
yet in their teens.

His efforts to improve his French would obviously be helped if he
lived with a French family. He ate most of his dinners with the Letelliers. The table conversation was lively, and although it often dealt
with family matters, his facility with the language rapidly improved.

In the morning Mme. Letellier brought him long slices of French
bread covered with butter and jam and a steaming mug of café au
lait. Often she found him struggling over the manuscript he had begun shortly after he arrived in Paris. He was writing a novel. The
book was heavily influenced by Thomas Wolfe at the beginning.
Gradually the original style Ferlinghetti was starting to carve out for
himself began to emerge.

From the moment of his arrival in Paris he had been keeping in
close contact with Mrs. Bisland, and he continued to correspond
regularly with her during the entire time he stayed there. Three
months after his arrival in France he wrote:

My French improves, by dint of four hours daily in class, and by
living with the French most of the rest of the day. But I am looking
for an apartment of my own since living with a French family costs

too much in proportion to living independently. If one actually finds an apartment at non-black-market rates, it is much much cheaper than hotels or pensions: i.e. about 2500 francs for rent for a month is only about 8 dollars, while I am spending $50 a month for my present lodgings and 2 meals a day. This 2 meals a day is deceiving, however, since one of them is breakfast, consisting solely of coffee and a piece of bread, so that it is necessary to spend more money for extra food. Speaking of food I have received all 3 of the packages I have ordered from Gristede to date, but I have not ordered any more since by the time I pay the postage (which amounts to about 25 percent of the food value) it is more expensive than buying meals in restaurants here. I may be able to finish writing a dissertation (required for the Doctorate here) in French by this September if I don't take any vacation this summer, but I doubt it, since most of the professors will be away for the whole summer and I have to have one professor supervise the work in its various stages. Then, too, I have hardly made a dent in French literature. At present I am translating Flaubert, Proust, and French Romantic poetry, but I am most interested at the moment in my novel in English, which I have now extended to over 10,000 words. The novel contest I spoke of before requires, I find, 20,000 words, instead of 10,000, plus a full synopsis, so that I have a long way to go on it . . . The vitamin tablets have not yet arrived. . . . I am sorry that I have come to the end of the page without getting off the subject of myself. I hope you are well again, and that no trouble will develop. My very best to everyone. . . . Affectionately as ever,

Lawrence

Just one week later, he wrote:

I have just finished copying the first 10,000 words of my novel, after recently receiving the actual facts of the contest from Doubleday Doran, via Justine Krug in Bronxville, who first wrote me about it. (The minimum number of words to be turned in is not

10 but 20,000 plus a complete synopsis of the rest of the novel, and there is no deadline, so that I am well-started and have plenty of time.) As for the idea of getting an "immediate" income from it, that is not my plan at all, since it is not *now* that I need money, but in about a year. . . . Thank you so much for going down to Columbia for my diploma, which must be very handsome. If you happened to see Philosophy Hall, that's where I went to class all that year. . . . Glad to hear that you are much better and that everyone at home is well, although whatever is wrong with "Sally's foot" I can't imagine from your letter. Maybe it needs a new shoe. I can find no aches, pains, ailments, abridgments, aberrations, or annihilations of my own anatomy to mention, and if I have foot trouble at all it would be probably from always putting it in my mouth. (Joke)

> Affectionately yours,
> Lawrence

Doubleday did not award the book a prize, but he did interest an agent in the novel. She sent it off to Simon & Schuster. The book was called *The Way of Dispossession*, a title taken from a line in T. S. Eliot's *Four Quartets*. He had read the poem in 1943 and kept it with him, constantly referring to some of his favorite lines, which included, from the "East Coker" segment of *Four Quartets*:

In order to arrive at what you do not know
        You must go by a way which is the way of ignorance
In order to possess what you do not possess
        You must go by the way of dispossession

Thirty years later Ferlinghetti would conceive the idea of writing a poem in four parts, each one of extended length, and modeling the project after *Four Quartets*.

Unfortunately Simon & Schuster rejected the book. In a letter to Mrs. Bisland, Ferlinghetti wrote: . . . it is just 50,000 words, but being (as it is) an 'interior monologue,' it is necessarily limited in length. However, this is just long enough for the new genre of novel which I am writing."

In fact, this description could be applied to *Her*, which Ferlinghetti started making notes for the following year, taking time off from his thesis.

During the winter in which he worked on *The Way of Dispossession*, Ferlinghetti met George Whitman, who was later to found the Mistral Bookshop in Paris. The store would take the name of the old Shakespeare and Company bookstore, founded by Sylvia Beach. Throughout the post–World War I period, Beach's place had been the gathering place for poets, artists, novelists, and intellectuals, offering a refuge to visiting writers, championing new books, and helping to set the tone for the literary life of that time. Sylvia Beach knew Ernest Hemingway, Ezra Pound, and James Joyce. In fact, she was the publisher of the first edition of *Ulysses*. When Whitman opened his store, he tried to carry on in the tradition of Sylvia Beach. Throughout the 1960s and '70s many visiting writers stopped in at Whitman's store. The poets and writers of the Beat Generation, Ginsberg, Corso, Burroughs, and Ferlinghetti himself, stopped in when they were visiting Paris.

Ferlinghetti had known George Whitman's sister at Columbia and she had told him about her brother's eccentricities, but he was not prepared for what he found when he visited Whitman's apartment for the first time. The place was tiny—there was hardly room for a bed and a small pathway to it—and the room was filled with books, which took up most of the floor and wall space. Like Ferlinghetti, Whitman was living on the G.I. Bill, which included a generous book allowance. He augmented his library further by judiciously selling and swapping books at the Sorbonne.

The two men became friends, and in the spring of 1948 with several others they took a trip into the French countryside. They traveled to Le Touquet, a seaside town near Bologne; to Amiens; to Baume; and to several other villages and towns. Ferlinghetti left the group after a few weeks in order to visit a family in the country town of Poix. As he wrote Mrs. Bisland: "I met a very charming family in

Poix . . . M. Rameau is a kind of squire who seems to spend most of his time riding to hounds, as they say in England, while Madame Rameau seems very much a lady. They plied me with hospitality and champagne and sent me off to Paris with preserves and butter (unobtainable in Paris) . . ."

Following this journey to the country, Ferlinghetti gave a report to Mrs. Bisland on the postwar condition of some of the churches she had seen on her own earlier tours of France:

> Travel notes: Chartres Cathedral is intact; Amiens cathedral is intact except for a window or two, although the buildings all around it are bombed out; Rouen is a ruin—the cathedral itself is half-destroyed, all the stained-glass is gone, though the great 465 ft. iron spire still remains—the Church of St. Ouen in Rouen is practically intact, although over half of its stained glass is gone—this church is more beautiful than the cathedral and is really much better Gothic—but you would hardly recognize Rouen—all along the Seine is a shambles.

Ferlinghetti was thinking of leaving the Letelliers during the summer of 1948, but because he was reluctant to give up the opportunity of daily French conversation with them, he did not leave until fall. He continued working on his novel and began a series of poems written in cantos—after Ezra Pound—and entitled *Palimpsest*. Ferlinghetti had come across a book by that name in a Paris bookshop. The author was the poet Hilda Doolittle, known as H.D., and her book had been published in an edition of seven hundred copies in 1926. A "palimpsest" is a parchment from which one writing has been erased to make room for another. Ferlinghetti's *Palimpsest* was a collection of poems that formed a kind of survey of his life to date, using very little of the pictorial imagery that marks his later work.

In the late summer of 1948, on a trip to Provence, he first came across the poems of René Char. He documents the occasion in "Poem 4" of *Pictures of the Gone World*:

In Paris in a loud dark winter
                    when the sun was something in
                                        Provence
        when I came upon the poetry
                        of René Char
            I saw Vaucluse again
                        in a summer of sauterelles
        its fountains full of petals
                    and its river thrown down
    through all the burnt places
                    of that almond world
and the fields full of silence
                    though the crickets sang
            with their legs
                    And in the poet's plangent dream I saw
    no Lorelei upon the Rhone
                        nor angels debarked at Marseilles
but couples going nude into the sad water
                            in the profound lasciviousness
            in an algebra of lyricism
                        which I am still deciphering

At the end of the summer, Ferlinghetti spent a few weeks with the Letelliers in their thatch-roofed cottage on an island in Brittany. Then he returned to Paris to arrange to move to his own place.

He found an old apartment in the basement of 89 Rue de Vaugirard in Montparnasse. Ferlinghetti thought it was like a cave with its two rooms and a kitchen beneath street level. Since the rent was only twenty-six dollars for the entire year, he felt he could stay there forever even though it was damp and dark and infested with vermin.

Because the apartment was situated only ten blocks from the Boulevard St. Germain and close to the Sorbonne, Ferlinghetti felt that he was living in "Hemingway country," the legendary area of old-time bohemians and post–World War I expatriates. Only a few blocks away was the Café Dôme, where Hemingway had spent so much time when he lived in Paris.

For a while Ferlinghetti shared the apartment with Ivan Cousins, an old Navy friend with whom he had also lived briefly in New York, while working for *Time* magazine. They had become friends at midshipmen's school in Chicago, had graduated together, and had both been sent to the Staten Island naval base. The two spent a lot of time together, and Ferlinghetti even took Ivan to Plashbourne. While Ferlinghetti was overseas, Ivan often visited the Bislands and he corresponded with them.

Cousins was living in Alaska when he received the letter from Ferlinghetti that painted an intriguing portrait of life in Paris and included an invitation to share the apartment on the Rue de Vaugirard. He quickly decided to join Ferlinghetti in France. Although he had no literary ambitions, he was drawn to the excitement of Paris and decided to use his G.I. Bill money to live there for a while.

Ferlinghetti met Cousins at the Gare St. Lazare on his arrival in October 1948. They immediately sped through the streets of the Left Bank, headed for the Café Deux Magots. "When I got off the train," Cousins recollects, "Ferlinghetti told me that I looked French. It was because I was wearing a blue shirt, very popular in Paris then. In the café, as he went on and on about what I had to see, I watched the cathedral across the street swaying up and down. I felt as if I were still aboard ship . . . Our rooms on the Rue de Vaugirard were very cold, and we kept a continuous pot-au-feu going on the stove. Ferlinghetti once added chocolate, ruining the dish . . . Our concierge looked upon us as Communists and treated us badly." If they came home after 10 p.m. they had to wait hours for the concierge to open the gates of the house for them.

In January 1949, Ferlinghetti wrote to Mrs. Bisland, addressing her in a new, affectionate way:

Dear Mother Bisland

I had the intention to write a longer letter this week, but I am in danger of writing no letter at all, so I will get this off . . . Hope all is going better for you since I last heard . . . Ivan is doing much of nothing, since he has not found a position as yet. In fact, he doesn't like Paris. This is mostly because of the lack of creature-comforts. I doubt whether he stays here later than this spring. I myself am coming along very well with my thesis, but it is a big subject and requires extensive reading of all modern poetry . . . I have not received Delia's package as yet, but intend writing her soon . . . With best wishes and thoughts to everyone.

Affectionately, Lawrence

For his thesis, "La Cité: Symbole dans la poesie moderne: À la recherche d'une Tradition Metropolitaine" (The City as a Symbol in Modern Poetry: In Search of a Metropolitan Tradition), Ferlinghetti read hundreds of texts, concentrating on T. S. Eliot's *The Waste Land*; Hart Crane's *The Bridge*; Mayakovsky's poem on the Brooklyn Bridge; Federico García Lorca's *The Poet in New York*; Whitman's *Leaves of Grass*; and other poetry by more obscure writers. He also read *City of Dreadful Night*, by Francis Thompson, and *The Tentacular City*, by French-Belgian poet Verhaeren. From a deep interest in Ezra Pound and T. S. Eliot and other American poets, he had gone on to search through all of world literature, not only for the thesis, but also for work that would assist his own development as a poet. In a very few years he would find in San Francisco that the poets there, far from being provincial, had kept in touch with contemporary world literature, as he had done in his Paris days.

The entire French capital was a school for Ferlinghetti. He might have finished the work on his thesis much earlier than he did, but his wide range of interests kept him from working on it steadily. In later years, when he was being interviewed about the past, he would often say that his thesis was called "Le Pissoir dans la littérature française." He did take it seriously, and yet his time was mostly taken up by his poetry, prose, and daily explorations of the city.

His notebooks were full of varying topics—perhaps suitable for a series of lectures—that interested him. A recurrent theme was the city. His thesis bibliography, with its urban poets, reflected his growing interest in the urban landscape. Even some of the people and places he knew and saw in New York City were finding their way into his Parisian notebooks. Later they would become a part of the poetry he wrote in San Francisco. He was interested in the varied responses poets had to the same terrain, some seeing life and hope in the city where others saw death and destruction. Several of Ferlinghetti's poems can be classified as city poems, which take a particular city as their theme. "London cross figured creeping with trams" and "midsummer New York and of myself back then reading that copy I found on the Third avenue El, the El with its flyhung fan and its sign reading SPITTING IS FORBIDDEN." City imagery laces Ferlinghetti's mature work and has become an abiding part of his poetic vision.

Proudly he wrote "Mother Bisland" about his progress both in his writing and at the Sorbonne. Presley Bisland certainly would have applauded his efforts. It was as if Ferlinghetti had inherited Bisland's own love of education and literature.

As he worked on the thesis, Ferlinghetti began to study Catholicism, an interest that developed as he toured the many cathedrals and churches of Paris. He read Thomas Aquinas and other Catholic thinkers and got to know a priest with whom he would argue almost weekly for a long period of time about Catholic doctrine. Much of his mature poetry reflects the arguments that raced through his mind back then.

Ferlinghetti became more serious about his painting and his poetry than he had ever been, finding in both forms of expression a strong outlet for all his emotions. His Sorbonne pass got him into most of the city's theaters at a low price and into the museums free. He discovered Picasso, La Comédie Française, and the mimes of Paris, and he was exposed to the new European writing. Years later he translated his appreciation of the avant-garde European writing into action when, as publisher of City Lights Books, he was one of the first to make these writers available to American readers.

Without registering, Ferlinghetti attended two different art schools that had what was called a "free studio." He simply walked off the streets carrying his own drawing materials and joined the other students as they painted from models.

Ferlinghetti summed up some of the interests he developed during that period in this passage from *Her*:

> . . . pausing briefly for the absorption of Jean-Paul Sartre and his flies, and Albert Camus and his rebels, and James Joyce and his blooms, and Pablo Picasso and his harlequins and horses and blueplates and Guernicas and doves, and Céline with Henry Miller in his pocket, and Fernand Léger with feet caught in a machine, and Antonin Artaud and his mother, and René Char and his bad boys, and Michael Mourre and his dead God in an Easter pulpit, and Marc Chagall on his horse, and Samuel Beckett and his unnamable selves, and their ranks further augmented by hundreds if not thousands of holdout members of underground Resistance movements, hundreds if not thousands of Maquis who had still hidden waiting for decades in backstreet caves all over the Left Bank, waiting for the true Liberation that they still believed had yet to arrive . . .

The work on his thesis—which was written in French—inspired Ferlinghetti to greater effort on his own poetry. But as the deadline approached, he began to spend most of his time in his apartment or at the Sorbonne Library. After the written thesis was submitted, there was an oral defense conducted by a panel of three professors in a lecture hall. The examination was open to the public, and several of Ferlinghetti's friends, including George Whitman, were in the audience to lend their support. All went well for a while, and Ferlinghetti was feeling quite confident that he was defending his thesis competently when he suddenly gave a poor translation of some lines from *The Waste Land*. One of the professors inquired sternly, "How can you make such an error?"

"I'd like to quote an old French adage," replied Ferlinghetti:

"*Une traduction c'est comme une femme. Quand elle est belle, elle n'est pas fidèle. Quand elle est fidèle, elle nest pas belle.*" (A translation is like a woman. When she is beautiful, she is not faithful. When she is faithful, she is not beautiful.) The audience burst out laughing and Ferlinghetti was awarded his degree.

CHAPTER FIVE

I N 1949, FERLINGHETTI went to America for a two-week visit
with Mrs. Bisland. It turned out to be the last time he saw her.
One day they drove out of town to the cemetery where Presley Bisland was buried and they talked about the old days at Plashbourne.
Ferlinghetti's attachment to Mr. Bisland and his fond memories of
the old man overcame the residual sadness he always felt when he
returned to the big house and to his room with its familiar furniture and the beautiful view of the gardens.

During this visit Ferlinghetti felt strongly that Mrs. Bisland was his
"real family." Although he saw his mother briefly, he found he had
little to share with her. Mrs. Bisland was still the regal Victorian ma-
triarchal figure she had always been. Her natural reserve continued
to keep Ferlinghetti at arm's length while he yearned for some kind
of emotional confrontation. In spite of that, Ferlinghetti felt closer
to his foster mother than he had ever been.

In 1952, two years after Mrs. Bisland died, he dreamed that his
wife had a child and that the first word it uttered was "Bisland." This
dream, along with several others in which Anna and Presley Bisland
appeared, was recorded in his journal.

On the ship that brought him back to France after his visit to
Bronxville, Ferlinghetti met Selden Kirby-Smith. Kirby, as she was
called, a graduate of Swarthmore College and Columbia, where she
had written her master's thesis on D. H. Lawrence in America, a
subject that interested Ferlinghetti greatly and which was the basis
of many of their first conversations on board ship.

In Paris, Ferlinghetti and Kirby began to see quite a lot of each
other, although they did not live together. Ferlinghetti introduced
her to the Left Bank people of the Café Mabillon and the other

St. Germain gathering places he frequented. He took her to the Comédie Française, and when she had been in Paris only a week he suggested that they go to his friend Marie Ponsot's house to have her portrait done by Claude Ponsot, Marie's future husband.

It turned out that Kirby had been in some of the same classes Ferlinghetti took at Columbia. She even described the tweed jacket that he used to wear to Lionel Trilling's class and the intense way his eyes followed Trilling as he moved about in front of the class. Kirby told him they also shared Marjorie Nicholson's class in seventeenth-century literature. "I had wanted to meet Lawrence at Columbia," she said later. "The occasion never arose."

In the summer of 1950, Ferlinghetti vacationed at Puerto de Andraitx, a small fishing village near Palma, Majorca. On the way he stopped in Madrid and went to the Prado and other museums. He was particularly impressed by the paintings of the great Spanish artist Sarolla, and he later wrote:

> Sarolla's women in their picture hats
> stretched upon his canvas beaches
>   beguiled the Spanish Impressionists
>   And were they fraudulent pictures
> of the world
>   the way the light played on them
>   creating illusions
>   of love?

He rented a beach house with two friends and Kirby came down for several weeks.

Inspired by Henry Miller's *The Colossus of Maroussi*, with its vivid descriptions of life in Greece, Ferlinghetti had planned to see Greece for himself that summer but he never got farther than Majorca. Ferlinghetti recalls: "I met someone who said I could buy a boat in Majorca. I didn't really have much money, but the idea was in me to get a boat and then go on to Greece. Once I was there I decided it was so beautiful that I'd stay awhile. I never did get the boat, but I did meet an old lady who wanted me to sail this old Bristol lumber schooner she had. I was to be the one-man crew that would take her to Rome. But that didn't happen either."

In Majorca, Ferlinghetti wrote most of his *Palimpsest* manuscript, which is full of allusions to the sea and to the fishing village in which he was vacationing. He continued to work on *Palimpsest* off and on during his remaining time in Paris. The manuscript, unpublished, still lies buried in his box of journals and notes. It provides a poetic record of his time in Paris as well as an indication of how his style of writing was developing.

There was a part of him that wanted to remain in Paris even after he received his degree from the Sorbonne, but his restlessness, his desire for new experiences, and a feeling that he had gone as far as he could, creatively, in his present environment finally convinced him to leave. While living in Paris he had finished one novel, written a series of poems, and was at work on another novel, *Her*. As he had hoped, like other expatriates he came to grips with his feelings towards his own country while abroad. Gertrude Stein once said that she didn't understand America until she came to Paris and had lived there for a while. Henry Miller found Europe a good proving ground for his own strong ideas about the United States. It was only after he returned home after living for several years in Paris that he was able to write *The Air-Conditioned Nightmare*, a journey through the Central States from east to west.

Similarly, Ferlinghetti had to play himself off against his native land. The vision of America he had found in *Look Homeward, Angel* remained with him, but he had, in fact, seen very little of America with his own eyes. Later, when he had been back in the States for a while, he would compare New York, Baltimore, and other cities he visited with Paris. Now, although he longed to return home, he could not imagine life without cafés, the red wine, the French bread, the camaraderie he had found in Paris. From what he had been told, he felt that San Francisco might offer a similar atmosphere, so although he had never been there, he decided to go to that new, still unknown yet potentially exciting city.

Ferlinghetti returned to America in December 1950, and Kirby arrived in New York about ten days later. They had decided to marry. Together they went to Baltimore, where they spent the night at the home of Ferlinghetti's brother Harry. There Ferlinghetti saw his mother, who was very withdrawn and shy and spoke only a few words. He also saw his brother Clement, who was, by then, retired from the New York prison system and was warden of a Maryland boys reformatory. Clement and he had little to say to each other. It was a meeting of strangers. Only when Ferlinghetti and Kirby spoke about their wedding plans did his mother display any interest.

Ferlinghetti never saw his mother again; Clemence died a year later. Their short encounter had little recognizable impact on him. So much had been buried and forgotten. His mother had been unable to speak to her sons about her own background, and it was not until a decade after her death that Ferlinghetti met some of his mother's relatives and finally came somewhat closer to the woman who bore him.

Kirby took a train from Baltimore to Jacksonville to stay with her family until the wedding, and Ferlinghetti left for the West Coast. As the Union Pacific's *California Zephyr* moved through the land, Ferlinghetti looked out the window, seeing, for the first time, his native American earth. He made no notes on the trip except for a description of a fellow passenger, a woman in her fifties who never stopped talking. Only when he arrived in San Francisco did he begin to describe the environment. He wrote that he saw the "Coitus Tower of San Francisco," a prominent landmark rising from Telegraph Hill in North Beach, which is easily visible far out in San Francisco's Bay.

Ferlinghetti's first few months in town were a blur of impressions. He traveled around the city exploring Chinatown, the Italian neighborhood, and the other colorful areas of the city, noting that although everything was compressed into a relatively small geographical space, it seemed, somehow, uncrowded. He felt comfortable in San Francisco and was convinced almost immediately that he had made the right choice in deciding to live there.

Kirby and Ferlinghetti were married on April 10, 1951, in Jacksonville, Florida. Ivan Cousins was Ferlinghetti's only guest, but Kirby's side of the family was well represented. Cousins felt awkward among the strangers, but he was happy to see Ferlinghetti again. It was not until several years later, when Ivan and his wife moved to San Francisco, that the two old friends were reunited.

After a two-week honeymoon at a fishing lodge owned by Kirby's mother at Lake Geneva, Florida, the newlyweds went to San Francisco. They rented an apartment owned by a Parisian woman, Germaine Schmidt, who operated a music school in the same building. Germaine was a congenial landlady. She added a little touch of Paris to their American home, and Ferlinghetti never tired of talking French to her, particularly when the subject was Paris or some aspect of French culture. Through her Kirby and Ferlinghetti met many members of San Francisco's French community.

Ferlinghetti devoted his time to working on translations of Prévert and on his novel *Her*. He also began to write art criticism for the *Art Digest* (later *Arts Digest*), an influential journal published in New York. The magazine featured art news from different areas of the country, and Ferlinghetti was responsible for the "newsletter" from San Francisco. His assignments—to cover art exhibits in San Francisco—put him in touch with the works of abstract expressionists working in the city at that time, and he got to know the painters themselves. The *Art Digest* paid Ferlinghetti only twenty-five dollars monthly for his reviews, but the pieces he wrote were short and the exposure in this rather prestigious cultural magazine was important to him.

In one of his first San Francisco reports, Ferlinghetti described an exhibition by Henri Michaux. Although Ferlinghetti had read Michaux's poetry, he had never seen any of his paintings. He was extremely interested in the fact that Michaux, a well-established poet, was also working as a painter. In the Michaux exhibit Ferlinghetti recognized that the poet was struggling to solve some of the problems he was trying to solve in his own work. He wrote: "The poetry of Henri Michaux has always been as much a necessary act of audacity, as much an attack on the 'congealed and established' as the statue of the Mannekin Pis which stands symbolically relieving itself in a street in Michaux's native Belgium. For this reason an exhibition of painting by Michaux such as the recent one at the Oakland Art Museum is one of curious interest."

Ferlinghetti found San Francisco to be a cosmopolitan city, as exciting as Paris and as up-to-date as New York. The pioneers of abstract expressionism were as hard at work there as on the East Coast. The exhibits Ferlinghetti covered reflected the fact that West Coast artists were bold experimenters, and the exhibits were harbingers of the later cultural ferment in which he was to play such an important role. All over the city art galleries flourished, museum exhibits were crowded, and experimental film events drew enthusiastic audiences. It was an extraordinarily exciting cultural environment in which to live.

Ferlinghetti was greatly influenced by the abstract expressionists. All his adult life he had been deeply interested in modern art, and it had a special impact on his poetry. While he was attending the Sorbonne, Ferlinghetti became acquainted with the work of Pierre Soulages, whose bold canvases started him thinking about new ways to present a poem on the written page. When he returned to the States he continued to be preoccupied with this idea. The bold black-and-white painting of Franz Kline, who helped pioneer New York's open-form art movement ("open-form" was just another way to describe abstract expressionism), seemed to Ferlinghetti to be related to this subject, and as he covered the art scene in San Francisco for *Art Digest,* he continued to concern himself with how the written word could be related to the new movements in painting. Many of the San Francisco artists Ferlinghetti met had taught at the California School of Fine Arts, not far from North Beach. Among these was Mark Rothko, who had come to San Francisco on a visit from New York during the 1940s. He and other New York artists helped encourage the development of the new West Coast movements in art. The West Coast painters included Clyfford Still, whose original style developed out of his courage to explore even beyond the new frontiers of art. Mark Tobey, who had once studied in the Orient, combined occidental art with Chinese calligraphy in a style that had an important influence on other painters. He often spoke of reaching higher states of consciousness in his paintings, and he was interested in the affinity between painting and music. Morris Graves, who like Tobey looked toward the Orient for inspiration, was fascinated with Zen Buddhism and with the simplicity of Chinese painting. Ferlinghetti wrote a poem about a Graves exhibit. It is included in *A Coney Island of the Mind*. It begins:

The wounded wilderness of Morris Graves
    is not the same wild west
            the white man found
It is a land that Buddha came upon
          from a different direction
It is a wild white nest
      in the true mad north
         of introspection
  where "falcons of the inner eye"
         dive and die
    glimpsing in their dying fall
      all life's memory
      of existence

Like the poets, the San Francisco painters were moving deep into their experiences, on various levels of consciousness, refusing to remain static and keeping independent of the artistic establishment. Ferlinghetti was impressed by the daring and clarity of emotion that these artists were able to express in their work. His contact with the art world encouraged him to rent a studio where he could further develop his own painting. The studio, located in an aged French-style building on the San Francisco waterfront, not far from the Ferry building, had belonged to Hassel Smith, another San Francisco painter. It had a view of the Bay and was heated by an old wood stove. Ferlinghetti spent several days a week there painting and writing.

He was obsessed with the idea that "style is a feeling for the weight and arrangement of words on a page." He wanted to learn how to put his poems on the page to achieve the maximum effect. His concern was for a pictorial perception formed by the printed word. He wanted to arrange the poem so that the way it *looked* helped express the message. Like the artists, he was looking for new visual forms. Instead of working from the left-hand margin and dividing the poem into stanzas, each word or group of words was to be placed on the page according to the poem's mood or meaning. He wanted to move the words around the page, to convey meaning through that movement. There were to be no commas, periods, or semicolons. The eye—unencumbered by punctuation marks—was meant to pause as the line was broken. A good example of this is "Poem 1" from *Pictures of the Gone World*. It is his first complete San Francisco poem, identified by Ferlinghetti as a North Beach poem. It was written in an apartment on Chestnut Street. As with many houses in the city, perched as they were on hillsides, there was a view of San Francisco Bay and of the rooftops of much of North Beach.

> Away above a harborful
>   of caulkless houses
> among the charley noble chimneypots
>   of a rooftop rigged with clotheslines
>   a woman pastes up sails
>   upon the wind
> hanging out her morning sheets
>   with wooden pins
>   O lovely mammal
>   her nearly naked teats
>   throw taut shadows
>   when she stretches up
> to hang at last the last of her
>   so white washed sins
>   but it is wetly amorous
>   and winds itself about her
>   clinging to her skin
>   So caught with arms upraised
>   she tosses back her head

                    in voiceless laughter
and in choiceless gesture then
                        shakes out gold hair
while in the reachless seascape spaces
                      between the blown white shrouds
stand out the bright steamers
                    to kingdom come . . .

His involvement in the art world also led to Ferlinghetti's first encounter with the forces of political reaction. In 1955 a battle developed over the murals of the painter Anton Refregier, who was known for his left-wing politics. When the murals were first commissioned by the Roosevelt administration and when they were unveiled at San Francisco's Rincon Annex Post Office in 1948, there was little adverse comment. In the early fifties, the political climate had changed drastically, and with the growing influence of McCarthyism, attacks on the murals gradually began to build up into a real storm of protest. Most of the criticism centered on the mural entitled "War and Peace," which included the flag of the Soviet Union among those of other nations. Under the onslaught of the criticism Refregier said that the inspiration for the mural had been a U.S. Treasury Department poster that had been used in War Bond drives. But the criticism continued. From May 1949 to July 1951, letters and resolutions of protest came from the American Legion, the Veterans of Foreign Wars, the Society of Western Artists, and others. Using such brave phrases as "definitely subversive" and "designed to spread Communistic propaganda," the protests charged that "the murals do not truly depict the romance and glory of early California history."

Ferlinghetti wrote in rebuttal that the murals with their portraits of "Indians, conquistadores, padres, nuns, miners, railroad and ship workers, businessmen, vigilantes, soldiers, patriots, judges, earthquake and riot victims, bridge builders, and builders of the United Nations . . . spoke out so blatantly that many different groups of citizens were aroused."

In 1955 the battle for removal of the murals surfaced again, with a congressional resolution sponsored by a California congressman calling for the removal of all twenty-nine panels. The resolution cited twenty-three instances of Refregier's association with Communist organizations or organizations of "fellow travelers." Ferlinghetti wrote that "it was all too evident then that the murals had become the latest battleground of intellectual and artistic censorship." A Committee for the Defense of the Refregier Murals was in the process of being formed. After a while the furor died down, however, and the murals remain to this day in the post office.

Earlier, Ferlinghetti had found himself the target of similar reactionary opinions. In the summer of 1952 he had taught two courses at the University of San Francisco, at that time a conservative Catholic institution. In a class on Shakespeare's sonnets, Ferlinghetti delivered a lecture of Shakespeare's alleged homosexuality. He was permitted to complete the summer's assignment, but he was not rehired, a fact he didn't regret since teaching did not sustain his interest. While enjoying the preparation of the lectures, he did not really like the role of instructor. He was so deeply involved in his painting and his poetry that the academic life simply interfered with his own work. So one of the shortest academic careers in history was ended.

Ferlinghetti's involvement in political causes, in combating the forces of reaction, was just beginning.

CHAPTER SIX

WHILE FERLINGHETTI WAS working for the *Art Digest* he began to write book reviews for the *San Francisco Chronicle*. Joseph Henry Jackson, the book review editor, asked him to concentrate on reviewing new books of poetry. Although he wasn't paid for these reviews, he enjoyed the work. "I consider criticism a secondary form of creation, but also an interesting one," Ferlinghetti has stated. In addition to reviewing books, Ferlinghetti occasionally wrote a piece about the San Francisco literary scene. In one of these he described a new kind of cultural event, poets reading their own poetry in front of an audience. His most extensive review of this sort was about Dylan Thomas's second San Francisco reading, in 1952. Thomas spent some time in Henri Lenoir's Vesuvio Café in North Beach, drinking and holding forth before and after his poetry reading. Ferlinghetti wrote, "There is no one like Dylan Thomas in modem poetry today," and gave a vivid description of his legendary style of reading.

Ferlinghetti wrote for several other publications, although not on a regular basis. In one review that appeared in *Counterpoint* magazine Ferlinghetti described a Kenneth Patchen reading that referred to Patchen's incredible "presence" and compared his reading to that of Dylan Thomas. A journal entry noted:

> A quiet man walked into the room and started reading. He read very slowly. He looked up very seldom. He read for a long time. This man was Kenneth Patchen reading his poetry. The room was a room in a museum, The San Francisco Museum of Art . . . When Dylan Thomas was at the museum last year, he said there were only two kinds of poetry—loud and soft. Kenneth Patchen's poetry

at the museum was both loud and soft. Henry Miller once said,
"The first thing one would remark on meeting Kenneth Patchen
is that he is the living symbol of protest." . . . As Patchen read at
the museum, the impression was the same: the anger and the light
came out—loud and soft, loud words in a quiet voice.

Ferlinghetti admired Patchen as a man who had resisted affiliation
with any of the schools of poetry. He had remained uncompromis-
ingly independent of trends and groups, although he paid heavily for
this independence. The academic world virtually ignored him. After
Patchen's death, in 1972, Ferlinghetti recalled that Stanford University and the other colleges in the area where Patchen had spent his last
years never recognized his presence. Ferlinghetti thought that Patch-
en's social protest poetry, his pacifist poems written during World
War II, and his explicit love poetry were too radical for the academic
world. Luckily for Patchen and his readers, James Laughlin of New
Directions kept most of Patchen's poetry and his short stories, novels,
and prose in print. Patchen was another painter-poet. New Directions
published a series of painted books by Patchen, and many of his other
works were illustrated with his sketches and drawings.

Ferlinghetti met Patchen in 1952. The older poet kept his distance
and made Ferlinghetti feel like a student in the presence of a great
master. "Patchen was difficult to get along with, and he always had a
young poet as a kind of messenger boy . . . some guy who was in love
with his poetry and who was willing to go around running his errands."

Patchen lived for a time with the printer David Ruff, who produced a limited edition of Patchen's work, and with Holly Beye,
who had been at Swarthmore with Kirby Ferlinghetti. They lived
in several North Beach lodgings. When, in 1956, Ferlinghetti published Patchen in the Pocket Poets Series, he chose some of the
poems he had known well since the early forties that he felt best
reflected the poet's wide-ranging style.

Holly Beye and David Ruff introduced Ferlinghetti to Kenneth
Rexroth, to whom Ferlinghetti was immediately attracted. The
older poet was involved in a nonstop commentary on American

culture that always emphasized the unity of the arts and the importance of total involvement, something Ferlinghetti had always espoused himself.

Rexroth was born in South Bend, Indiana, and had spent much of his youth in Chicago. He was a part of the Chicago Renaissance, a literary movement made up of such writers as Carl Sandburg, Edgar Lee Masters, Vachel Lindsay, Ben Hecht, and Maxwell Bodenheim, lasting from around 1912 to 1923. He attended the Chicago Art Institute, the New School for Social Research in New York, and the Art Students' League. Rexroth had also been a farmworker and a factory hand, as well as a conscientious objector during World War II. His first book of poetry, *In What Hour*, was published in 1941.

Since coming to San Francisco, Rexroth had been the focal point of a group of poets, painters, and other artists who regularly met at his house. In a real sense he helped an entire generation of San Francisco writers find their own identity. Older than many of the new writers, he was sympathetic to their aims and ready to teach. Rexroth became the guiding spirit—a creative father figure—for this new generation of poets, who later became known as the poets of the San Francisco Poetry Renaissance.

Ferlinghetti attended the evenings at Rexroth's house. He says, "I was very timid in those days, and I must have gone for a couple of years to his house without ever daring to open my mouth . . ." He learned a lot, nonetheless, just by listening to the poets, artists, filmmakers, and political activists. The atmosphere was charged with Rexroth's personality. He seemed to know everyone, and could rattle off names and schools, movements, and trends. Within the space of minutes he could cover an incredible number of subjects, and he was truly knowledgeable. In addition he loved San Francisco passionately. He looked on the rest of the country as a ruined landscape in need of immediate and vast repair, and was happy to view the world from the vantage point of the city on the Bay, which he could see from the window of his house.

Rexroth's gatherings brought Ferlinghetti in touch with most of the San Francisco–Berkeley poets. He met Thomas Parkinson,

Philip Lamantia, and James Broughton there. Parkinson was a Berkeley poet who taught at the University of California. Lamantia was a native San Franciscan whose poetry had been praised by André Breton, the French surrealist. Broughton was a California poet and filmmaker.

It was at Rexroth's that Ferlinghetti met Robert Duncan, whom he liked immediately. "He is a man of enormous intellect. I believe he has the finest ear of any poet around, and he is a brilliant talker," was Ferlinghetti's assessment of Duncan. Duncan also had gatherings at his home, not far from Ferlinghetti's apartment, at which he read his poems and expounded, like Rexroth, on a wide range of subjects. Like Rexroth too he was a fascinating raconteur and was knowledgeable about painting and the other arts. His insights into Gertrude Stein, Ezra Pound, William Carlos Williams, and H.D. were profound. Ferlinghetti didn't share Duncan's enthusiasm for Charles Olson and Robert Creeley, but they agreed about the merits of the poetry of Denise Levertov, and Ferlinghetti eventually published the first collection of her work.

Most of all Ferlinghetti admired the older writers, Rexroth, Patchen, and Henry Miller, for their independence and their refusal to be classified. He became, in a sense, their spiritual godson, receiving from each of them an aspect of his literary, political, and social education. He was gratified later to be able to publish the two Kenneths. Miller, to whom he wrote frequently, never gave him a manuscript.

While Ferlinghetti was still teaching at the university, he and Kirby moved into an apartment on Chestnut Street that had belonged to Gordon Onslow-Ford, an artist associated with the California School of Fine Arts, now known as the San Francisco Art Institute. In his journals Ferlinghetti refers to Chestnut Street as the "Rue de Seine" of San Francisco. It was here that he began to write his "painter-poems."

After settling into his new apartment, Ferlinghetti began to send poems to a North Beach magazine called *City Lights*, a title that had attracted him because the name of this new popular culture journal was the same as one of Ferlinghetti's favorite Charlie Chaplin movies. Leafing through the journal that he found, Ferlinghetti was impressed. The articles dealt with film, drama, literature, and the cultural scene in general. Peter Martin, the editor, was a transplanted New Yorker who while living in San Francisco was constantly thinking about returning East. *City Lights* was an attempt to give voice to the cultural ferment he found developing in the San Francisco Bay area. Martin, the son of Italian anarchist Carlo Tresca and nephew of U.S. Communist Party leader Elizabeth Gurley Flynn, was a political radical who had remained independent of any groups and was therefore attracted to the freedom he discerned in San Francisco's artists and writers. Martin published the new ideas that were the hallmark of the San Francisco poets. Robert Duncan, for example, wrote of the need to create poetry out of the street, the need to learn to appreciate the spirit of the city, the necessity of understanding one's own neighborhood. In short, Martin's magazine reflected what was new and innovative in the cultural worlds of San Francisco, Berkeley, and the surrounding area.

Martin accepted five of Ferlinghetti's translations of the poetry of Prévert for publication in *City Lights*. Soon after they appeared, he and Ferlinghetti met. Martin thinks that it may have been Rexroth who brought the two of them together.

Shortly after they met, Martin shared an exciting idea with Ferlinghetti. He wanted to open a bookshop specializing in paperback books. The only thing stopping him was money. Few of his friends believed that a shop handling only paperbacks could thrive. Martin believed that paperbacks were the coming thing, and although the idea hadn't been tested, he wanted to be the first to open such a shop. Ferlinghetti, remembering the bookstands along the banks of the Seine and the bookstores in Paris, agreed that the idea was entirely feasible. He and Martin decided to go into partnership, and they rented a location in the building where Martin had his magazine offices.

Ferlinghetti and Peter each put in five hundred dollars, which in those days was enough to stock the store. They organized the shelves according to their personal tastes. Martin, interested in popular culture, began a film section. Ferlinghetti made sure there was plenty of literature, and they both worked on the political section. The *City Lights* offices were on the second level of the store in a small space reached by a narrow, winding staircase. The books were jammed into an equally small space at ground level.

In June 1953 the City Lights Bookstore opened. If it was not an instant financial success, it certainly looked a thriving enterprise. The store was always jammed with people. Rexroth was a frequent visitor, and many of San Francisco's writers began to drop in almost as soon as news of the first paperback bookstore was out. Almost immediately Ferlinghetti thought about expanding the store's scope. He wanted to publish a series of poetry books under the City Lights imprint. Martin did not think the idea was realistic. "I told Ferlinghetti that operating a bookstore was difficult enough. Publishing would be a next to impossible task, especially if the main focus was on poetry. Time, of course, would prove me wrong. Ferlinghetti never really came across as a poet. I thought of him as a translator. He never showed me his poems except for one I published in *City Lights* about a Dylan Thomas reading he attended. I wasn't surprised that he wanted to publish poetry, though. He certainly had an interest in it. I knew that. I just didn't know that he'd been working on his own poems for so long a time. He was very quiet. A good person to work with, but we never really got to know each other well."

Shortly after they opened, a young man came into the store and announced that he wanted to work for City Lights Books. His name was Shigeyoshi Murao. Martin told him that they had no money to pay any help; Murao said that was no obstacle. He wanted to work anyway. He'd been offered a job at Vesuvio's, a popular North Beach bar, but would feel more at home in a bookstore. The two partners decided to give Murao a job. After a few days they felt they had to pay him something. "How else could we call ourselves radicals and go to sleep with a clean conscience each night?" Martin recalls. Murao stayed at *City Lights* for more than twenty years.

In 1955, Martin sold Ferlinghetti his interest in the store and moved back to New York, where after working for several magazines he opened the New Yorker Bookstore on Manhattan's Upper West Side.

Within a few months of taking over sole ownership of the bookstore, Ferlinghetti realized his ambition and on August 10, 1955, published his *Pictures of the Gone World* under the City Lights imprint. The small volume was printed in letterpress by David Ruff and collated and saddle-stitched by Ferlinghetti, Kirby, David, and Holly Beye. With the publication of his first book of poetry, Lawrence Ferling took back his father's name and became Lawrence Ferlinghetti. The book documented the struggles Ferlinghetti had gone through in the maturation of his political philosophy, the development of his literary aesthetics, and his work as a painter. In addition, it was a travel journal of the places in which he had lived. The design of the book reflected Ferlinghetti's continuing concern with the way the poem looked on the page. Although the spread on the page never got as unorthodox as Cummings's work, Ferlinghetti was satisfied that the arrangements of the words enhanced the meaning of the poem.

The poems in *Pictures* are intensely lyrical. The music of the lines blends harmoniously with straightforward pictorial imagery. There are "fields full of silence"; "a face which darkness could kill in an instant"; and "a horse at night standing hitched along." Ferlinghetti weaves in and out of the tragedy and comedy of daily existence. His language moves through "their stone eyes staring thru three thousand years" that "allay our fears of aging" and remains consistently simple: "Just as I used to say love comes harder to the aged because they've been running on the same old rails too long." There is a whimsical sense to the poems, foreshadowing later well-known Ferlinghetti works such as "Dog" and "Underwear." By the mid-fifties his humor was being applied to biting social and political commentary. In these early poems he is exploring death, age, love, beauty, and the tragicomic in every-day life. In a few poems, however, the future social critic emerges. Ferlinghetti had finally come into his own with a unique style, owing more to E. E. Cummings and Kenneth Patchen than to either Eliot or Pound, his great influences of the 1940s. There is a refreshing lack of profundity to the work. It is as if the language were an integral part of the streets of San Francisco. Perhaps Ferlinghetti's interest in con-temporary European literature derailed him from Eliot and Pound. In the works of Apollinaire he saw how useful it was to focus in on the wonder of ordinary life, and from the surrealists he learned how to reflect the ordinary in new ways.

In his first book Ferlinghetti had established himself as a lyrical poet, an artist committed to common language, and a writer who can both laugh and cry beautifully. The fact that he painted helped him develop a sense for the poem as picture, creating an impression of something more than merely language on the page. The first line of the poems in *Pictures* is "Away above a harborful." Space is established. The poet creates a scene.

Ferlinghetti had sent a number of his Prévert translations to New Directions. His first communication from the publishing house reads:

> Thank you for sending us some of your translations from Prévert. We would like to hold them for consideration later when our Prévert project gets underway and hope you will have patience with us until that time.

James Laughlin wrote to Ferlinghetti on December 2, 1956, about the possibility of New Directions publishing *A Coney Island of the Mind*, a collection of poems written after *Pictures*. Laughlin's letter reads, in part:

> . . . I am only just now getting down to selecting material for ND 16, and I want to tell you that one of the most interesting things I found in the manuscript box was your "A Coney Island of the Mind" collection. You are certainly getting to be a very good writer of poems. I'm impressed.
>
> Might I pick out a couple of these poems for use in ND 16? Please let me know right back by air because the printer is breathing down my neck. The financial arrangement would be the usual for

ND annuals (it will be a paperback distributed by Meridian again this year) . . .

May I keep the rest of the collection a bit longer? I'd like to think more about it for a possible little book, something along the line, perhaps, of your wonderful little Pocket Poets Series, which I greatly admire.

The letter went on to ask about the whereabouts of Jack Kerouac and of Allen Ginsberg, whom Laughlin wished to represent in New Directions. Laughlin also mentioned two new Rexroth titles, *In Defense of the Earth* and *100 Chinese Poems*, published by N.D., and asked to display them prominently at the bookstore.

To be praised twice in one letter by James Laughlin, founder-publisher of the publishing house that Ferlinghetti most admired, was, to say the least, a cause for celebration. Naturally, Ferlinghetti wrote a quick reply giving permission for a selection of his work to be represented in the New Directions annual of prose and poetry.

For your own poems it is terribly difficult to choose because I find them all quite irresistible (or able, I could never spell that word). I don't know when I have felt so drawn to a new poet, not that you are just beginning to write, but, what with other pre-occupations, I haven't before really registered. We really must try to think up some larger project for you. I think you could have here the kind of success that Prévert has had in France if one could just think up the formula for getting it across. But more of that later.

For the annual Laughlin chose three poems from the *Coney Island* group. They were titled from their first lines: "In Goya's greatest scenes"; "Sometime during eternity"; and "See, it was like this." In the credits for the New Directions annual, Ferlinghetti is described as being of French, Italian, and Puerto Rican background because at this time he believed that part of his family, on his mother's side at least, came from Puerto Rico.

James Laughlin appreciated Ferlinghetti's openness of language and his evident warmth of heart. He was impressed with Ferlinghetti's ability to say directly and exactly what he had to say and no more. He admired the way he captured a clear, precise pictorial image on the page. "I was so tired of involuted poets tied up in complicated syntax . . . You can always form a quick judgment as to what Ferlinghetti is saying," Laughlin said later. "Rexroth had told me about him. He took me around to City Lights Bookstore and I took to him immediately. He is a very lovable person. I guess I probably saw *Pictures of the Gone World* while I was there." A year later New Directions released *A Coney Island of the Mind*. It became Ferlinghetti's best-selling book.

James Laughlin had begun his publishing career in the 1930s, while still a student at Harvard, by publishing excerpts from one of Henry Miller's *Tropics* in a college publication. This erotic fragment produced quite a storm on the staid Harvard campus. It was only the first of many that Laughlin would face as a pioneer of the avant-garde. He is a tall, conservatively dressed individual whose appearance and natural gentility belie his publishing activities.

Because Laughlin was himself a poet, his praise of Ferlinghetti's work was even more important to Ferlinghetti. Although he had brought out the first collection of his own poetry, Ferlinghetti didn't want to continue to publish his own work. After the selection of his poems for the New Directions Annual, it became increasingly evident that a book with New Directions was going to be a reality. Laughlin didn't overlook the fact that national publicity was beginning to focus on Ferlinghetti and the other so-called Beat poets. On September 16, 1957, he wrote to Ferlinghetti:

Dear Ferlinghetti:

Please forgive my delay in answering your interesting letter of August 28th. Things have been in a terrible crush these weeks, my having been away so long. But I have been meaning to write you from day to day, as I am really enthusiastic about your poetry and, of course, with all this publicity breaking (the good piece in *LIFE* on your poets group there in San Francisco, and the preview of Kerouac's book) the time is ripe to do something.

I must say, however, that I am very lukewarm on the idea of doing just another poetry book in the usual format, with all the limitations of the customary poetry market. I understand that Grove Press has had pretty good success doing new poetry in paperback form and I think we ought to experiment with this, and that you are just the man to begin with, because you are so lucid, not to mention your wonderful wit and verbal color.

Now such a book ought to be at least 96 pages, I think, and that means that there isn't enough material in the "Coney Island," so what have you got that we could add to it to bulk it out? What would you think of picking up again the poems which you had in your "Pocket Poets" selection, which both I and my wife liked so much. What has the sale on that volume been? To what extent has it been around in the same channels that our paperbacks would reach? I see no reason why such a volume should not also contain some bits of prose. So why don't you turn it over in your mind and shoot on to me whatever you have ready that you think might fit in well. To capitalize on the present publicity, we ought to get going right away. And there might, of course, be a few hundred copies bound up in hard covers, which you might sign, or something, to justify the considerably higher price that would be necessary to float the binding.

I am very much interested in what you told me about the other books that you are working on, and I hope that if we can get off the ground successfully on this first venture, a long and mutually interesting publishing relationship will develop. Not, of course, that you haven't already made a fine start for yourself with the first book, but I suppose any poet likes best to be published by somebody else. Which reminds me to say that I appreciated very much the nice things you had to say about my own little book of poems, and will send a few out to you for sale—many thanks—when we get our stock on them from Italy in a month or so.

Kenneth brought me a copy of your Fantasy record to Wyoming, and I enjoyed it very much. Extremely powerful stuff, and this kind of mounting will obviously create an enlarged poetry public. The only thing I didn't like was the monotony of the verbal tone. Both you and Kenneth seemed to have your voice at the same pitch all the way through. Good old Dylan, as I recall, used to put a lot of variation into his readings, almost as if he were an actor acting the lines, and I think that helped to put it across. Not that I like very soupy readings of poetry, but I think some variation in pitch and force would help . . .

One other thing. As you know, we use photographic jackets on our paperbooks, so perhaps you might be thinking about a good photo, or a montage of different photos, which might be suitable.

What about your Prévert translations? Did anything ever get done about them? Would there be any point in putting some of them into the paperback volume, if he would give permission, or would that detract? I have always been interested in his work, but was never quite sure how meaningful it would be to readers in this country, because so much of it seems to depend on the tradition of French popular song, local color, and local references.

With best wishes,

As ever,
J. Laughlin

JL:SB

Ferlinghetti agreed to include a selection of work from *Pictures*, as Laughlin had suggested in his letter. The Prévert translations did not go into *Coney Island*, but were published by City Lights Pocket Poets Series, with an introduction by Ferlinghetti. Some of them later appeared in a Penguin anthology of Prévert's work, which also included translations by others.

The Fantasy record Laughlin had referred to was the recorded result of the series of jazz and poetry readings Rexroth and Ferlinghetti had done in North Beach at a club called The Cellar, located on Green Street, not far from the bookstore. Rexroth promoted the combination of jazz and poetry as a means of helping make poetry more accessible to the public. He had successfully read poetry to jazz accompaniment as a young man in Chicago, along with Black poet Langston Hughes, and with Maxwell Bodenheim in Greenwich Village. Coupled with his commitment to social and political change, Rexroth felt strongly about giving poetry a more public surface. He had always felt stifled in conventional, elitist literary circles, and cautioned younger poets about the dangers of becoming too withdrawn from the world around them. Rexroth's poems ranged from love lyrics and beautifully descriptive nature poems, comparing natural landscapes to the workings of the mind, to the angry protest works that influenced the younger poets. One of his poems in the latter category, "Thou Shalt Not Kill," ostensibly a tribute to Dylan Thomas, memorialized many poets: suicides, neglected geniuses, tortured lyricists. His own political activism was partly an outgrowth of his belief that the artist and the writer should be involved beyond the studio or the typewriter. When he began performing with Ferlinghetti at The Cellar, he had obtained the backing of The Cellar Jazz Quintet, a group made up of two of the owners of the club, plus three other San Francisco musicians. Kenneth Patchen also read poetry to jazz during the same period. After the venture was an apparent success, Fantasy recorded a 12-inch LP of Rexroth and Ferlinghetti reading. Ferlinghetti read selections from the "Oral Messages" section of *Coney Island* and poems from the title section of the book. From the very beginning, the Cellar readings attracted big crowds. On the first night the fire marshal had to be called to clear the hallway. The club held only about one hundred, but there were nearly five hundred people waiting to get in.

The "Oral Messages" section of *Coney Island* is prefaced with the remarks:

> These seven poems were conceived specifically for jazz accompaniment and as such should be considered as spontaneously spoken "oral messages" rather than as poems written for the printed page. As a result of continued experimental reading with jazz, they are still in a state of change.

But actually, the poems remained as they were first spoken, and appeared that way in the New Directions book published in 1958. The poems were a dramatic departure from Ferlinghetti's conception of the poem arranged on the page with the eye of the reader in mind. He was comfortable now about moving into newer forms, influenced by the excitement around him stirred up by the new poetry. His work in "Oral Messages" is loose and fluid, although lacking the sensitive lyricism of *Pictures of the Gone World* and the *Coney Island of the Mind* grouping of poems. In "Autobiography," from "Oral Messages," he writes: "I have heard the Gettysburg address and the Ginsberg address," and, echoing *Howl*, "I too have ridden boxcars boxcars boxcars." Much of what he wrote in *Coney Island* became part of the culture of rebellion that was growing throughout the country, generally under the label of "Beat Generation." He wrote:

> I'm a good Joe.
> I'm an open book
> to my boss.
> I am a complete mystery
> to my closest friends.

The poems also include allusions to the writings of Djuna Barnes, William Butler Yeats, and the Romantic poets.

Rexroth and Ferlinghetti both picked up on the street lingo of the Beat culture. Rexroth began referring to the "squares," as did Ferlinghetti. The elder poet turned his often acid tongue to jazz lyricists and stated, "Almost all poetry written for jazz is strictly corn. That's true of the Negro poets, too. You can go into any Fillmore Street record shop and pick up a record with better lyrics than the pseudo-jazz poems." At any rate, the poetry and jazz readings began to be popular forms of entertainment in the coffeehouses that were then flourishing all over the country in an imitation of popular North Beach hangouts.

A Coney Island of the Mind opens with a statement by Ferlinghetti that the title is taken from Henry Miller's *Into the Night Life*. He explains that the phrase "expresses the way I felt about these poems when I wrote them—as if they were, taken together, a kind of Coney Island of the mind, a kind of circus of the soul." The first poem in the book reflects Ferlinghetti's enduring interest in Goya's "Disasters of War" series. The experimentation with form continues as in *Pictures*, and Ferlinghetti's social consciousness is in full force:

In Goya's greatest scenes we seem to see
                                        the people of the world
        exactly at the moment when
                they first attained the title of
                                        "suffering humanity"
        They writhe upon the page
                        in a veritable rage
                                of adversity
        Heaped up
                groaning with babies and bayonets
                                under cement skies
                in an abstract landscape of blasted trees
                bent statues bats wings and beaks
                        slippery gibbets
                cadavers and carnivorous cocks
                and all the final hollering monsters
                        of the
                                "imagination of disaster"
        they are so bloody real

it is as if they really still existed

And they do

Only the landscape is changed

They still are ranged along the roads

plagued by legionnaires

false windmills and demented roosters

They are the same people

only further from home

on freeways fifty lanes wide

on a concrete continent

spaced with bland billboards

illustrating imbecile illusions of happiness

The scene shows fewer tumbrils

but more maimed citizens

in painted cars

and they have strange license plates

and engines

that devour America

Ferlinghetti had never seen the original of Goya's "Disasters of War" series, but he was struck by their force in reproductions he saw while at Columbia University. In this series of brutal etchings Goya, who was known for his beautiful portraits and soft lyrical canvases, was depicting the savagery of war as graphically as possible and illustrating how the Church as well as the State was deeply involved in war's horrors. The pictures cried out for an end to human slaughter.

A Coney Island of the Mind as well as the earlier *Pictures of the Gone World* were testaments of Ferlinghetti's having found himself a permanent home as much as they were reflective of the emergence of a new, original poetic voice. San Francisco was literally the "crossing-over" for him. He had taken the train West as far as Oakland, but the San Francisco Bay had to be crossed. He boarded the ferryboat at First and Broadway in the East Bay city, carefully observing the low-lying buildings of his new home, and then he disembarked at

San Francisco's old Ferry Terminal. The chemistry of the city began to work on him almost immediately.

In his writing he seemed to be following Mr. Bisland's example. The bookstore and publishing house may have been inspired to a certain extent by the memory of Mrs. Bisland's success in business. Ferlinghetti, however, had become his own person and was fulfilling some of the dreams that were his alone. The publishing business began to take more and more of his time and energy. He and Kirby even postponed starting their own family while Ferlinghetti got City Lights Books off the ground.

He had been disappointed that neither E. E. Cummings nor Henry Miller responded positively to his requests for manuscripts for City Lights Books, but he was excited that William Carlos Williams gave his enthusiastic approval to the idea of Ferlinghetti reissuing *Kora in Hell: Improvisations*, which had originally been published by the Four Seas Press in 1920. The book had been unavailable since the early twenties. Williams expressed excitement that the edition would not be an expensive one, but would be made available to a wide number of people. Williams gave Ferlinghetti the idea of numbering the volumes in his Pocket Poets Series, advice which he accepted.

Like Miller, Rexroth, and Patchen, Williams had been largely ignored by the academic community. He was an intimate of Ezra Pound and Marianne Moore. During his lifetime he brought out a massive body of work: poetry, novels, autobiographical sketches, and essays while maintaining a thriving practice as a physician.

Williams did not write much political poetry. His work broke new ground, and he was a pioneer in the forms of contemporary poetry. Recognition came to him late in life. His Pulitzer Prize for his last collection, *Pictures from Breughel*, was posthumously awarded.

In one of his letters to Ferlinghetti, Williams wrote about the necessity of breaking out of the habit of setting poems on the page "as if they were composed behind a straight-edged ruler." That simple statement says as much about Williams as several pages of criticism might. He broke away from tradition. That is what *Kora in Hell* was all about back in the twenties, deliberately defying the rules and insisting on a new awakening to American speech among poets—echoing Whitman's call for an indigenous American poetry. Williams believed there were too many poets who still looked to English and European poetry for inspiration to guide them forward instead of seeking their material in their own neighborhoods and on their own streets. Although he was of a different generation, he felt a kinship with young poets like Ferlinghetti and Ginsberg because he saw that they faced their environment and interpreted it without concern for the conventions of poetry as they had been handed down through the ages.

CHAPTER SEVEN

B Y 1955, FERLINGHETTI was well established in San Francisco. He had realized his dream of painting in his own studio. He
was writing art and literary criticism, and he lived in a community
of creative people who were changing the form and content of the
American literary scene.

The bookstore was a going concern, although it was not a great
financial success. Ferlinghetti was committed to keeping it open,
and almost overnight it had become an important San Francisco literary landmark. City Lights Books had been launched with
the Pocket Poets Series, of which *Pictures of the Gone World* was
Number 1. Next he published *Thirty Spanish Poems of Love and
Exile*, a collection of twentieth-century Spanish and Latin American poetry translated and edited by Kenneth Rexroth.

One day in 1955 a young poet wandered into City Lights Bookstore. His name was Allen Ginsberg. He offered Ferlinghetti a
manuscript of his early poems. Ferlinghetti read them but polite-
ly turned them down. A few weeks later Allen showed Lawrence
a poem in progress. It was titled "Howl." Unfortunately, although
Ferlinghetti liked the poem, City Lights didn't have the money at
the time to publish it. Nonetheless, the two men found that they had
a great deal in common, and they began to see more of one another.

In the East (Ginsberg was from Paterson, New Jersey, and had
attended Columbia), Ginsberg had come into contact with several
writers with whom he shared ideas, and he was almost as excited
about their writing as he was about his own. One of these was Jack
Kerouac, who had published a novel in 1950 called *The Town and
the City*. William Burroughs, whose book *Junkie*, written under the
pseudonym of William Lee, had also been published, and was an-

91

other close friend. Ginsberg needed the stimulation of other poets and writers, and found that he could not work as well when isolated from other creative minds. Both Allen and Lawrence respected and learned from older writers who had encouraged them. Rexroth had fulfilled this function for Ferlinghetti; William Carlos Williams had been one of Ginsberg's mentors. Ginsberg's roots were deeply embedded in many traditions, but it was Williams who helped him realize the value of sounding out the poem, recognizing the richness of native American speech, and using it to express his ideas.

In addition, Ferlinghetti and Ginsberg helped to stimulate the creativity of their contemporaries. This made them public figures. Their role was to be out in the arena, involved in the life around them, and as time would show, that is how both functioned—as poets in the world.

Unlike Ferlinghetti, however, Ginsberg was not a shy person. He was a perpetual questioner as well as a good listener. He didn't hesitate to ask if he wanted to know something, and he had enormous energy.

Partly as a platform for his own poetry, Ginsberg planned a reading at the Six Gallery in San Francisco shortly after he and Ferlinghetti met. Ginsberg had also met several of the young San Francisco poets and a few who were living in Berkeley: Philip Lamantia, Michael Mc-Clure, Gary Snyder, and Philip Whalen. He invited them to read their poetry. Ginsberg dropped into City Lights to tell Ferlinghetti about his plans for the reading. Rexroth had agreed to introduce the poets.

On the night of the reading the Ferlinghettis invited some of the poets to ride with them. Ginsberg, Kerouac, Kirby, and one or two others managed to get into the car and off they sped. About seventy-five people had crowded into the small gallery. After Ginsberg read the first part of "Howl," the audience reaction was amazing. They seemed to know that they had heard a great poem, demonstrating that fact by their applause. A party was held after the reading, and most of the poets attended. The Ferlinghettis were tired and went home. Ferlinghetti immediately sat down at his typewriter and composed a telegram that he sent to Ginsberg. The message paraphrased one that Ralph Waldo Emerson had sent to Walt Whitman upon receiving a copy of the 1855 edition of *Leaves of Grass*. The telegram to Ginsberg read: "I greet you at the beginning of a great career. When do I get the manuscript?"

Ferlinghetti and Ginsberg worked well together. Ferlinghetti was impressed with the clarity of Allen's mind and the power of his poems. Ginsberg had read *Pictures of the Gone World* and was taken with the warmth and lyricism of Ferlinghetti's poetry. In addition, he liked the way the Pocket Poets books looked; he liked their size and shape. He found it comfortable working on the publication of "Howl" with his new publisher and friend. City Lights Books was radically different from the world of the New York publishers he had encountered in the early fifties, when he had helped friends with their manuscripts. He was at home in North Beach with its cafés and friendly bars. The Ferlinghetti-Ginsberg friendship and working relationship suited both men well.

"Howl" was in four sections when Ginsberg first brought it to Ferlinghetti. After some discussion, the two agreed that the fourth section didn't work as part of the poem and it was taken out. (Ginsberg published it later under the title *The Names*.) A "Footnote to Howl" was included. This also had been part of the poem until Ginsberg had read it to Rexroth, who said, "No, No, that's enough," and so it had been separated from the body of the poem. Ferlinghetti and Ginsberg sorted through some of Allen's early poems and finally agreed on eleven of them. The book—Number 4 in the Pocket Poets Series—was called *Howl and Other Poems*.

William Carlos Williams responded enthusiastically to a request from Ferlinghetti for a foreword to Ginsberg's book. He requested that a copy of the poem be sent to him, and judging by what he wrote, he must have been very excited when he first read it: "He avoids nothing but experiences it to the hilt. He contains it. Claims it as his own—and, we believe, laughs at it . . . Hold back the edges of your gowns, ladies, we are going through hell."

Williams agreed with Ferlinghetti that this was the beginning of a great career. He had followed Ginsberg from his first poems, where he was still developing his own voice, and now had been given the opportunity of helping him. Neither Williams nor Ferlinghetti could have predicted the kind of hell Ferlinghetti, let alone the ladies, would go through when *Howl and Other Poems* began to be circulated. Within a short time after publication the book, its author and its publisher were a *cause célèbre*. The poems were branded "obscene" and were put on trial in a proceeding that tested the definition of that word in a court of law. It also gave *Howl*, Ginsberg, Ferlinghetti, and City Lights so much national publicity that sales boomed and word spread about the new poetry that was being developed on the West Coast.

Howl was printed by Villiers in Great Britain, a company with long experience in setting type and printing works for small presses at reasonable prices. City Lights had a relationship with Villiers that continued into the middle sixties. Villiers printed fifteen hundred copies of *Howl and Other Poems* in a saddle-stitched letterpress edition. This first edition came into the country through customs without incident. Part of the second printing, which consisted of three thousand copies, ran afoul of the San Francisco office of the U.S. Customs department. Five hundred copies were confiscated by the U.S. Collector of Customs, Chester McPhee, an old hand at determining what was proper reading material for the citizens he served. In an earlier seizure he had stopped *The Miscellaneous Man*, a poetry magazine edited by William J. Margolis, from entering the country. In regard to *Howl*, McPhee declared, "The words and the sense of the writing is obscene. You wouldn't want your children to come across it." The seizure of *Howl* took place on March 25, 1957.

Fortunately, in anticipation of such problems, Ferlinghetti had taken the precaution of submitting the manuscript of *Howl* to the American Civil Liberties Union before sending it to Villiers. The ACLU informed McPhee that they were prepared to fight the seizure and that they did not consider the book obscene. At this point Ferlinghetti printed a photo offset edition of *Howl* identical to the original text and placed it on sale. Since it was printed in San Francisco, the book was out of the jurisdiction of Customs. However, McPhee still had the five hundred and twenty copies he had seized.

William Hogan, book review editor of the *San Francisco Chronicle*, offered his Sunday column to Ferlinghetti so that he might write about the seizure in defense of *Howl*. In the article Ferlinghetti recommended that McPhee be awarded a medal for helping to make *Howl* famous. He wrote that he considered the title poem "the most significant single long poem to be published in this country since World War II, perhaps since T. S. Eliot's *Four Quartets*. He pointed out that "it is not the poet but what he observes which is revealed as obscene. The great obscene wastes of *Howl* are the wastes of the mechanized world, lost among atom bombs and inane nationalisms . . . Ginsberg chose to walk along with Nelson Algren, Henry Miller, Kenneth Rexroth, Kenneth Patchen, not to mention some great American dead, mostly in the tradition of philosophical anarchism." He then said that Ginsberg wrote his own best defense of *Howl* when he wrote the poem "America," which is included in the collection of *Howl* and which conjures up the specter of an America devoid of love and poetry, a "sphinx of cement and aluminum."

Ten days after Ferlinghetti's article appeared in the *Chronicle*, McPhee released the copies of *Howl* he had been holding. The United States attorney in San Francisco refused to move against the book.

It then became the turn of the San Francisco Police Department, specifically the Juvenile Division, headed by Captain William Hanrahan, a zealous smut hunter who publicly announced that he hoped that *Howl* would open the door for a host of book seizures he wanted to initiate.

Two of Hanrahan's officers walked into the City Lights Bookstore, where Shig Murao was calmly manning the sales desk. Kirby was also in the store. Kirby recalls that the two officers looked like well-groomed college students. When they announced their reason for being there and handed over the warrants for the arrest of Ferlinghetti and Shig, Kirby told them that there were a lot of so-called obscene works in bookstores, referring to books by Henry Miller, the Marquis de Sade, and others.

The warrants charged Ferlinghetti with being the publisher of *Howl* and the owner of the shop selling it. Shig was arrested as the actual seller of the book. He had sold a copy to one of the officers.

But the charges against Shig were eventually dropped since it could not be determined if he had read the book and knew whether or not it was obscene. So Ferlinghetti stood trial alone.

The complaint against him alleged that he willfully and lewdly printed and sold obscene and indecent writings: *Howl and Other Poems*. The prosecution attempted to isolate certain words and show them to be obscene. In a copy of the book, the allegedly obscene words were underlined. The ACLU defense asserted that, according to the law, individual words could not make a particular book obscene. The book as a whole had to be judged. As an example of how society's attitudes about words change with time, the defense cited the word *syphilis*, which at one time could not be uttered in polite society but was now considered perfectly proper.

The ACLU considered the *Howl* trial a test of the fundamental constitutional rights to freedom of speech and press, and they assigned a celebrated trial lawyer, J. W. K. "Jake" Ehrlich to the case. Ehrlich had practiced law in San Francisco since 1922. He had been the attorney for Caryl Chessman, the condemned murderer who became famous for his appeals from death row, but he rarely handled cases that had any political implications. Also participating on the defense team were Lawrence Speiser, an old hand at civil rights cases, and Albert Bendich, a lawyer with a strong labor law background who was staff counsel for the ACLU.

Like Captain Hanrahan, the prosecutor, Ralph McIntosh, was a zealous smut hunter with a long history of action against pornographic movies and nudist publications. He was an assistant district attorney who had worked his way through law school by working nights as a linotype operator on a paper.

The judge in the case, Clayton Horn, was one of the city's four police magistrates. Just prior to the *Howl* trial he had received national publicity when he sentenced five women shoplifters to see the film *The Ten Commandments* and to write essays on the moral lesson of the movie.

The defense assembled an impressive list of distinguished witnesses for the trial. They were Kenneth Rexroth; Mark Schorer, author, professor of English, and chairman of the Department of Graduate Studies at the University of California at Berkeley; Luther Nichols, book review editor of the *San Francisco Examiner*; Walter van Tilburg Clark, professor of language arts at San Francisco State College; Leo Lowenthal, professor of speech at Berkeley; author Vincent McHugh; and three other professors from San Francisco State College: Mark Linenthal, Herbert Blau, and Arthur Foff. The prosecution had only three witnesses: Russell Woods, a San Francisco Police officer; David Kirk, an English professor at the University of San Francisco; and Gail Potter, a teacher.

Ginsberg, who was out of the country in Morocco when the trial opened, wrote to Ferlinghetti:

> Received your letter today with clippings. I guess this is more serious than the customs seizure since you can lose real money on this deal if they find you guilty. What does it look like? I guess with the ACLU it should be possible to beat—except this is local law—does that give police complete discretion to decide what's obscene? If so, that may make it difficult.

> Presumably a matter of local politics—therefore can anything be done to call off police through politicians at city hall thru state college thru poetry center thru Witt Diamant? If it is a matter of purely local law & juvenile bureau, perhaps somebody at Berkeley & State Coll . . . but arrest and formal charges have been filed already, so I guess open showdown is inevitable.

Statements in support of Ginsberg's poem poured in from Kenneth Patchen, Robert Duncan, James Laughlin, Thomas Parkinson, Barney Rosset of Grove Press, the Northern California Booksellers Association, novelist Eugene Burdick, and William Hogan of the *San Francisco Chronicle*. Hogan wrote: "*Howl and Other Poems*, according to accepted, serious contemporary American literary standards, is a dignified, sincere and admirable work of art." Numerous articles appeared locally and nationally. One of the most aptly titled was "How Captain Hanrahan Made Howl a Best Seller." Written by David Perlman, it ran in *The Reporter* on December 12, 1957.

All through the summer of 1957—with a few weeks between each day in court—the trial of *Howl* went on. It began with the testimony of policeman Russell Woods. He told how he had gone into the City Lights Bookstore and purchased a copy of *Howl and Other Poems* from Shigeyoshi Murao. The book was identified by the officer and marked as People's Exhibit One. So there it was. The poems stood unabashedly naked before the entire courtroom.

McIntosh read into the record the publication material listed in the book. When he read the phrase Ginsberg had used to characterize the works of his friends Burroughs, Kerouac, and Cassady, "All their books are published in heaven," he said, "and I don't quite understand that, but let the record show anyway, your honor, it's published by the City Lights Pocketbook Shop."

After Officer Woods testified, Ehrlich picked up a copy of the book and looked at the cover. "Is there anything about this book that indicates that there is something in it which would lead to a moral breakdown of the people of this city, to say nothing of Police Officer Woods?" he asked, and then continued, "We are confronted with the manner in which this book is to be evaluated by the court. As I understand the law, the court must construe the book as a whole. I presume that I could take the classic *Leaves of Grass* and by cutting it to pieces find a word here or there or an idea that some people might not like. But in *Leaves of Grass* there is the intent of the poet to convey a certain idea, not lewd and lascivious or licentious or common, but a story, laying out a certain format concerning life itself."

It seemed fitting that Ehrlich chose "Leaves of Grass" as an example since the poem had been one of the strongest influences on Ginsberg's own development, not merely stylistically but philosophically as well. In the author of that long epic of the nineteenth century, Ginsberg saw a poet who understood the necessity for a true human community of love and mutual understanding, but one that could come about only when the old ethics had broken down and when people could freely and openly express their sexual preferences and also not be locked into humiliating jobs and lifestyles. *Leaves of Grass* was never officially put on trial, but it did raise a great many eyebrows when it was published. A few people guessing at Whitman's homosexuality, which was well hidden until quite late in the twentieth century, attacked the poet himself. Others attacked the poem for presenting a repugnant view of society because it treated life on the streets and not life in "proper" society.

Judge Horn stated, in a discussion of the admissibility of expert witnesses such as literary critics:

> . . . it is obvious that you are never going to get unanimous consent on anything that is involved in this case. That's the reason why the freedom of the press should be so stringently protected, so that no one segment of the country can censor to the injury of the rest, what they can read, see and hear and so forth. That is why this case is such an important one, why I am giving it such a lot of time and consideration.

Ferlinghetti had been listening closely, and smiled at what the judge was saying, but the prosecution was somewhat crestfallen. McIntosh said:

> You can see how far this thing can get out of hand, both sides bringing down all kinds of expert witnesses and telling your Honour how you should decide when your Honour has your own set of rules there. I think your Honour can fairly and conscientiously interpret the rules as set down, trying to take an objective view of it through the whole community and decide it yourself.

McIntosh knew that the defense would be calling an array of well-placed, well-groomed, and articulate witnesses. That was just what he didn't need.

Mark Schorer was sworn in as first witness for the defense. He was asked what sort of writing he had done and answered: "I have published three novels, about seventy-five short stories, thirty-two of them collected in one volume, more pieces of literary criticism than I know the number of, in practically every periodical one might name." He then mentioned that he read books as an adviser to the Harvard University Press and Princeton University, and was a paid consultant to the Army, who used his expertise when choosing textbooks for educational programs. It was a formidable record. Schorer was also at that time writing his definitive biography of Sinclair Lewis, and this was put into the record. When he was asked to name colleges where he had taught he was able to provide a long and impressive list.

The defense asked: "Do you have any opinion as to the literary value of Exhibit One, to which we refer as *Howl and Other Poems*, by Allen Ginsberg?" And Schorer responded:

> I think that "Howl," like any work of literature, attempts and intends to make a significant comment on or interpretation of human experience as the author knows it. And to that end he has devised what we would call an esthetic structure to sort of organize his material to demonstrate his theme . . . The theme of the poem is announced very clearly in the opening line, "I saw the best minds of my generation destroyed by madness, starving hysterical naked." Then the following lines that make up the first part attempt to create the impression of a kind of nightmare world in which people representing "the best minds of my generation," in the author's view, are wandering like damned souls in hell. That is done through a kind of series of what one might call surrealistic images, a kind of state of hallucination. Then in the second section the mood of the poem changes and it becomes an indictment of those elements in modern society that, in the author's view, are destructive of the best qualities in human nature and of the best minds. Those elements are, I would say, predominantly materialism, conformity and mechanization leading toward war.

Schorer's statements had touched on the deepest concerns of the San Francisco writers community—and, indeed, of counter-culture people for generations, whether they were called bohemians, hippies, or beatniks. The *Howl* trial was becoming not only a forum on the meaning of obscenity and the right of free speech but also a platform for ideas that would be of widespread concern in the sixties.

Schorer went on to interpret the meaning of the third part of *Howl*:

> And then the last part is a personal address to a friend, real or fictional, of the poet or the person who is speaking in the poet's voice—those are not always the same thing—who is mad and in a madhouse, and is the specific representative of what the author regards as the general condition, and with that final statement the poem ends.

Schorer then spoke of Ginsberg's use of language. "To write in the language of the streets really meant not to write in the language of poetry; this is the language narrowly determined by critics to be the proper language for poetry. One must always be in rebellion. Each person had to determine his or her own language—from the level of their own mind and their own body."

The defense then asked: "So that the use of a particular word, which some think offensive, is necessary to paint the picture which the author tries to portray?" The answer was "Definitely."

In cross-examination McIntosh asked Schorer if the defense had given him a copy of *Howl* to read. He answered that he had bought a copy at the U.C. Book Corner in Berkeley.

McIntosh tried to demonstrate that parts of the poem were incomprehensible. In answer to a question about the meaning of "angel-headed hipsters," Schorer told McIntosh: "You don't understand the individual words taken out of their context. You understand the whole impression that is being created . . . You can no more translate this back into logical prose English than you can say what a surrealist painting means in words . . . Poetry is a heightened form of language through the use of figurative language. . . ."

McIntosh then took Schorer on a journey through what the prosecution considered to be the most damaging parts of the poems,
specifically the words *cock, pubic beards*, and *balls*. Then he went
on to where, in his own words, "there are just little dots in there."
He asked if the lines "Who blew and were blown by those human
seraphim, the sailors, caresses of Atlantic and Caribbean love" were
necessary. Schorer answered affirmatively, saying:

> The essence of this poem is the impression of a world in which
> all sexuality is confused and corrupted. These words indicate a
> corrupt sexual act. Therefore, they are part of the essence of this
> picture which the author is trying to give us of modem life as a
> state of hell.

Luther Nichols, the *San Francisco Examiner* book reviewer, at the
beginning of his testimony, offered this opinion:

> Mr. Ginsberg is expressing his personal view of a segment of life
> that he has experienced. It is a vagabond one; it's coloured by ex-
> posure to jazz, to Columbia, a university, to a liberal and Bohemian
> education, to a great deal of traveling on the road, to a certain
> amount of what we call bumming around. He has seen in that ex-
> perience things that do not agree with him, that have perhaps em-
> bittered him. He has also seen things at a social level concerned
> with the atom bomb, and the materialism of our time. In sum, I
> think it's a howl of pain . . .

McIntosh asked: "You are familiar with the San Francisco Renaissance, are you?" Nichols said, "Yes." He had recently read *On the
Road*, by Jack Kerouac, which he called "a prose representation, I
think, of this same segment of the American population."

McIntosh asked if he understood Ginsberg when he wrote: "who
howled on their knees in the subways and were dragged off the roof
waving genitals and manuscripts." Nichols said: "Not explicitly. I
would say he's attempting to show the lack of inhibition of the per-

sons he's talking of, the members of his group, you might say."

And then he spelled out for the prosecution what group Ginsberg was speaking for, in his estimation: "Of the younger liberals. The post–World War II generation; those who returned, went into college or went into work immediately after World War II. . . .

When Walter van Tilburg Clark took the stand, he was asked by Mr. McIntosh, after a few questions about *Howl*, if he considered himself a liberal. The defense objected, and the judge sustained his objection.

Then it was the prosecution's turn. The prosecution called Gail Potter. Some of the spectators in the courtroom laughed when, in listing her qualifications, she said that she had rewritten Faust. ". . . Took three years to do that, but I did it; I rewrote *Everyman!*"

She also stated, "To have literary style you must have form, diction, fluidity, clarity. Now, I am speaking only of style, and in content, every great piece of literature, anything that can really be classified as literature, is of some moral greatness, and I think this fails to the nth degree."

The defense had no questions for Ms. Potter. The *Howl* trial was over. The judge ruled in favor of the defense.

In his decision Judge Horn stated:

"I do not believe that *Howl* is without even the slightest redeeming social importance." He then reiterated much of what Mark Schorer had said about the structure of the three parts of the poem, and of "Footnote to Howl" said that it seemed "to be a declamation that everything in the world is holy, including parts of the body by name. It ends in a plea for holy living."

In a decision that is still the basis for most of our present obscenity law, the judge set out specific guidelines for the future in the form of twelve rules. The first was:

If the material has the *slightest redeeming social importance* it is not obscene because it is protected by the First and Fourteenth amendments of the United States Constitution and the California Constitution.

In Rule Twelve the judge said:

In considering material claimed to be obscene it is well to remember the motto: *Honi soit qui mal y pense* (evil to him who thinks evil).

During the trial the City Lights Bookstore featured a display of books that had been banned through the centuries. It was a formidable collection of great literature: *Ulysses, Lady Chatterley's Lover, Huckleberry Finn, The Odyssey, Gulliver's Travels,* and, of course, *Howl and Other Poems.*

By the trial's end, there were more than 10,000 copies of *Howl* in print. To date *more than 400,000* copies have been sold.

.

CHAPTER EIGHT

FERLINGHETTI HAD NOT testified at the trial, but his public statements certainly were felt throughout the proceedings. His clearly written defense of *Howl* attracted widespread attention. He was convinced that this was only the beginning of a new awakening in American poetry, and that the San Francisco poetry renaissance (which he always insists must be spelled without capitalization) would be around for a long time to come.

The old coffeehouses of North Beach, The Black Cat Café, Vesuvio's, The Iron Pot, and 12 Adler Place, were as busy as ever. In some cases the clientele had changed, but new places were opening up all the time. Henri Lenoir of Vesuvio's, a man whom Ferlinghetti admired as one of the true San Francisco bohemians, advertised "booths for psychiatrists," and more to the tempo of the times, he offered "beatnik kits" for sale.

City Lights Pocketbook Shop, with Shig manning the front desk, prospered. Murao kept true to the tradition of Bohemianism. He had seen the lines being drawn by the forces of oppression during the *Howl* trial, and made sure that the original character of the bookstore didn't change.

There were now seven volumes in the Pocket Poets Series. Numbers 5, 6, and 7 were *True Minds*, by Marie Ponsot; *Kora in Hell*, by William Carlos Williams; and *Here and Now*, by Denise Levertov, whose later poetry was published by New Directions. Levertov's work came to Ferlinghetti's attention from Rexroth. City Lights had also issued a pamphlet by Norman Mailer called *The White Negro*.

In the year following the *Howl* trial, Ferlinghetti published *Gasoline*, by Gregory Corso. He had first become familiar with Corso's writing through *The Vestal Lady on Brattle*, a collection of early

poems, and wrote to Corso, who was living in Cambridge, Massachusetts, expressing his admiration and his desire to publish a new
collection of his poetry. *Gasoline* began with an introduction by
Ginsberg, who was as excited as Ferlinghetti by Corso's humor and
direct language. Corso was rapidly becoming recognized nationally,
along with Ginsberg, Kerouac, and Ferlinghetti. He joined Ginsberg
in giving readings and he appeared in national journals that focused
on the new writing.

Not long after meeting Ferlinghetti, Ginsberg had talked to him
about the possibility of publishing works by Kerouac. City Lights
had been offered the manuscript of *On the Road*, but Ferlinghetti had turned it down. Ferlinghetti was also given the opportunity,
which he passed up, of publishing some of Kerouac's poetry, including *Mexico City Blues* and a collection of poems written in San Francisco in 1954. Ginsberg suggested a book of Kerouac poems to be
published after *Gasoline*, but Ferlinghetti said no to this proposal.
In 1961, however, Ferlinghetti published Kerouac's *Book of Dreams*.
And in later years he admitted that he regretted not having published Kerouac earlier. He had been determined to follow his own
course, becoming increasingly sensitive to critics who were calling
City Lights Books the house organ of the Beat Generation in the late
fifties. Still, Ginsberg continued to write to Ferlinghetti and to talk
to him about new writers he felt City Lights should publish.

Ginsberg had been instrumental in helping William Burroughs
publish his first book, *Junkie*. When he gave Ferlinghetti a copy of
Burroughs's *Naked Lunch* (which was not yet in its final form), Ferlinghetti was at first repelled by it. He suggested that Ginsberg edit
a section from the book and submit it to him. Ginsberg never got
around to doing it, and Ferlinghetti did not publish Burroughs until
the early sixties. *Naked Lunch*, later published by Grove Press, went
on to become a contemporary classic.

Ginsberg and Ferlinghetti discussed many of the writers of the San
Francisco Renaissance/Beat Generation such as Gary Snyder, Philip
Whalen, and Michael McClure. As early as 1956 Ginsberg urged him
to publish Whalen and Snyder, gently attempting to persuade Ferling-

hetti as to their merits. In a letter to Ginsberg in 1959, Ferlinghetti wrote that he just wasn't very interested in what Snyder was writing at the time and that he'd like to wait for other work from him. When Snyder's first book was published by poet Cid Corman of Origin Press, Ferlinghetti cooperated closely on the sales and distribution. In 1960, Snyder's second book was published by Corinth Press of New York.

Meanwhile Ferlinghetti's own book was doing well. James Laughlin had been prophetic in regard to *A Coney Island of the Mind*. It was New Directions paperback #74, with a cover photograph of Coney Island at night. Over the years, the collection has sold more than 900,000 copies.

M. L. Rosenthal wrote in *The Nation* that in *Coney Island*, Ferlinghetti showed that he had "learned some useful things, and gladly, from various European and American experimenters," and he called him "a deft, rapid-paced, whittling performer. He has a wonderful eye for meaning in the commonplace." Harvey Shapiro, writing in the *New York Times*, was not as wholehearted about the book. He found Ferlinghetti "highly readable and often very funny . . . his book a grab bag of undergraduate musings about love and art, much hackneyed satire of American life and some real and wry perceptions of it." Hayden Carruth, the critic for *Poetry*, found nothing to like in *A Coney Island of the Mind*. He wrote that Ferlinghetti had "no trace of understanding for language's capacity and no sensitivity to sound."

At about this time, Grove Press publisher Barney Rosset and Donald Allen established the *Evergreen Review*. The second issue of the nationally distributed magazine appeared in 1957 and was devoted to the San Francisco scene. The cover showed a nighttime photo of a downtown scene over which were superimposed the words *San Francisco* and the names of Ferlinghetti, Miller, Rexroth, Ginsberg, Kerouac, Duncan, Josephine Miles, and Michael Rumaker.

Rexroth led the issue with a San Francisco letter in which he spoke of what he termed "the San Francisco Renaissance and the New Generation of Revolt and Our Underground Literature and Cultural Disaffiliation." He wrote about how San Francisco was like no other place in the United States. It was easy to live there, and in fact, he said, if he couldn't live in San Francisco he'd have to think about someplace like Aix-en-Provence. "I always feel like I ought to get a passport every time I cross to Oakland or Berkeley," he wrote, echoing sentiments that Ferlinghetti had at other times expressed.

In his article Rexroth took a long swipe at doctrinaire leftists, at capitalist society, and at the literary establishment. Then, in the first essay ever to define the San Francisco poets as a movement, he gave geographical place and spiritual space to the "new San Francisco writers." Of Ferlinghetti he said: "He is a lazy-looking, good-natured man with the canny cocky eye of an old-time vaudeville tenor." Of Ferlinghetti's poetry he wrote:

> His verse, so easy and relaxed, is constructed of most complex rhythms, all organized to produce just the right tone. Now tone is the hardest and last of the literary virtues to control and it requires assiduous and inconspicuous craftsmanship. Ferlinghetti is definitely a member of the San Francisco School—he says exactly what Everson, Duncan, Ginsberg say.

The magazine included several selections from *A Coney Island of the Mind*. Ginsberg was represented with "Howl."

The interest in the literary events in San Francisco was growing. The *Chicago Review*, edited by Irving Rosenthal, author of a much neglected, brilliant novel called *Sheeper*, featured ten San Francisco poets in the Spring 1958 issue. Ferlinghetti wrote a piece called "Note on Poetry in San Francisco," and had one poem in the issue. The essay partly reads:

> I have no very specific idea just what poetry the *Chicago Review* will select from San Francisco. This is not a school nor does it have any definite regional characteristics. There are all kinds of poets here, writing very dissimilar types of poetry (as this issue ought to show). But I should say that the kind of poetry which has been making the most noise here is quite different from the "poetry

about poetry," the poetry of technique, the poetry for poets and professors which has dominated the quarterlies and anthologies in this country for some time and which of course is also written in San Francisco. The poetry which has been making itself heard here of late is what should be called street poetry. For it amounts to getting the poet out of the inner esthetic sanctum where he has too long been contemplating his complicated navel. It amounts to getting poetry back into the street where it once was, out of the classroom, out of the speech department, and—in fact—off the printed page. The printed word has made poetry so silent. But the poetry I am talking about here is spoken poetry, poetry conceived as oral messages. It "makes it" aloud. Some of it has been read with jazz, much of it has not. A new "ashcan" school? Rock and roll? Who cares what names it's called. What is important is that this poetry is using its eyes and ears as they have not been used for a number of years. "Poetry about poetry," like much nonobjective painting, has caused an atrophy of the artist's senses. He has literally forgotten (taken leave of) senses. (I walked thru Chinatown recently with a famous academic poet, and he never saw the whole schools of fish gasping on counters, nor heard what they breathed.)

The other poets in the *Chicago Review* were Burroughs, Kirby Doyle, Duncan, Ginsberg, Kerouac, Lamantia, McClure, Whalen, and John Weiners. This was one of the first appearances of selections from *Naked Lunch*. Gary Snyder was noticeably missing from the list. In the next few years these poets, sometimes called San Francisco Poets and other times Beat Poets or Poets of the Beat Generation, were widely published in quality magazines and establishment presses all over the country.

Soon there were poetry readings going on all the time in San Francisco. The late fifties brought an era of coffeehouse readings, especially in North Beach at places like The Cellar, the Place, and the Co-Existence Bagel Shop. Tour buses poured into North Beach. Ferlinghetti and his friends found themselves accosted by scores of tourists, would-be beatniks, journalists, interviewers, and others demanding his time. He was reading both in San Francisco and in other cities. Shig Murao was in charge of the bookstore on a full-time basis, and Ferlinghetti, when he wasn't on tour, could usually be found at the store.

By 1958–59 City Lights Books was an institution in San Francisco. As of August 1958 there were nine titles in the Pocket Poets Series, with two more on the way. One was called *New Young German Poets*, edited by New York poet Jerome Rothenberg. A project called *A Marianne Moore Sampler* was planned, but much to Ferlinghetti's disappointment, it never saw print. It was to have been his homage to a poet who profoundly influenced him in the 1940s, and the publication of the text would have emphasized the true nature of City Lights, which wasn't limited to new writings of the Beat Generation.

Ferlinghetti's Prévert book, *Paroles*, published in 1958, was the result of careful planning. The book included the poems that had appeared in *City Lights* magazine and some that had never been published. This was the first extensive selection of the French poet's writings in English. Ferlinghetti wrote an introduction to the poems that gave remarkable insight into his own writing, as well as that of Prévert. He stressed that Prévert paid attention to the ordinary occurrences of life and that he wrote as one talks. Also, that Prévert was more of a see-er than a seer. Prévert, said Ferlinghetti, was not a prophetic writer. His poetry was grounded in the perceivable, in what the eye sees. Using the language of ordinary speech, the poet illuminated his vision without a grand plan or program. Each poem was meant to be heard separately and each poem distinctly isolated a specific aspect of life.

Meanwhile, the media continued to focus on the writers of the San Francisco Renaissance. Most of the poets ignored the insensitivity that so much of the coverage displayed. Ginsberg used his newfound fame/notoriety to expound upon other writers, the world's social-political situation, and a wide range of topics. He took seriously Whitman's admonition that poets should assume an active role in their country's life. Ginsberg was now a truly public poet. Ferlinghetti applauded Ginsberg's efforts, and he himself remained committed to public presentations of poetry. He scoffed at attempts to write off the San Francisco scene with labels like "Beat Generation." He saw the labeling as just another attempt to suppress a growing body of literature that was causing people to think in new ways, in ways they had previously been afraid to confront. The media were perversely fascinated by the "Beat" phenomenon, and vicious articles appeared in the popular press. Some even found their way into literary journals. A few of the poetry reviewers went to incredible lengths to castigate an entire generation of writers.

On May 23, 1959, a poetry reading made the first page of the *San Francisco Chronicle*. In a story headlined BEAT POETS APPEAR EN MASSE: A MESS, the journalist Donovan McClure wrote: "North Beach poets had their finest hour last night in a monster (or was it monstrous) poetry reading before an audience of longhairs (mostly uncombed) at Garibaldi Hall. There was a smattering of heckling, cheering and wild applause and cautious indifference among the five hundred who paid a buck each for the privilege. Such Beatnik literary giants as Allen Ginsberg, Jack Spicer, Robert Duncan and James Broughton took their turns . . ." The reading had been one of a number of benefits held for small literary journals. In this case the beneficiary was *Measure* magazine, edited by poet John Weiners (author of *The Hotel Wentley Poems*), whose work was a major contribution to the new poetry.

At the reading Ginsberg had read "Kaddish," one of his most famous poems—many think it his best poem. The article in the *Chronicle* failed to mention that Ginsberg had read the poem, and in response he wrote a letter to the editor, which was printed a few days later. In his letter he pointed out that Jack Spicer, a poet who had been around San Francisco for years and considered himself independent of literary trends, would be dismayed to see himself classified as a "Beat poet." So would Robert Duncan and James Broughton. Ginsberg took the paper to task for not mentioning that he had read his first major work since *Howl* and for neglecting to mention that "Kaddish" had received an enthusiastic reception.

Ferlinghetti sent his own response to the article:

May 27, 1959

Dear Editor:

It's a crying shame when a major American poet has to write to you
to point out the importance of his own poetry as Allen Ginsberg did
yesterday in a letter to the *Chronicle*. He said the *Chronicle* perhaps
had completely missed the major news item in its report of last Saturday's benefit poetry reading in North Beach, this item concerning
himself. He said: "I gave a very extraordinary reading of the first major poem I have written since 'Howl.' This is an event of considerable
importance to San Francisco."

As his publisher, I want to say that, far from being a conceited evalua-
tion of himself, Allen Ginsberg's statement is really an understatement
of the facts. It was a very great reading and, luckily, it was recorded
by Max Weiss of Fantasy Records who plans soon to issue it on an LP.
But the *Chronicle*'s sneering report only underlined the ignorance of
many literate San Franciscans as to the most important development
in modem poetry both here and across the country today. If the words
of a small publisher such as myself have no effect, perhaps various
New York publishers (New Directions, Grove Press, etc.) would be
able to enlighten you. Any of their editors would be glad to let San
Franciscans know what is going on in their city.

Lawrence Ferlinghetti
CITY LIGHTS BOOKS

Negative commentary and an uninformed press could not stop the
new poets from bringing their poetry to the people. The readings
continued to draw large audiences. There were massive readings on
the East Coast and in the Midwest, as well as in San Francisco.

By 1960 there were thirteen books in the Pocket Poets Series and twenty-three titles in the City Lights list as a whole. Ginsberg was preparing his second collection, *Kaddish and Other Poems*, which was to be Pocket Poets Number 14, issued in 1961.

Ferlinghetti's novel *Her* was published by New Directions in 1960. He had continued writing the novel during the fifties, sometimes putting it away for long periods and picking it up, changing things around, taking out whole sections and adding new ones. Some parts of the book reflect the Beat scene and show the influence of both Kerouac and Ginsberg. This is especially apparent in the section that talks about the Poetry Police:

> the Poetry Police were coming to save them, the Poetry Police were coming to save them all from death, Captain Poetry was coming to save the world from itself, to make the world safe for beauty and love, the Poetry Police had arrived to clean up the mass mess, the Poetry Police were about to descend in parachutes made from the pages of obscene dictionaries, the Poetry Police were about to land simultaneously in the central squares of forty-two major cities, having chartered all the planes in the world and being furnished with free seats for an endless passage since all were poids net, the Poetry Police were about to land simultaneously on the tops of the tallest buildings and bridges and monuments and fortifications of the world and take complete command of the rapidly deteriorating world situation, the Poetry Police were about to invade Geneva and decide once and for all what the shape of the table should be at all future peace conferences, the Poetry Police were about to consolidate their positions simultaneously in all parts of the world by climbing onto the backs and hanging onto the necks of everyone and shouting true profound wiggy formulas for eternal mad salvation . . .

Ferlinghetti called the novel "a surreal, semi-autobiography blackbook of a semi-mad period of my life, in that mindless, timeless state most romantics pass through, confusing flesh madonnas with spiritual ones." The novel's lack of critical success did not deter it from having wide sales. On the cover was a section from one of Ferling-hetti's paintings.

Her comprised numerous sketches, memory notations, dream journal entries, spontaneous diatribes, and careful recountings of Ferlinghetti's experiences—transformed by his imaginative pow-ers—and is a kind of document of his deepest emotions. The nar-rative is not dependent on characters, but on stream-of-conscious-ness associations. In a sense, it is a poem in prose; this is certainly true of the Poetry Police section—it is not difficult to think of it arranged on the page as a poem might be. Ferlinghetti goes deep into the pool of imagination that lies both near at hand and far off in the distance. There is a constant tug-of-war between that which is immediately discernible and that which is struggling for the light of the mind to take hold of the incorporate. *Her* is really a note-book of consciousness, a book of spiritual exercises. The sections on Paris, where he makes long lists of the painters he admired and the books he read, are an attempt to incorporate the diversity of things that interested him. He was exorcising all his influences by assimilating them into his own style, refined and made strong through the discipline of shaping the poems that make up his first two books of poetry.

As the novel was finalized, Ferlinghetti became increasingly en-thusiastic about the possibilities of the Beat writings. In his notebook in 1959 he noted:

> Beat Generation writings are vituperations—the only thing that will stand will be the narrative "i"—whether in prose or poetry—the voice of him sounding thru the American experience, first Whitman, then Thomas Wolfe, then Kerouac . . .

Ferlinghetti had finally come to the same realization about Ker-ouac that an increasing number of critics and readers had, that he was a major new voice in American letters. It was Kerouac who had coined the term "Beat Generation." As he remembered it, he was sit-ting with John Clellon Holmes, and he described himself, Holmes, and their contemporaries as a beat generation. The account is given in a speech Kerouac delivered to a Brandeis University seminar at Hunter College, and subsequently printed in *Playboy* magazine.

As always, Ferlinghetti tries to de-emphasize the term "Beat Generation," which has been used by many as a coverall for what Ferlinghetti defines as "an early phase of counter-culture poetry re-generation in America." In interviews he constantly emphasizes that the new poetry that surfaced in San Francisco is part of an ongoing movement of writers who are interested in new forms and in working independently of traditional literary trends.

CHAPTER NINE

IN 1958, FERLINGHETTI realized the dream of owning his own home. Beforehand he had lived in places that were not his. He had always been a "guest" or a renter. Now he found a dilapidated Victorian house on Potrero Hill, a quiet residential area overlooking the city and the Bay. Kirby agreed with him that it would be a great place to settle—close enough to North Beach and yet removed from it. As the years passed, they would be able to watch as high-rise buildings were constructed in downtown San Francisco, erasing the original view they had of Telegraph Hill and Coit Tower. The neighborhood gave the impression of being a city separate from the rest of San Francisco, perched as it was on a hill. Like many Victorian residences, the house had been allowed to fall into near rains. Ferlinghetti got caught up in the idea of doing his own repairs. He hired a carpenter and together they spent several months making the place habitable.

Meanwhile, City Lights Books continued to grow. Ferlinghetti published two broadsides by Bob Kaufman in 1959. Kaufman had joined the merchant marine at age sixteen and served for fourteen years. He was a devotee of saxophonist Charlie Parker, one of the pioneers of the new jazz. He knew jazz musicians, abstract expressionist painters, and poets on both the West and East Coasts. Kaufman loved the music of Eliot's "The Love Song of J. Alfred Prufrock" and recited poems from *The Poet in New York*, by Federico García Lorca, from memory. In much of his poetry, Kaufman employed the same humorous energies that Ferlinghetti himself was so adept at handling when attacking social and political injustices. One of his poems so offended a local anti-beatnik policeman, William Bigarani, that the policeman tore the poem off the wall of the Bagel Shop where it had been posted, promoting a local controversy.

The two broadsides published by City Lights were *Second April* and the satirical work *The Abomunist Manifesto*. Both were suffused with the spirit of jazz. When Kaufman read them aloud it was with an originality and exuberance that electrified people. New Directions later published his first collection of poems, *Solitudes Crowded with Loneliness*, in which the two City Lights broadsides were included. His second collection, *Golden Sardine*, was published by City Lights in 1967.

Word about the new poetry began to spread to other parts of the world. In January 1959, Allen Ginsberg and Ferlinghetti were invited to attend a fifteen-nation writers conference at the University of Concepción, Chile. Kirby went along. A Chilean poet then teaching at the University of California in Berkeley had been instrumental in getting them invited, but he had neglected to tell the two American poets that most of the conferees would be doctrinaire communists. For those writers, revolution was a very real goal, not just something they wrote about symbolically in their poetry. Ginsberg often talked about rebellion, and Ferlinghetti characterized artists and writers as socio-political rebels, but they were not ready to see the total change of society as they knew it, and certainly not with Stalinist countries as models. Neither Ferlinghetti nor Ginsberg could be called a revolutionary in the sense that neither advocated violent or total overthrow of government.

The conference was held during the Cuban Revolution. Fidel Castro had entered Havana on January 8, 1959, just a few days before the conference got under way. In Concepción, Ferlinghetti and Ginsberg were able to hear from new sources about events in Castro's Cuba. Their perceptions of the Cuban Revolution were different from those of most North Americans. For the people at Concepción, the United States represented a powerful force that established contact only with the elite of the Latin American countries and on the whole supported those who needed the least help. In Chile, for example, U.S. corporations controlled vast holdings and little of the money filtered down to the poor. Ferlinghetti got a chance to see this firsthand on a visit to the Lota Coal Mines, where working conditions were unbelievably wretched and primitive and there was no visible progress for the average laborer.

The poverty in Lota contrasted sharply with the enclave of wealthy tourists who came to the town's resort area to enjoy the beauty of the botanical gardens and to bask in the sunshine. In his journal Ferlinghetti noted that "working conditions were like those in the United States seventy or eighty years ago."

The atmosphere at the conference was casual. There was a lot of arguing. Debate was encouraged. Ferlinghetti felt himself a kindred spirit to this new generation of South American writers. They were engaged in society. They did not hide behind the walls of institutions, but often stood before them to either change them or bring them down. Writing was, for them, not only a means of expressing their own subjective needs but also a way of going out into the world with a call for change to better the lives of all people.

After the conference Ferlinghetti and Kirby traveled around Latin America. He wrote in his journals of the all-pervasive influence of North American industrialists on the economies of the places he visited. Everywhere, a double standard existed. Freedom and a leisurely lifestyle existed only for the affluent minority. Neither was available to the vast majority of people. The Ferlinghettis were struck by this on their first stop, Bolivia's capital city, La Paz. In spite of its great industrial complex, its rich mines, and abundant oil reserves, the people are among the most pathetically illiterate and deprived in all of Latin America.

From Bolivia the Ferlinghettis traveled by steamer across Lake Titicaca to the sparsely inhabited southeastern tip of Peru. Again, Ferlinghetti found much poverty, illiteracy, and an economy almost completely controlled by outside interests. But he was tremendously impressed with the great beauty of Lima, which, though surrounded by desert areas, is nestled amid green valleys. "Lima has a spirit and sense of being in the manner of Vienna, Paris, Madrid—one of the few cities in the entire Western Hemisphere that seem to have that certain Parisian or Continental soul. Certainly the only such city in South America I've seen," he wrote in his journal. He went on to contrast Lima with Concepción. Concepción had been virtually destroyed by an earthquake in 1939, and had been almost entirely rebuilt—the buildings were all new and modern. In Lima, on the other hand, despite many new buildings, much of the past was retained. Especially impressive to Ferlinghetti was the Plaza de Armas, where huge colonial buildings stand. At one time Lima had been the wealthiest city in the Western Hemisphere, and it still retained a regal atmosphere.

After some short trips to a few of the Central American countries, Ferlinghetti and Kirby arrived in Mexico City. While there, they walked through the pathways of Chapultepec Park, the city's equivalent of New York's Central Park and San Francisco's Golden Gate Park.

While Ferlinghetti and Kirby traveled through Latin America, Ginsberg had chosen to stay on for a while in Chile. One of the reasons Ginsberg stayed behind was his unusual ability to develop friendships and his ease in getting to know small details about the people he met and places he lived. Ferlinghetti had the same insatiable curiosity, yet found it difficult to break through his natural shyness, so he admired Ginsberg's ease with people. At the conference the two had become acquainted with Nicanor Parra, a mathematics professor at the University of Chile and a noted poet. He offered Ginsberg the use of his home during his post-conference stay in Chile.

Ferlinghetti decided to publish a selection of Parra's poetry in the Pocket Poets Series, introducing him to American readers. When he returned to San Francisco that was one of his first undertakings. The book was called *Anti-Poems*, the poetry of an iconoclast, blasting the old institutions of Chilean society, including the Church and clerics. Parra was humorous, satirical, and straightforward. He had broken from neo-Romanticism and traditional poetic forms. His temperament, like that of Ferlinghetti and Ginsberg, was more that of a rebel than of a revolutionary. He didn't call for the destruction of his society, but pointed out that it must change because it was burdened with ponderousness and injustices. His role was to level barrages at hypocrisy, and in his poetry he strove to speak out for the oppressed in society.

In 1960, Ferlinghetti added the satirical sketches *Hiporama of the Classics* of Lord Buckley to the City Lights list. Buckley, a comedian, had been performing ever since the speakeasy days of the 1920s. In the nightclubs of North Beach and elsewhere he attracted an appreciative younger audience with his translations of the classics into the new Beat and hip jargon.

Ferlinghetti was one of the editors of a small mimeographed poetry journal, *Beatitude* magazine. It had been jointly founded by Bob Kaufman, John Kelley, William J. Margolis, and Allen Ginsberg. The editorship revolved, and when it came to Ferlinghetti's turn, he corrupted the names of himself and his contributors. He published *Beatitude Anthology* in 1960, a selection of poems that had appeared in various issues of *Beatitude*.

While the publishing was thriving, Ferlinghetti was busy with both his own writing and his life with Kirby. He and Kirby owned a small cabin in Bixby Canyon, an isolated area some two hundred miles south of San Francisco. During the summer of 1960 they bought a small parcel of land near the site of the old cabin, hoping to build on it in the future.

Big Sur was a little-known area in 1960. To travelers on California State Highway 1, Bixby Canyon is nothing more than another break in the rugged Big Sur coastline spanned by a bridge. At the north end of the bridge there is a narrow dirt road leading into the canyon. A small collection of rural mailboxes is the only indication that anyone lives nearby. The road hugs the wall of the canyon for about three quarters of a mile, then it descends to the canyon floor. It crosses the creek at the base of the canyon, then winds southward toward Big Sur. The road was originally part of the old coastal highway, before the bridge was built. At the point where the road approaches the creek, there is a large wooden gate leading to several homes, each on a separate parcel of land. Together the property owners decide on how large any building can be and how many are allowed on each parcel. They are united against any large-scale building in the canyon, preserving its rustic atmosphere and disturbing the natural habitat as little as possible.

Ferlinghetti's cabin was located next to the creek, not far from the point where the road leads into a footpath that goes directly to the beach. He kept it simple, heating the cabin with a fireplace. Various guests who lived in it over the years made gradual additions. Since he and Kirby first began going to the canyon, it had been a refuge from city life, a place of escape. Here he could spend his hours in solitude, walking down to the beach, following the tree-shaded stream to where it empties into the sea in a quiet pool carved into the sand—a pool that changes shape quite often, depending on the caprice of the stream and the ocean. By the late sixties Bixby Canyon began to appear in Ferlinghetti's writings. In "After the Cries of the Birds" he says, ". . . mixed with trips to my cabin Bixby Canyon Big Sur and its wild beach of white sand rocks and kelp, far way below the highway's great arched bridge . . . and further on, . . . to write out the true poem of my life, after the cries of the birds had stopped one strange evening on Bixby Beach and later in redwood cabin by Bixby Creek rushing with spring rains . . ."

With the birth of his children, Bixby became even more important to Ferlinghetti. Kirby remembers how he liked to go there frequently for the sake of the kids. There, out of the way of the urban landscape, he spent hours with his children, playing with them and watching them grow.

During one of his visits to Bixby, in the late fifties, Ferlinghetti went to see Henry Miller, who lived at Partington Ridge, fifteen miles away in Big Sur. Ferlinghetti wrote in his journal: "I arrived at his place with a bottle of French wine. That was the only way an outsider would be welcome." Still Miller had no interest in City Lights publishing company. The San Francisco Poetry Renaissance seemed a distant thing to him. He didn't care much about what was happening to the north of him.

Ferlinghetti's own attention was being drawn south, to the Caribbean. He had become increasingly interested in the Cuban Revolution, heightened both by the trip to Chile and because of the growing press attention. This concern, coupled with the fact that he had found out that his mother's family (on her father's side) came from the Caribbean, resulted in a trip to the Virgin Islands and to Cuba on what was a personal fact-finding mission.

Ferlinghetti had thought about the history of his family from time to time. He had rarely verbalized these thoughts and the feelings they aroused. While corresponding with William Carlos Williams over *Kora in Hell* and "Howl," he learned that Williams knew of a family named Monsanto and that his parents had been married at Monsanto's residence in Brooklyn. Williams wrote to Ferlinghetti that his mother's family, who had come from Puerto Rico, knew several Monsantos there.

Ferlinghetti had been in touch with Tram Coombs, a San Francisco poet who had since moved to Charlotte Amalie, on St. Thomas in the Virgin Islands. Through Coombs, Ferlinghetti discovered that his relatives might be living on St. Thomas. There had been Mendes-Monsantos on the island for many years. Coombs located Mrs. Gladys Woods of St. Thomas, who was the local telephone operator. Her father was Jean-Baptiste Mendes-Monsanto, and she was Herman Monsanto's half sister. A missing link had been found to Ferlinghetti's past, and one that excited him. He talked to Gladys Woods over the phone from San Francisco at great length, and told her that he would soon go to the Virgin Islands to meet her.

The Caribbean trip began in November of 1960, and included a stopover at the University of North Carolina, Chapel Hill, where Ferlinghetti gave a poetry reading. He was introduced to the students by his former English professor Phillips Russell, and received an enthusiastic response from the large audience. In Chapel Hill, which was little changed from his college days, he had a reunion with Anne Oakes Scarborough, Presley and Anna Bisland's granddaughter. She and her husband were living in Chapel Hill, and she had been corresponding with Ferlinghetti on and off through the years.

From Chapel Hill, Kirby and Ferlinghetti traveled south to Florida, where they visited with Kirby's family, and then went on to Puerto Rico. From San Juan they took a boat to the Virgin Islands. Ferlinghetti noticed that the port of Charlotte Amalie looked very much like Palma de Majorca in Spain. They immediately got in touch with his great-aunt Gladys, who invited them to stay at her home. She gave them a complete rundown of local history, paying particular attention to details pertaining to the Mendes-Monsanto family.

Ferlinghetti and Kirby saw old photographs of his great-grandfather Jean-Baptiste, and of his grandfather Herman. He learned that there were Monsantos throughout the Caribbean, but that the Mendes-Monsantos remained in the Virgin Islands. Much to his surprise, Ferlinghetti also found out that he had another aunt, Gladys's sister, Mrs. Jean McGrath, who lived in the seaside community of Bolinas, just north of San Francisco on the coast of Marin County. He would get to know her and talk with her about the family.

Since Gladys was the island's telephone operator, she knew practically everyone on the island. As she walked with Ferlinghetti and Kirby through the quaint streets of Charlotte Amalie, Gladys gave a running commentary about everything they saw and everyone they met. It was a fortunate time for them to have visited, because the island was not yet the commercialized tourist center it is today. They visited an old mansion that had been the home of Ferlinghetti's great-grandfather and went to Thatch Quay, which had been owned by the family. He left the Virgin Islands with warm feelings for the Mendes-Monsanto family—Gladys would play a key role in Ferlinghetti's life years later when he and Kirby were having marital difficulties, and during his long divorce. She visited her sister in the early 1970s and spent quite some time with Ferlinghetti, acting, as he put it, like a mother would have.

From St. Thomas he and Kirby went to Haiti, arriving in Port-au-Prince on November 29, 1960. At that time Haiti was ruled by the U.S.-supported dictator François "Papa Doc" Duvalier. A portion of the Haitian journals that Ferlinghetti wrote in the two days he spent there were published in the magazine *Journal for the Protection of All Beings*. He and Kirby had never seen such poverty and degradation as they witnessed in Haiti:

The great iron market of Port-au-Prince, casbah of the Caribbean, this Iron Market an enormous native mercado (as in Guadalajara, La Paz, Cuzco, any Indian town)—a whole city block of death and dung and pissing desperation, an Exposition of it, everyone on their own hunger-hanger. Some Desolation Photographer should come and do a real Death Magazine job on the Market of Iron, huge hive aswarm with obsidian natives, all hawking, pulling at you, running after you with wares, shouting, crying, laughing, eating, and smoking St. Ange leaves. Take picturesque postcard photos of stringbean children with rubbertire shards tied to feet . . . Third Avenue Elevated terminal fallen into jungle, a Meccano Erector set, all girders and iron plates . . .

The coins all read LIBERTÉ, EGALITÉ, FRATERNITÉ. These noble savages are all absolutely equal, except for the six percent who own everything not owned by foreigners. If money's the blood of the poor, in the Port of the Prince, the blood has black corpuscles. The Prince has long washed his hands of it . . . Ah, but our guidebook tells us, "Tourists beset by beggars, fresh children, arrogant young men and petty thieves will do well to remember that the first and last belong to the declassed riffraff found in any large city, and the others are insecure members of a rising and still unaccepted middle-class." Our guidebook is written by a noted American poet. It goes on to say that the average cash income of the Haitian is under $75 a year.

They stayed only two days and then, with great anticipation, they flew to Cuba, arriving on Sunday, December 3.

Ferlinghetti had become active in the Fair Play for Cuba Committee, which was made up of old-line Socialist Workers Party members and a great many unaffiliated people like himself. The group staged demonstrations in support of U.S.–Cuban dialogue against the background of a growing anti-Castro sentiment, which was widespread around the country. The Committee tried to counter the prevailing views of official Washington, which saw Castro's revolution as part of the worldwide Communist conspiracy. Ferlinghetti felt that no one in power in Washington wanted to admit the real grievances that had led to the Castro movement. He drew a parallel between the civil war in Spain in the thirties and the Cuban Revolution. In the Spanish war, Ferlinghetti noted in his journals, the United States also wore blinders and did not care to see that the Spanish people were defying fascism. Truth was cast aside for political and economic convenience. Now, in the case of Cuba, it was happening again.

The first thing to catch Ferlinghetti's eye when he and Kirby arrived in Havana was the huge red lettering on the side of the airport building:

CUBA TERRITORIO LIBRE DE AMERICA—PATRIA O MUERTE.

In translation this was a dramatic reminder that Castro and his revolutionary forces were now in control of the country.

In his journal Ferlinghetti wrote:

> . . . not a single question asked us at Airport . . . Sixteen-mile drive from Airport to Havana—Dramatic waterfront in Havana—Sea beating great long seawall Northside of city—Morro Castle at one end—Didn't see an armed soldier all the way to the city. Just saw two young ones. Two others in new-looking jeep without arms. Had on black boots. Beautiful city! Beautiful trees on the Pasea del Prado—We get hotel on Prado—$5 for two—First we meet a Greek in the lobby who says he's been here a month and "everybody's happy and like brothers." Outside our windows in hotel, the trees that line the center island of the Prado are filled with starlings. They fill the air with their cries—just as in the big trees in the main square of Ogden, Utah. We have a tiny white room with a marble balcony above the avenue and the trees. Taxis toot, birds drown them out. Four soldiers in berets go by below.
>
> No weapons—The first night we go to a Cow Fair (Feria de la Vaca) on the grounds of the Capitol in the center of Havana—It

costs ten cents to get in and there are all kinds of booths and
galleries as at any fair—including ones selling magazines, pam-
phlets, and info about "the New Cuba"—some in English, including speeches by Fidel. Here there are many soldiers but not
in disciplined groups and the ones with rifles have no bayonets
on them. Just wandering around, rather—And here's a big band
on a long bandstand—all soldiers—about to give a concert—
Man with little pistol in holster is rigging up the microphones
on stage—At the back of the stage is a huge picture of the head
of a cow—This Fair must be sponsored by INRA (the Agricul-
tural Reform Agency). Two soldiers, one looking a little like Jean
Louis Barrault in his teens, with revolvers in holsters, couldn't
be more than 20 yrs old. There's a good-size crowd waiting for
the band to start in the balmy night air—lots of kids and mothers
and all kinds of interesting looking young cats of various colors,
hardly any pure white, hardly any beards—See one young soldier
now with big black beard looking like Allen Ginsberg in Chile—
Everyone sitting on wooden chairs looking very peaceful. Notice
there aren't any people who look like the usual well-dressed upper middle class. Everyone in the park looks like the working
class; tho some wear suits with ties and white shirts, mostly it's
leather jackets, plaid shirts, etc. A few berets. . . . Something that
sounded like a bomb just went off a few blocks away . . . Concert starts—It's like a big band concert anywhere—This band in
Castro hats and fatigues—playing something like Sousa strained
through a Cuban moustache . . . Crowd now has overflowed
the seats and there are many standing on all sides and strolling
around. The people have really taken over the Capitol grounds.

The Capitol building itself and others on the great Plaza next to
it are all floodlighted . . . as are statues . . . as is Head of Cow. At
11 p.m. tomorrow night the money from the Fair will be used to
present a cow to every farmer.

He continues, in the same journal:

This young hotel clerk—sort of like a belligerent CCNY student—is the first scratch under the surface—and not very far under. He's confident Fidelista (others later told me the clerk was a "nut") non-communist, angry with uncomprehension by U.S., point at N.Y. Times Story of Eisenhower allotting one million for "resettlement of refugees from Reds." Reading this aloud from the paper, he interjects, "What Reds?" N.Y. Times says "resettlement" of refugees—(but does it say where resettlement is to be?). The inference is that the resettlement would be in the U.S.—in Miami area?—but Cubans take it to mean "resettlement" of exiled Batutianos in Cuba—or—Cuban paper "Il Mundo" reports it as One Million Aid to *Counter-Revolutionaries*. . . . In Chile at Writers' Conference last January, Cuban delegate said that Cuban writers are Revolutionary poets whereas American Beats are Rebel poets. Still he admitted a parallel in their dissent writing. Young hotel clerk here in Cuba now is Angrier than any Angry Young Man or than any Beat Poet—(U.S. Beats not angry with anyone—too cool for that—And Jack Kerouac told me before I left for Cuba, "I got my own Revolution out here in Northport—the American Revolutions." His is a typically selfish view. Other writers in U.S. today—older ones especially—mostly not interested in coming down here to see for themselves—I tried to get Rexroth interested—He wouldn't go—put down the whole idea of reporting it.)

Cuban taxi driver told us the Cubans like Americans very much—but this scratch under surface in form of this hotel clerk shows very belligerent recalcitrance, if not hatred, for American press and government, if not for individual Americans, directly due to U.S. slaps in face and policies under Eisenhower. Earlier in evening, at cafe, young hipster came up, started conversation, wouldn't sit down after he found we were Americanos. Coming up in elevator to hotel room later, I told kid driving elevator that we were "Americanos pero no yanquis." He smiled, shook my hand, enthusiastic. Turns out he is from Venezuela, arrived three months ago from there, aged fourteen and illiterate. Now he is in third grade here, goes to school half time, since there aren't enough schools to go full time, works in hotel in evenings—can now write—

The next day, Ferlinghetti continues in his journal:

All I've seen so far indicates Havana, and Cuba in general, are much, much better off economically than all other Caribbean countries, including even British Jamaica, U.S. Puerto Rico (whioh is considered a U.S. imperialist colony here), and U.S. St. Thomas—the latter and Jamaica being dependent on tourist trade almost completely—(Here in Cuba now tourist trade is almost practically at zero, all the big hotels empty, whole tourism apparatus stalled)—U.S. press having scared everyone to death—). But the real scene is: one woman with a rifle sitting in a camp chair guarding each bank on Sunday—Her sign says that the bank belongs to the people. . . . Went out to offices of newspaper *Revolución* at ten p.m. on Plaza Civica—a huge empty space with modernist buildings spaced far apart—walked across it and down a smaller plaza in the dark to get to the newspaper building—No one fired at me in the night—as I was led to expect by U.P.I. and A.P. dispatches—I saw only one soldier—sitting down guarding a garage—And one at entrance desk of *Revolución* escorted me upstairs. Over entrance is sign: PRENSA LIBRE.

In lobby is bust of Jose Marti with quotation: "No Hay Monarca Como Un Periodista Honrada"

Literary Assistant Editor I come to see was out. Made appointment for tomorrow at 5 p.m. Carlos Franqui, editor of *Revolución*, just returned from trip to Russia and other countries. . . . Back on the great square by the Paseo del Prado at midnight, I came upon a group of about 35 or 45 campesinos from the cow fair—of various colors—in the midst of a big political argument.

On Monday, December 5, he noted that he couldn't accuse anyone of allowing him to see only what was on a "guided tour." He came and went according to his own wishes and his own interests and ideas.

Wandering through the city, Ferlinghetti came upon a poster announcing a reading by Pablo Neruda. He had missed Neruda in Chile, and now saw an opportunity to meet him. About the same time, he was contacted at his hotel by a member of the Writers' Union and was introduced to several younger Cuban poets. Almost immediately he thought about publishing a collection at City Lights. In the meantime, they told him that Neruda was staying at the Cuba Libre, the former Havana Hilton. Ferlinghetti called Neruda at the hotel, and he and Kirby were invited to come and see him. On their arrival they were greeted by the poet and his wife, Matilde. Since Ferlinghetti knew little Spanish, they spoke together in French, the one language they had in common. They spent several pleasant hours together until a driver arrived from the sponsors of Neruda's reading, the House of the Americas. The reading was to be held in the old National Assembly building. Although Ferlinghetti thought that he and Kirby were not properly dressed for the occasion, Neruda insisted that they drive with him to the Assembly building and they all climbed into a massive car. On the way, the Chilean poet recounted a story of the first time he had gone to a big city in Chile. He checked into an inexpensive hotel and spent the night fighting the bedbugs, using lighted matches as a "weapon." Ferlinghetti complained that he was having a similar problem at the hotel where he was staying in Havana.

At the reading Neruda established immediate rapport with his audience. Ferlinghetti understood some of the Spanish, but was as impressed with the listeners as with Neruda himself. There was a revolutionary fervor in the old Assembly Hall. Most of the people there were soldiers. Neruda's poems praised revolution and attacked U.S. imperialism.

On December 8, Kirby and Ferlinghetti left Cuba for New Orleans, and then went on to San Francisco. Ferlinghetti's first project after his return was the writing and publication of a City Lights broadside, *One Thousand Fearful Words for Fidel Castro*. On the back of the broadside he wrote:

> There are not one thousand words here. The author has left room for a happier ending, in case the relentless hostility of government and press in the U.S. should somehow not triumph in the end. The poem in its present form was first read by Ferlinghetti at a rally in San Francisco one week before the end of the Eisenhower Era. . . .

This fragment does not appear in subsequent reprintings of the poem.

The rally referred to was sponsored by the Fair Play for Cuba Committee and held in San Francisco's Civic Center. The atmosphere was tense. Thousands of Castro supporters turned out, and many people attended who simply believed that he was not being given a fair chance by the United States. When Ferlinghetti read the poem, much of the tension broke. The poem addresses itself to the root of the problem between the two governments. By setting the narrative in San Francisco, Ferlinghetti was able to avoid the editorializing that the poem might otherwise have done. The poem begins in North Beach and Mike's Place is the anchor or vantage point from which the poet looks out into the world. He speaks in his usual easygoing straightforward manner as if he were sitting around Mike's Place, commenting on the U.S.–Cuban situation. The use of irony is very strong. Ferlinghetti utilizes common objects in his poem, as well as common language, to make his point clear.

> I am sitting in Mike's Place trying to figure out
> what's going to happen
> without Fidel Castro
> Among the salami sandwiches and spittoons
> I see no solution
> It's going to be a tragedy

I see no way out
among the admen and slumming models
and the brilliant snooping columnists
who are qualified to call Castro psychotic
because they no doubt are doctors
and have examined him personally
and are also qualified to call him Communist
with a capital C . . .

After his return from the Caribbean, Ferlinghetti was anxious to get back to work in his publishing business. Three of the most important City Lights books were published in 1961: Kerouac's *Book of Dreams*; *Kaddish and Other Poems*, by Ginsberg; and *Bottom Dogs*, by Edward Dahlberg.

Kerouac's book was a collection of his dreams just as he remembered them, dreams that are peopled by all the figures who became characters in his books. By this time Jack was a legend. He had been pursued by journalists, colleges, and universities, and there were already entire armies of Kerouac imitators eager to write their own *On the Road*. *Book of Dreams* quickly became a City Lights best seller.

Kaddish and Other Poems began with Ginsberg's moving elegy to his mother, Naomi, who had died in 1956. The title poem documents Ginsberg's relationship with, and feelings toward, his mother. "Kaddish" is the name of the Hebrew prayer for the dead. This new collection of Ginsberg poems soon rivaled *Howl* in sales.

Bottom Dogs had originally been published by Simon & Schuster in 1930. Ferlinghetti reprinted the book by photo-offset from the original in an edition of five thousand copies. The author had a large following in the underground for both *Bottom Dogs* and *The Sorrows of Priapus*, which was published by New Directions. In publishing Dahlberg, Ferlinghetti continued to stand by his commitment to publish authors with widely varying styles and interests, not limiting his list to the Beat Generation, in this case a man who had been largely neglected by the major publishers, and yet one who had made a substantial contribution to contemporary American letters.

Michael McClure and a young poet, David Meltzer, came to Ferlinghetti with the idea for a magazine called *Journal for the Protection of All Beings*. The first issue, published by City Lights, had Ferlinghetti, McClure, and Meltzer as coeditors and was subtitled the "Love-Shot issue." The effort was conceived as "A Visionary Revolutionary Review." Contributions on this theme by Thomas Merton, Bertrand Russell, Gary Snyder, Gregory Corso, Robert Duncan, and Norman Mailer were all gathered. The editors' statement read:

> We hope we have here an open place where normally apolitical men may speak uncensored upon any subject they feel most hotly & coolly about in a world which politics has made.

> We are not interested in protecting beings from themselves, we cannot help the deaths people give themselves, we are more concerned with the lives they do not allow themselves to live and the deaths other people would give us, both of the body & spirit.

The copyright page held the terse announcement: "Due to the transitory nature of life on earth this Journal is not sold on a subscription basis."

Norman Mailer's piece, "An Open Letter to JFK & Castro," was a scathing attack on U.S. policy toward Castro. Mailer talked of his own involvement in the Fair Play for Cuba Committee, and that of his fellow writers, and of the reaction of the North American press and the U.S. government toward Castro, how they seized on every opportunity to distort the facts in order to make Castro look bad. (By the time of the magazine's publication, Castro had denounced the U.S. and Eisenhower had broken all ties with Cuba.) Also in the *Journal* was a series of documents: "The Surrender Speech of Chief Joseph," the great Nez Percé Indian leader; a "Declaration of Rights," by Percy Bysshe Shelley, which began with the statement: "Government has no rights; it is a delegation from several individuals for the purpose of securing their own."

It was a journal in the anarchist pacifist tradition, and showed the poet as rebel. The second edition did not appear until seven years later, and was a photo essay on the "temporarily aborted revolution of May 1968 in France . . ." On the back cover was a statement from Herbert Marcuse, reading in part: "I think there is a common ground between the American movement and the French movement. It is a total protest against specific evils and against specific shortcomings . . . against the entire system of values . . . practiced in the established society." The issue was called "On the Barricades." The third and final issue of the *Journal*, entitled *Green Flag*, appeared one year later, and contained an anthology of work both documenting events of and demonstrating support of the People's Park rebellion in Berkeley.

New Directions brought out Ferlinghetti's third collection of poems, *Starting from San Francisco*. The book was dedicated to "Phillips Russell, Professor Emeritus, in return for some seeds he perhaps didn't know he sowed." The poems in this collection lack the surrealist quality of Ferlinghetti's earlier work. They are not as intensely lyrical, and are more indicative of the direction Ferlinghetti was going in the "Oral Messages" section of *A Coney Island of the Mind*. The colloquial Ferlinghetti is still very much present. For example, in the poem "Starting from San Francisco," he begins:

> Here I go again crossing the country in coach trains
> back to my old lone wandering.

After a series of ten poems, which included two very popular ones, "Overpopulation," and "Underwear," and a lyrical work called "Come Lie with Me and Be My Love," are four of Ferlinghetti's broadside poems. These are "The Great Chinese Dragon"; "Tentative Description of a Dinner to Promote the Impeachment of President Eisenhower"; "Special Clearance Sale of Famous Masterpieces"; and "One Thousand Fearful Words for Fidel Castro." "Starting from San Francisco" originally included a recording of Ferlinghetti reading three of its poems. The record was slipped into a pocket in the back cover of the book, but it was dropped in future reprintings.

A San Francisco poet, James Schevill, reviewed the book, pointing out that "Ferlinghetti is perfectly aware of the risk he is running in using political-topical themes . . . yet one cannot deny the excitement he stirs up in an audience. Entertainment in the true sense of that corrupted word . . ." X. J. Kennedy, also a poet, was less sympathetic. In the *New York Times Book Review* he wrote, "Ferlinghetti has won a large audience, apparently made up of people who wish poetry, like TV, to be bright, laden with gags, and undemanding . . . Listening, I wonder: shouldn't an oral poetry oftener have interesting sounds in it? Ferlinghetti reads flatly; there are few audible patterns. Lacking such patterns, his product seems mostly an amusing talk." On the other hand, Alan Dugan, a poet-critic writing in *Poetry* magazine, says, "Oral poetry has to fit the speaker's voice . . . Mr. Ferlinghetti's verse is perfectly suited to his style, and his style of delivery is effective and engaging . . . He treats political problems with wit, insight, and frankness, and reads it well on the record."

CHAPTER TEN

THE FERLINGHETTIS' DAUGHTER, Julie, was born on February 15, 1962; their son, Lorenzo, was born July 5, 1963. The rambling Victorian mansion on Wisconsin Street in the Potrero Hill area became more of a real home, well lived in, despite the trips Kirby and Lawrence had been taking. The pressures of Ferlinghetti's newfound fame often overwhelmed him. There were times when the barrage of journalists, photographers, and interviewers was too much. Now, with a family to raise, Ferlinghetti began to stay home more. He wanted his kids to have the kind of security that he never experienced as a child.

One of his later books, *Back Roads to Far Places*, is dedicated to Julie. When he talks of his daughter, he thinks of her special kind of strength, saying, "Julie reminds me of Anne Scarborough. They are both strong characters, as well as being strong physically. They are really solid emotionally. They both know exactly what they want out of life, and really seem to have it all together." Julie is a more outgoing person than her brother, Lorenzo. He reminds Ferlinghetti of his own introspective nature, and the two had a close relationship, a strong intuitive bond. (Father and son spent a great deal of time together.) "When Lorenzo was ten years old and attending school in Bolinas, he wrote in the school paper that his father treats him like a person," said Ferlinghetti—pleased. *The Mexican Night*, Ferlinghetti's Mexican journal, is dedicated "To Lorenzo should he ever come upon himself in that labyrinth of solitude."

In addition to the children, there was the family dog. Ferlinghetti, talking of him, said, "The fifth member of my family was a dog, named Homer. He was very important for me. I still miss him. He was a greathearted dog, and sort of like the dog of Ulysses, sitting on the porch while his master wandered around the world. He was always there when the master returned. Homer just kept waiting for me to come back. Always waiting. He died in 1973."

In 1962, City Lights published *A Hundred Camels in the Courtyard*, a collection of short fiction by Paul Bowles, author of *The Sheltering Sky*, *Delicate Prey*, and *Let It Come Down*. Bowles, who lived in Tangier, Morocco, was a masterful short-story writer, as well as a composer of music for film and ballet.

Red Cats appeared in 1962 as Pocket Poets Series Number 16. Edited and translated from the Russian by the poet Anselm Hollo, it contained work by three Russian poets, Andrei Voznesensky, Yevgeny Yevtushenko, and Simyon Kirsanov. It was the first American appearance of these poets in book form. Voznesensky, born in 1934, was a protégé of Boris Pasternak. He had studied to become an architect, but gave it up to devote full time to poetry. Before *Red Cats* appeared, his work was included in three separate collections in the Soviet Union. He and Yevtushenko were the acknowledged leaders of a Russian poetic renaissance. Yevtushenko was an outspoken critic of some Soviet policies. His poem "Babi Yar," written in 1962, was a eulogy for thousands of Jews killed at Babi Yar, Russia, during World War II. The poem came under stern criticism from the Kremlin, which accused the poet of hinting that the Soviet Union was anti-Semitic. He attracted gigantic crowds to his readings in Moscow and other cities. Kirsanov was, like the other two, politically concerned and representative of young Soviet poets who, like their American counterparts, were seeking new ways to express their ideas.

Following the publication of *Red Cats*, Ferlinghetti published Ginsberg's *Reality Sandwiches*, poems written from 1953 to 1960 excluded from previous collections. Two of the most notable poems, "Siesta in Xbalba" and "Love Poem on Theme by Whitman," compared favorably with his earlier work. Ginsberg was carrying on the Whitmanic call for a bond of love and sensuality between all Americans. The love he was writing of, as in *The Sleepers*, by Whitman, was not only that between a pair of lovers, heterosexual or homosexual, but universal love that could be experienced among all people. The theme was carried on in later Ginsberg collections from City Lights.

In 1963, City Lights' *The Yage Letters* appeared. The back-cover commentary of this sixty-eight-page book sums up the concerns of some of the Beat Generation writers. It reads:

> *The Yage Letters*: an early epistolary novel by William S. Burroughs, celebrated author of *The Soft Machine* & *The Ticket That Exploded*. Burroughs' 1951 account of himself as *Junkie*, published under the pseudonym of William Lee, ended "Yage may be the final fix." In letters to Allen Ginsberg, an unknown young poet in New York, his journey to the Amazon jungle is recorded, detailing picturesque incidents of search for telepathic-hallucinogenic-mind-expanding drug Yage (Ayahuasca or Banisteriopsis Caape) used by Amazon Indian doctors for finding lost objects, mostly bodies and souls. Author and recipient of these letters met again in New York, Xmas 1953, pruned and edited the writings to form a single book. Correspondence contains first seeds of later Burroughsian fantasy in *Naked Lunch*. Seven years later Ginsberg in Peru writes his old guru an account of his own visions and terrors with the same drug, appealing for further counsel. Burroughs' mysterious reply is sent. The volume concludes with two epilogues: a short note from Ginsberg on his return from the Orient years later reassuring Self that he is still here on earth, and a final poetic cut-up by Burroughs, "I am dying, Meester?"

Ferlinghetti, though satisfied with the progress of the publishing house, was restless to travel again. His prophecy concerning Ginsberg had been justified. Allen had begun to establish himself as a permanent presence in contemporary American literature—a true heir to Walt Whitman. With the publications of works by William Burroughs and Jack Kerouac he had recognized two other important writers. Ferlinghetti's own poetry and prose were having a remarkable influence on an even younger generation of writers, and his work was making inroads into the lives of people who rarely read poetry. He felt a return to France at this time in his life, even for a short visit, was vitally important for him. A lot of activity had been going on there in the past years. Although he didn't like the idea of leaving his family behind, he knew he must go. On May 30, 1963, just arrived in Paris, he writes of the trip in his journal:

> Thus returned to Paris thirteen years later . . . still the loneliest city in the world, now buried in a welter of automobiles, traffic lights and neon; seems much larger and brighter than before . . . I remembered it much smaller and darker, much in the same manner I remembered an unhappy poem I wrote one afternoon in Greenwich Village as having been written late at night. . . . So I was lost on that unreal Paris of 13 years ago. . . . Walked about in the night city—(Arrived at 11 PM at the Gare du Nord, from London via Calais.)—For about three hours I wandered around, bag in hand, finally settled for a hotel near the Sorbonne, slept well, petit déjeuner in room at nine, moved to another hotel, after walking around Left Bank for another three hours—Hotel de Seine, rue de Seine—Already I'm getting used to this new brighter Paris and already hardly remember the image of the old Paris. . . . (Pense—tv!) Thirteen years later, treize ans plus tard, take up my walking again. . . . the women just as beautiful. . . . always the City of Youth. . . . beautiful youth. . . . dark times gone. . . . struck into light. . . . 13 years to get back. . . . thru the knot-hole. . . . je suis voyeur-toujours (et je vois). . . . Même histoire. . . . over and over. . . . on voit ce qu'on peut pa prendre. What happens when one calls up a mistress of 13 years ago? Would she find it easier to recognize the face or the voice? Do the eyes grow older?

> It really is all still an illusion. The city itself doesn't exist. It's a dream I once had. It's a dark place, lost in memory. . . . like all the dark parks in Paris, after the gates are shut. . . . I've been walking the streets for two days, all those changed places, the map of Paris still stamped upon my brainpan. . . . The whole two days the papers on street corners have been reporting the sickness of the

Pope, it's obvious the cat's going to die. What day is it? Friday, perhaps. Everybody's Paris exists in everybody's brain. On top of which a flood of cars has descended. Tranquillity is gone from this town. . . . And such a city of wild loneliness. . . . does strange things to people. . . . bright sun. . . . warm air. . . . the statues must be turning in the Tuileries gardens. . . . the leaves laughing. . . . "The sex Musicians drift through streets of music trailing melodious propositions. . . ." (Burroughs' *The Ticket That Exploded*). . . . Impossible that everyone in Paris could be as lonely as I always am when I am here! All of a sudden, each time, I become aware of a great lump of loneliness which seems to have been growing inside of my body for years and years and only now I discover its real presence and enormous size. Impossible to cut it out! It's too immense, it's too boney, too supple, too aqueous, being the body itself. . . . toujours rôdant. . . . Walked another day and night thru the circular streets. . . . Shades of Dr. Matthew O'Connor no more, gone for good, not even the echo or smell or mood of *Nightwood* here anywhere anymore. And a good thing too. Dark street of a life forgotten. . . . J'ai passé par là. . . . Walked into the dark courtyard of 89 rue de Vaugirard, where I had my two room cave those years, pressed the minuterie, and the hall and courtyard lights came on. Saw the shuttered window of my room on the courtyard, felt the new front door. The lights go off again. Not a sound anywhere, not a light in any of the flats, dark buildings all around. . . . Walked out thru the black cobblestoned yard, past the shuttered concierge's lodge. Out in the street, directly in front, is a huge plastic yellow sports car, at least 25 feet long and low and very soft-looking. . . . Which I hadn't seen upon entering. I persist in believing it wasn't there two minutes before, though there is a black canvas hood fastened down all around the driver's plastic cockpit bubble and it's obvious it hasn't moved in a long time; a dream auto washed up, phantom chariot. . . . Even seeming much taller and more "business like," though it is obvious they haven't moved in a long time and are the same old buildings. Ghost feet of a hundred children (who used to go up and

down some inside escalier next to my pad) still sound; like mice.
. . . Another chapter finished, in a senseless journey, exorcising
old phantoms, ghost cars that sit driverless and covered, pointing
two ways, nothing under the hood, while elsewhere silent motors
race. . . . Claude Beigbeder is with Marc Toujours, teaching in
Tunisia. . . . the girl who once wrote "A mort@" on my Vaugirard
door and it was months later before I figured out who did it, or
why. The "why" shall remain a secret. (In any case, it had nothing
to do with Algeria where "the Arabs asked terrible questions"!)

The journal entry is written in the style of *Her* and of his poetry.
The phrase "Dark street of a life forgotten" is an echo of the theme
of the hidden door in his poem called "Hidden Door." He expresses
anew his sense of nostalgia and déjà vu. "Ghost feet of a hundred
children" is an expression of his feeling of distance now from what
had once been familiar surroundings. Yet, for all the symbolism,
throughout this piece of writing he remains as accessible as he is in
his published works. His descriptions are concrete. Every thought,
every abstraction is anchored in the buildings and streets of Paris.
And over all there is an aura of wonder that is also evident in *Pictures
of the Gone World*. When he writes about the huge plastic yellow
sports car and says, "I persist in believing it wasn't there two minutes
before," calling it a "dream auto washed up, phantom chariot," the
approach is surrealistic as well as rooted in reality.

On his way from Paris, Ferlinghetti traveled south through Spain,
revisiting the Prado.

At the Prado, the Bosch paintings with their people all sinking or
burning or caught by weird machines or animals. And in another room an unknown painting of three women in straw hats with
flowers being rowed from a revolution . . . Then back to Bosch,
"El Bosco"—his world one huge Gothic hell and medieval inferno
of people and creatures doing things to each other. (So too W.
Burroughs "unlocked his word horde") . . . The world of the Bosco of the Bosco kid: A man-woman being eaten by a blue insect

and Goya's Monstre Panic (huge man figure) in the skies, towering over fleeing people and wagons . . . Fire!

Back in San Francisco after the trip, Ferlinghetti edited the first issue of *City Lights Journal*, a project he'd been thinking about for several years. It was the culmination of a great deal of planning, and included avant-garde writing from the United States and elsewhere. One of the most important international contributions was a short introduction to the poets of the "Hungry Generation" by Ginsberg. These were poets Ginsberg had met while traveling in India in 1962 and 1963. In fact, the cover of the *Journal* showed Ginsberg, somewhere on the Indian subcontinent, without a beard, draped in a blanket. There was also a piece by Gary Snyder entitled "A Journey to Rishikesh & Hardwar." Ginsberg and Snyder were influential in the sixties in sparking an interest in Indian lifestyles among the young counter-culture people.

The *Journal* included work by people who would later be published by City Lights or by other firms but who were, at the time, largely unknown. One of these was Ed Sanders, whose *Poem from Jail* was published a few months after the *Journal* appeared. *Dawn Visions*, by Berkeley poet Daniel Moore, first published in the *Journal*, reappeared in 1964 as a Pocket Poets book. There were works by Kerouac, Burroughs, San Francisco poet Al Fowler, *Afrique Accidentale*, by New York poet Ted Joans, and *The Death of 9 Rue Git le Coeur*, by Harold Norse. (The address refers to a hotel in Paris in which many of the Beat Generation figures lived in the early sixties.) A selection from *Trout Fishing in America*, by Richard Brautigan, also appeared in the *Journal*. Brautigan, a North Beach habitué, soon gained a reputation rivaling that of Ferlinghetti and Ginsberg's for *Trout Fishing* and other novels.

City Lights Journal Number 2 came out in 1964; its dramatic cover showed Ezra Pound walking, cane in hand, sinister-looking hat on head, and an overcoat draping his body like a cape. The *Journal* was widely discussed because of a controversial interview with Pound by Grazia Livi, an Italian journalist. In *Journal* Number 2 there was an account of the arrest of Maurice Girodias, publisher of the Olympia Press, Paris. Ferlinghetti noted in the preface:

> We have not heard a single publisher (in either England or America) raise his voice above a low mumble against the censorship of the Olympia Press in Paris, original publisher in English of books by Jean Genet, Beckett, Durrell, Nabokov, Burroughs, Henry Miller, Corso, and others now famous or infamous. "The Arrest of Maurice Girodias" is published here as received from Olympia Press. Since this story was set in type, Girodias' prison terms have been increased to over 80 years and the fines imposed have mounted to almost $80,000.00. His appeal is now scheduled for November 17, 1964. There are two camps in the De Gaulle administration: the people around Andre Malraux (who are sensible to the asinine figure France is cutting in this matter) and the dumb Catholic bigots who consider Girodias the most virulent public menace since Communism. Girodias writes: "I will certainly welcome any help, any article, any petitions which can be engineered in America or England, as this appears my only chance . . ."

The second *Journal* featured "A Few Bengali Poets," introduced by Ginsberg, including a long work by Malay Roy Choudhoury, one of the leaders of the Hungry Generation. Ginsberg wrote:

> The poems were translated into funny English by the poets themselves & I spent a day with a pencil reversing inversions & syntax & adding in railroad stations. The poems are interesting in that they do reveal a temper that is international, i.e., the revolt of the personal. Warsaw, Moscow, Calcutta, the discovery of feeling.

In this spirit—the discovery of feeling—Ferlinghetti printed works by Miroslav Holub, a Czechoslovakian poet, and an article on Louis-Ferdinand Céline, the controversial French writer who was the author of *Death on the Installment Plan* and *Journey to the End of the Night*. A selection of prose from *Happiness Bastard*, a novel written by poet Kirby Doyle and published later by Essex House in North Hollywood, California, was an important inclusion. Also in the *Journal* were poems from *Lami in Oakland*, by a talented young poet, Alden van Buskirk, who died in 1962 at the age of twenty-three. There were also four poems by New York poet Frank O'Hara, author of *Meditations in an Emergency*. O'Hara was friend-teacher to John Ashbery and other New York poets. Ferlinghetti had long wanted to publish a book of his work, and in 1964 O'Hara's *Lunch Poems* became Pocket Poets Series Number 19. Another poet included in the second *Journal* was Julian Beck, the founder of the Living Theatre. In the contributor's notes Ferlinghetti wrote that City Lights would someday publish Beck's *The Life of the Theatre*. The promise was fulfilled in 1971.

The *City Lights Journal* was conceived by Ferlinghetti as a continuing collection of the most significant new writing. After the San Francisco Renaissance, there had been a kind of literary lull. The concern with Cuba and the emergence of a generation of college-age political activists, beginning largely in Berkeley with the Free Speech Movement of 1964, consumed a great deal of energy. It seemed that most of the efforts of the underground were being directed to political areas. But there were still young writers everywhere, hoping to be heard, as Kerouac, Ferlinghetti, and Ginsberg had been before them. A staggering number of little poetry magazines began proliferating around the country, in every big city and in many small towns. Some were finely bound, beautiful hand-set letterpress editions; some were photo-offset editions; and others were mimeographed, crudely stapled collections. The majority included poetry, prose, and short reviews, and some were illustrated. Many of them found their way into the City Lights Bookstore. Shig Murao had to turn a few of them down, yet there were enough to fill several long shelves of the basement poetry section, and they crowded the magazine racks upstairs.

In 1963, New Directions published a book of plays by Ferlinghetti entitled *Unfair Arguments with Existence*. The plays were written at a back table in the Caffè Trieste, one of the coffee houses located a short walk from City Lights Bookstore and frequented by writers.

The plays were heavily influenced by Samuel Beckett and Eugene Ionesco, who were doing in theater what the new American poets were achieving with their poetry. Ferlinghetti had long been interested in the theater and openly acknowledged the influence of Beckett and Ionesco. He writes: "My play, 'Mother Lode,' is pure Beckett . . . If you look at it as a Beckett play like 'Waiting for Godot.'" Ferlinghetti hoped that, through theater, ". . . we may yet discover some seeking action for life itself."

One year later New Directions brought out another book of theater works by Ferlinghetti, *Routines*. Ferlinghetti describes a routine as ". . . a song & dance, a little rout, a routing-out, a run-around, a 'round of business or amusement': myriads of people, herds, flowerbeds, ships & cities, all going through their routines, life itself a blackout routine, an experimental madness somewhere between dotage and megalomania, lost in the vibration of a wreckage (of some other cosmos we fell out of) . . ." *Routines* consists of a series of *happenings*. Ferlinghetti was searching for a theater "as genesis of creation, working (or playing) toward revolutionary solutions, or evolutionary solutions, acting out aspirations to some ideal existence. This was not always accomplished through speech itself but through acting as a paraphrase of thought even in pure miming an 'inner speech' to be heard . . ." There are thirteen "routines." One, called "The Center of Death," is a satirical fantasy on dying. It begins with a billboard sign on a tropical island, reading:

COME HERE TO DIE
CENTER FOR DEATH
TERMINAL CASES ONLY
Not for everyone

"Servants of the People" is another routine. Much longer and more substantial than the others, it explores Ferlinghetti's reaction to superpatriotism and latter-day McCarthyism.

In 1962, Ferlinghetti first mentioned, in a letter to Ginsberg, that he expected to put out a large volume of the selected works of Antonin Artaud in collaboration with Jack Hirschman, who was producing seven Artaud programs for KPFK radio. Hirschman and his wife had collected every available published English translation of Artaud and many unpublished translations. The *Artaud Anthology* appeared in 1965, edited by Hirschman, and introduced American audiences to one of the most original voices in European theater. His two books, *The Theatre of Cruelty* and *The Theatre and Its Double*, had contributed substantially to the development of contemporary theater. Artaud broke away from the constraints of both traditional French literature and those contemporary trends that demanded obedience to a particular set of rules. For Artaud, the rule derived from his mind and body working in unison, at the moment of creation, owing responsibility only to the artist's immediate subjective needs.

It is not surprising that it had taken so long to finish the ambitious Artaud project, and it was understandable that Ferlinghetti did not have time to edit it himself. He was increasingly involved with City Lights Books, and although he had plenty of help in the bookstore—particularly from Shig—City Lights publishing company continued to be primarily a one-man operation. Ferlinghetti guarded the right to make the publishing decisions. Ginsberg has said that Ferlinghetti was often stubborn in his selection of books for the City Lights list. He sees this as both a virtue and a vice, inasmuch as it helped Ferlinghetti maintain his independence, but negative because he sometimes missed out on superior work. Ginsberg goes on to note that City Lights should be seen in relationship to other small publishing operations committed to the new writing, such as Totem Press, Corinth, New Directions, and Jargon. Taken together, they were able to publish an incredible variety of contemporary writings from the U.S. and around the world. Ginsberg cites as an example of Ferlinghetti's stubbornness the poem "Power," by Gregory Corso, which he considered fascist in some aspects. (Ferlinghetti emphasizes it is fascist with a small *f*.) After Ferlinghetti turned the poem down, Corso decided to have his later books published by New Directions. Ferlinghetti couldn't be persuaded that Corso was writing against those who use power to exploit others. However, Ferlinghetti did welcome suggestions for books and new publishing ideas from Shig Murao, Mary Beach, Jan Herman, Gail Chiarrello, and Nancy Peters. Through the years, and although he didn't always agree with Ginsberg, he respected Ginsberg's ideas and often followed up on his suggestions.

In letters to Ginsberg, Ferlinghetti mentioned various projects he was excited about. Some of these became a reality, some were modified, and many were completely forgotten. Yet by the end of 1965 there were forty-eight books bearing the City Lights imprint.

The list was doing well, due in large part to Ginsberg's books, so Lawrence and Kirby took the children for an extended trip to Europe. They decided to go to Spain. Once there they rented a house in the small coastal town of Nerja, thirty miles east of Málaga, and stayed for four months. There were walks on the beach, plenty of reading and writing, and some excursions elsewhere in Spain. While in Málaga, Ferlinghetti came across the poems of Pablo Picasso in a Spanish magazine. It was the first time he had ever heard of them, and he brought them back to the States, eventually publishing them in the Pocket Poets Series.

Ferlinghetti began a long poem, "The Free Spirit Turning Thru Spain." It was at least twenty manuscript pages in length. The work was never completed on it, and the poem remains in his notebooks along with several other long poems and some prose pieces. It is a forceful attack on Franco, written in the spirit of the early broadside poems.

On February 21, Ferlinghetti wrote in his journal:

> We are settled in a tiny house/White walls, tile floors, dirt street full of big rocks and broken cobbles, on cliffs over the beach . . .

In a more extended journal entry written the following day:

> reading Orwell's *Homage to Catalonia* about the political alignment of the Communist Party in the Spanish Civil War to the right

of such parties as the Anarchists, a position much closer to the fascists than the humanitarian and libertarian left. I am struck with the similarity to the position of the Cuban Communist Party at the time of the Cuban Revolution, 1959 or earlier, when the Communists were much to the Right of the Revolutionary (25 of July Movement) Party of Fidel Castro whose barbudos were true revolutionaries in the sense that the working class militiamen in Barcelona were in the early days of the Spanish Civil War.

In May 1965, Ferlinghetti read at the Spoleto Festival of Two Worlds in the Italian town of the same name at the invitation of Gian-Carlo Menotti, Festival Director. He made the following notes after arriving there:

> . . . there is an awful lot of bullshit being passed around this Spoleto Festival. First the gossip had it that Yevtushenko had refused to come because Ezra Pound was coming and he considers Pound still a Fascist (but he did come . . .). It was rumored that Pound wouldn't come because he did not want to meet Ferlinghetti who had recently published in City Lights Journal an English translation of an interview Pound had given to the Italian picture magazine *Epoca* . . . yet Pound is now coming.

Kirby, meanwhile, had become very ill and had to return, with the children, to San Francisco. Ferlinghetti then went to stay in Paris. While there, he heard that a massive poetry reading was being hastily organized in Great Britain and that it would be billed as an international reading. Ferlinghetti and Corso were asked to come, along with Allen Ginsberg, Andrei Voznesensky, German poet Ernst Jandl, and several English poets, as well as the English novelist Alexander Trocchi. It was held June 11, 1965, in the Royal Albert Hall, London, and attracted seven thousand people. Ferlinghetti's contribution for the evening was a long work with a long title: "To Fuck Is to Live Again (Kyrie Eleison Kerista) or The Situation in the West, Followed by a Holy Proposal." The poem later appeared in a new

edition of *Starting from San Francisco* (New Directions, 1967), under the somewhat expurgated title, "The Situation in the West, Followed by a Holy Proposal." Written in the Potrero Hill house from
the vantage point of Ferlinghetti's study and its magnificent view of
San Francisco and the Bay, the poem was a celebration of love and
anarchy, beginning with the visionary dream:

> Dreaming of utopias
> where everyone's a lover
> I see San Francisco from my window
> through some old navy beerbottles

That is a very accurate description of what it was like for him on
the top floor of the Wisconsin Street Victorian, in his workroom. He
could see enough of the city to write:

> the earth a turbine
> storing sexual energy
> turning and turning into the dark
> under the skyscrapers with their time on top
> tickertape time tick tick
> civilization and its crickets
> the dark thread
> draws us all in
> into the wind-up labyrinth
> undischarged sexual energy
> not mine the city's
> There's the Fairmont phallus
> There's the Mark masturbation
> There's the park there's the cement works
> There's the steam brewing factory
> There's the actor's workshop
> There's the Bay there's that Bridge
> There's that treasured island the Navy doesn't need
> we need it but we don't need the Navy

Shortly after "reporting on the situation in the West" (the poem eventually moves out of San Francisco and wanders all over the world), Ferlinghetti came home. It was time to publish another *City Lights Journal*. Like the first two, the third journal reflected Ferlinghetti's eclectic tastes. In the introduction he wrote: "This issue (A kind of International Retrospective of the past two years) begins too close to home with a bird imagined by Barbara Garson in Berkeley (out in Left Field) . . . We have to go to Europe for The Living Theatre. (At this moment, there is no avant-garde theatre in San Francisco) . . . The San Francisco poetry scene continues potent, as witness the second section herein." The "bird" Ferlinghetti refers to is "MacBird," an anti–Vietnam War and anti–Johnson administration satirical play.

There was also a sampling of poetry from Spoleto in the journal. Ferlinghetti's contribution, "Pound at Spoleto," had appeared in an earlier version on the pages of the *Saturday Review*. It captured the venerable, and still controversial, old man of contemporary poetry and was later published in Ferlinghetti's *Open Eye, Open Heart*. It begins in a straight journalistic manner, but it becomes increasingly poetic, building up a fast-paced cadence by the end. In part, it reads:

> The hall had gone silent at a stroke. The voice knocked me down, so soft, so thin, so frail, so stubborn still. I put my head on my arms on the velvet sill of the box. I was surprised to see a single tear drop on my knee. The thin, indomitable voice went on. I went blind from the box, through the back door of it, into the empty corridor of the theatre where they still sat turned to him, went down and out, into the sunlight, weeping . . .

In a letter to Ginsberg in 1966, Ferlinghetti wrote about some new plans for City Lights:

> We are taking on newer dimensions in the City Lights publishing: Colin Wilson was here and gave me *The Outsider* for a paperback!

(If only his agent doesn't get in the way.) And I've written Charles Olson about loving to do his *Call Me Ishmael*. Don Allen says Grove gave it up. And probably will do Rexroth's *Beyond the Mountains*.

Call Me Ishmael, Olson's brilliant work on Herman Melville and his classic novel, *Moby Dick*, was published in 1966. Olson was a leader of postwar (W.W. II) American poetry, the author of the revolutionary projective verse essay included in Donald Allen's *The New American Poetry: 1945–1960*. He was a moving force behind Black Mountain College, where many poets studied, and was acknowledged by Robert Creeley and Edward Dorn as a prime influence on their own poetry. A collection of his poems, *The Distances*, was in print from Grove Press, and Corinth had brought out the first volume of Olson's American epic, *The Maximus Poems*. Ferlinghetti did not care much for Olson's poetry, often commenting that he found it too lugubrious for his taste.

The idea of publishing *The Outsider* in a paperback edition never got any further. It was merely one more example of how Ferlinghetti, as he had years earlier with Cummings and Miller, tried to develop his list in many directions. Often, as in the case with Wilson, an agent got in the way.

In 1967, Ferlinghetti was invited to the Berlin Literary Colloquium, where he was to read with Andrei Voznesensky. Nearly five thousand people attended the reading. A German critic, commenting in a large daily newspaper, wrote that the Russian Voznesensky looked like an American college boy, clean-shaven and with a youngish-looking face, while the American (Ferlinghetti) looked like the average person's image of a Russian revolutionary, with a whitish beard. After the reading Voznesensky pulled some strings for Ferlinghetti, who wanted to travel in the Soviet Union. The Russian poet did not accompany him, although they were becoming friends.

On February 9, 1967, late in the afternoon, Ferlinghetti landed at the Moscow airport. He noted in his journal, ". . . dusk descending—Metropole Hotel—great snow world wand white birches." The next day, armed with addresses Ginsberg had given him, he began to look up some people. He visited the Writers' Union on Voronsky Street, where he met notable poets and novelists, including Andrei Serge-yev, who had been in *Red Cats.* He also visited Zoya Voznesensky, wife of the poet, and had a lively discussion concerning American lit-erature. She said that Ferlinghetti's poems translated well into Rus-sian. He went to the Drama Theatre on Taganka Square, where he saw a dramatization of John Reed's *Ten Days That Shook the World.* It was a brilliant production and included some strong criticisms of Stalin, who was mercilessly satirized by the actors, causing waves of laughter in the audience. Voznesensky had told him of the theater and its experimental nature.

It was one thing to criticize Stalin, but Ferlinghetti found that few Russian writers, Voznesensky and Yevtushenko among them, were able to speak out against the oppressive Soviet regime. Yevtushenko had given in to government pressure, and he was less critical in his present work than he had been when he first gained public notice. Ferlinghetti sensed that Soviet poets were afraid both of physical punishment and of not finding an outlet for their work.

He met Zoya Voznesensky and a group of writers for lunch at the Writers' Union. They asked him questions about his own poetics, politics, and the state of American literature, and were especially interested in John Steinbeck, whom they had all read, but they were bitter about the statements Steinbeck had been making in support of U.S. government policy in Vietnam. Ferlinghetti told them that Steinbeck had sold out, had gone soft and far to the right. He also pointed out that Hemingway had lived in Cuba during the Batista dictatorship, never speaking out against the brutality of the dicta-tor's rule or the evil of U.S. collusion with it. When they asked him who were his favorite writers, he listed Whitman, Emily Dickinson, Ezra Pound, William Carlos Williams, Hart Crane, E. E. Cummings, Kenneth Patchen, and Allen Ginsberg. Zoya mentioned that she had met Ginsberg in 1965, and on the basis of the talks she had with him and from reading his poetry, she felt that Ginsberg was more con-cerned with the interior world while Ferlinghetti was committed to the outside world. Therefore she found Ferlinghetti's poetry more comprehensible. Ferlinghetti, who knew what an extrovert Ginsberg was, especially when compared to himself, felt that Ginsberg's work was very much about the outside world.

Ferlinghetti noted, sadly, that Boris Pasternak's portrait was missing from the authors gallery in the Writers' Union. He realized that membership in the union depended on publication and notice, and that writers who were no longer allowed to be published were not members of this "closed shop."

Few of Ferlinghetti's works were printed in the Soviet Union, and Ginsberg's work had appeared only rarely. So he was not particularly well known there. And since he was not on any kind of official mission he was able to wander around Moscow anonymously. Just from his conversations at the Writers' Union he had a lot to think about. Moscow caught him in its grip and he was eager to explore more of the Russian land.

Outside on the streets of Moscow he felt much freer than he had in the stifling atmosphere of the Writers' Union. He wandered through Red Square, past a great statue of the Russian revolutionary poet Vladimir Mayakovsky, a writer whose works influenced modern American poets, including Ginsberg and Corso. He walked through residential areas, fascinated by being able to wander freely. Generally, however, he sensed a melancholic mood among the people, a lack of joy, as if a massive weight were oppressing the populace, almost as if he had stepped into the pages of a long, brooding Russian novel.

In Moscow, Ferlinghetti boarded the trans-Siberian train to visit that frozen part of the country he had heard so much about. En route he made extensive journal entries, and two days into the trip he wrote he was on "The great Siberian Plain. It's like the sea—too huge to write about—nothing but birch trees like the froth on endless white groundswells—sometimes thin lines of black forests on the horizon, forlorn towns, rail junctions, with switchmen standing outside of sentry houses . . . I had the strong feeling that I was going to freeze to death in the Mongolian Mountains." A day later, February 14, he wrote: "So we ride through Siberia on a First Class train with white tablecloths over the land which bled and bled its white blood and its red blood." The writing matched the brooding quality of the land:

> Night outside now. Train stops in some big railroad yard on a snow plain. It's snowing lightly. It's ten below and the flakes drop into the white railroad yard under platform lights and floodlights. On the ground walking along at the same rate as our train is a man in a fur cap and a railway greatcoat. He is a young man, striding along in the snow night, holding a little flashlight and shining it into the Russian winter night. On the loudspeaker in our train, some old Russian music is coming across, something slow and reminding one of long winters and the Russian steppes. Maybe Prokofiev. The young man keeps striding along in the dark outside the train, hearing only the sound of our train. He looks in at me (I am standing in the corridor). He keeps striding along abreast, not hurrying or altering his stride. He keeps coming on and on in the night. The train picks up speed and he drops out of sight, still striding along, eternal over the Steppes.

Further, in the same notebook, a humorous description of Ferling-hetti's view of life in the land of Lenin is found:

> This is a description of a hotel dining room in the town of Nak-hodka, a forlorn port near Vladivostok, which is the end of the train journey across Siberia. After seven days and nights, I arrived at this hotel dining room, which might be described as the epitome of the height of this Worker's Paradise. A long, narrow ballroom-type scene, graced by a five-piece Western-type orchestra. It doesn't deserve to be called a group. Sometimes it sounds like Tommy Dorsey warming up and running down, sometimes like Guy Lombardo about to get constipated, accompanied by a Russian Jean Sablon bellowing into a mike. The musicians are as joyless as anyone else—not a smile, or a clown. All very serious in public. They look like they might be "cats" if allowed to escape for a few years. A dozen or so misshapen waitresses, mostly on the truck-horse side, all hefty and serious. The customers come in, and

on Saturday night a festive crowd it was, indeed. Dancing: the couples get up when the music starts, very sedately. They face each other straight, and put their arms up expressionlessly. Usually the man puts one arm around the woman, and the other he rests on her shoulder or upper chest. She puts both her paws on his chest, and they march and wiggle around like that, expressionless, looking away from each other. Some one or two daring types tried the late Western style of dancing without touching each other, even whirling about a bit. Really wild! . . . It is my last dinner here. I sit alone, staring at the band. The drummer is an older man with thick glasses and an implacable beat he must have picked up from a grandfather clock. He starts—It's "Melancholy Baby," believe it or not. The sax man gets right in there, he wouldn't call his horn an "axe," not he. The Jean Sablon–type singer probably can't face it. He doesn't even get up and sing "Melancholy Baby." He just sits there with his head hanging. The pianist holds up his end. You wouldn't call him a piano-player—he's a pianist, and he's melancholy, baby. And when it's all over, he actually hangs his head over the keys, puts his arms up and cradles his head in them. There's a middle-aged, very plain and straight waitress sitting alone at one of the tables, looking at the musicians and then looking away with a sad, sad look. She just sits there unmoving after the music stops. There is nothing whatever to be done . . .

The *Russian Winter Journals* are, in their entirety, a detailed and penetrating portrait of the Soviet Union. They contain poems as well as prose descriptions, but the major poem to come out of Ferlinghetti's journey to the Soviet Union is "Moscow in the Wilderness, Segovia in the Snow," originally published as a foldout broadside by Beach Books, Texts, and Documents. It was begun in Moscow and finished in San Francisco. The poem is an attempt to capture the foreboding sense of the Russian landscape and to present Ferlinghetti's personal vision of Russia as he saw it on his brief trip. In the poem he asks: "Is Lenin listening after fifty Octobers?" And of his wanderings through Moscow:

down the black boulevards
past Kremlin lit & locked
in its hard dream
in the great Russian night
past Bolshoi Ballet & Gorky Institute
John Reed at the Drama Theatre
Stalyagi & heroin at Taganka
Stone Mayakovsky stares
thru a blizzard of white notes
in Russian Winter light . . .

In 1975, City Lights would publish *Adventures of a Young Man*, by John Reed, short stories by the author of *Ten Days That Shook the World*. In a preface to the text Ferlinghetti writes: "In February 1967 I saw a brilliant new dramatization of his *Ten Days That Shook The World* at the Drama Theatre in Moscow. Yet in the USA, in his own country he has not been such a hero much of the time since his death."

While Ferlinghetti traveled through the Soviet Union, Shig Murao kept the bookstore operation going. He had been Ferlinghetti's partner since the late fifties, and the bookstore had gradually become a reflection of his own interesting personality. With his ever present smile, long black beard, dressed usually in a T-shirt, Shig had become a quiet, but strong and abiding force in the life of North Beach and the San Francisco literary community. He had a positive influence on the entire Beat scene as it developed. Murao cared little for publicity. In fact, he avoided the spotlight that journalists, tourists, and poets attempted to focus on him. For him the City Lights Bookstore was a work of art, surviving year by year without any of the advertising gimmicks or marketing techniques that were beginning to become a part of book selling. It was a "people's business." To Shig the store was a poem to which he was continually adding lines, asking for no help in the process, revising whenever he felt it necessary.

Shig's sense of humor, his ability to listen to the problems of others, and his uncompromising sense of what a bookstore should be gained him respect that went far beyond the boundaries of North Beach. Invariably when people talked about the San Francisco writing renaissance taking place there, they mentioned Shig Murao. His knowledge was staggering. He was extremely well read and his mind was encyclopedic. Many arguments around the cash register were solved by a quick word of authority or a well-placed joke from Shig.

Secure in the knowledge that Shig had the bookstore operation in control, Ferlinghetti was able to leave the store, and when he was at home continued to concentrate on the publishing end of the business. The City Lights list continued to grow in 1967. Two major publications were added: Philip Lamantia's *Selected Poems* and *Golden Sardine*, by Bob Kaufman.

Lamantia's book brought together work covering a twenty-five-year span, starting with his earliest poems, written in 1943, when he was only fifteen, and published by the surrealists, some of whom were living in exile in New York City during the war years. Lamantia's first book, *Erotic Poems*, was published by Bern Porter; later came *Narcotica* and *Ekstasis*, both published in 1959. *Destroyed Works* came out in 1962 and *Touch of the Marvelous* in 1966. He had lived in New York, Mexico, Greece, Spain, France, and North Africa. Ginsberg said of him: "An American original, soothsayer even as Poe, genius in the language of Whitman, native companion and teacher to myself."

Kaufman's publication, *Golden Sardine*, was edited by Mary Beach, the publisher-editor of Beach Books, Texts, and Documents, and a close friend of Ferlinghetti's. The poems had been scrawled on scraps of paper and stuffed into a portfolio. *Solitudes Crowded with Loneliness*, published by New Directions in 1965, had already brought Kaufman a wide audience in the U.S. and in France, where he was hailed as an American Rimbaud. The City Lights book was reissued in 1976.

Ferlinghetti's poetry was, by the middle sixties, well known among college students, though his books were still being scantily and usually negatively reviewed by the literary critics. The best-selling Ferlinghetti volume was still *A Coney Island of the Mind*, which brought him many readings. In 1968 six long works of his were published in a volume called *The Secret Meaning of Things*. It included "Moscow in the Wilderness, Segovia in the Snow." The most introspective of the poems in that collection was "Bickford's Buddha," which had been written on the back of a map of Harvard College while he was there for a reading: "I take a trip to the Harvard Co-op and overhear a bird ask for 'books by Ferlinghetti' They didn't have none."

Another poem in the book, "After the Cries of the Birds," which he had read at the Berlin Literary Colloquium, had been published as a separate pamphlet by Dave Haselwood Books, San Francisco. The Haselwood publication included a prose piece by Ferlinghetti explaining the "genesis of" the poem. It was as poetic as the poem itself.

"After the Cries of the Birds" was written in the mid-sixties, in the days of the big folk-rock concerts. It begins:

Hurrying thru eternity
        after the cries of the birds has stopped
I see the "future of the world"
          in a new visionary society
        now only dimly recognizable
        in folk-rock ballrooms
      free-form dancers in ecstatic clothing
          their hearts their gurus
           every man his own myth
          butterflies in amber
              caught fucking life
  hurrying thru eternity
          to a new pastoral age
      I see the shadows of that future
        in that white island
              which is San Francisco
      floating in its foreign sea

Ferlinghetti hoped that the youth rebellion, as reflected in a counter-culture lifestyle, rock music, and antiwar/anti-establishment protests might help move the world closer to an abolition of the nation-state. At a time when many people were seeking gurus who might help them liberate themselves from the morass of American culture, the poet writes the line "their hearts their gurus."

Assassination Raga was first read at Nourse Auditorium, a large hall in San Francisco. The occasion was a mass reading organized by poet David Meltzer. The poem was written a few days earlier when Ferlinghetti heard the news that Robert Kennedy had been killed in Los Angeles. He was shocked that his was the only poem at the reading dealing with the assassination. The work typified Ferlinghetti's public surface, oral poetry. It dealt directly with an event of the moment. In one section is his recollection of John Kennedy's assassination: "They lower the body soundlessly into a huge plane in Dallas and soundlessly the United States of America takes off & wings with that body."

By the mid-sixties Ferlinghetti was deeply involved in the anti–Vietnam War protests. He read at demonstrations and, with Robert Bly, did several large antiwar readings in the Pacific Southwest. He lent his name to organizations combating government policies, and did not hesitate to personally speak out against U.S. involvement in Southeast Asia.

A prose poem, *Where Is Vietnam?*, was issued as a broadside. In this poem Ferlinghetti characterizes President Johnson as Colonel Cornpone, who "got out a blank Army draft and began to fill in the space with men and Colonel Cornpone got down to the bottom of the order where there is a space to indicate just where the troops are to be sent to and Colonel Cornpone got a faraway look in his eyes and reached out and started spinning a globe of the world and his eye wandered over the spinning globe . . ."

CHAPTER ELEVEN

THE 1960s WERE years of turmoil. Ferlinghetti was personally involved or sympathetic to the demonstrations against the
House un-American Activities Committee hearings in San Francisco, the CORE and SNCC Freedom Rides of 1961, civil disobedience
against bomb-shelter programs in 1961, the great civil rights demonstrations of 1963, the Free Speech Movement of 1964 in Berkeley,
the beginning of the anti–Vietnam War movement in 1964 and 1965,
sit-ins against the draft in 1966, the Black rebellions in Cleveland
and Chicago in 1966, exposure of CIA involvement in the National
Student Association in 1967, and formation of massive draft resistance, a national movement that began in San Francisco. He didn't
find it surprising at all that much of the anti-establishment feeling
that grew in the country during the sixties came out of the city he
had chosen as his home. He and Kirby had both been radicalized in
San Francisco.

In the poem "Starting from San Francisco," Ferlinghetti writes from
the perspective of being on a train heading East, "crossing the country in coach trains," purposefully taking the train in order to see "one
small halfass town followed by one telephone wire and one straight
single iron road." The land hadn't changed much since he first crossed
it from Portland to New York after discharge from the Navy in 1945.
The poem conjures up images of bleakness: "All hiding? White man
gone home? Must be a cowboy someplace . . ." At the end of the poem
Ferlinghetti asks the question "Who stole America?", an appropriate
thing to ask from the vantage point of San Francisco.

In the summer of 1967, the first Human Be-In was held at Golden
Gate Park. Ferlinghetti, Ginsberg, Gary Snyder, Michael McClure
were among those poets in attendance. The Be-In was an attempt

at experiencing a sense of tribal community. It was a public celebration of the ideals Ferlinghetti had been personally celebrating in his poetry, and so it was natural for him to be involved. Ginsberg had become a leader of the youth movement. He was much sought after by the media to articulate what was happening among young people, particularly in San Francisco and New York City. Ferlinghetti was amazed at how well Allen handled the media. Ferlinghetti, in fact, remained somewhat in the background. He recognized that much of the new spirit among the young had been formulated in the Beat era of the previous decade, and was content to watch the many changes that were taking place have their effect on American society. But he was involved enough and spokesman enough that the FBI had begun compiling quite a sizable file on his activities; the same was happening with Ginsberg.

All the protests had given fuel to a growing sense of rebelliousness. People were being forced to look at their country in a new way because of the havoc created by the growing escalation of the Vietnam War. "Colonel Cornpone" was living up to Ferlinghetti's portrayals of him. And the discontent was being felt at the highest levels of society and filtering down, and the process worked in reverse as well. A lot of people who had been content with listening and believing their leaders were beginning to question them.

The Be-In was a reaction to the violence that was infecting American society. For Ferlinghetti it offered an opportunity to share with the new generation who were growing up in a time of an unpopular war a belief in the capacity of people to grow independently of predetermined social and political values. It eloquently expressed rebellion against materialistic, military America. That is what the *Journal for the Protection of All Beings* was about. In *The Situation in the West, Followed by a Holy Proposal*, Ferlinghetti wrote: ". . . so let's everybody love it up in the sun which won't burn forever." That's precisely what was happening at the Be-In.

The Be-In took place at the height of national interest in the new "hippie" culture. The Haight-Ashbury, adjacent to Golden Gate Park, a few miles southwest of North Beach, was descended upon by journalists out to document the counter-culture that had overtaken the area. The rambling old Victorian houses were filled with young people who rented low-cost apartments and were experimenting with a new lifestyle. There had been a community of young people in the area for a number of years, living what came to be known as the hippie lifestyle, but they hadn't been "discovered" by outsiders. Now it was often difficult to tell the old-timers from the newcomers. There were psychedelic shops and posters proclaiming peace and love. The new philosophy of Tune In, Turn On, and Drop Out was spreading, popularized by Timothy Leary, former Harvard professor and an early LSD experimenter. Later, when Leary would be hassled by the government, and literally had to escape the country in order to gain freedom from the harassment that had landed him in prison, Ferlinghetti was among those who came to his defense.

Ferlinghetti did not read at the Be-In. At one point Gary Snyder placed a string of Oaxacan beads around his neck.

The Summer of Love, of which the Be-In was a symbol, was followed by a long winter of dissent. After the celebration of the Be-In, or gathering of the tribes, a new mood swept San Francisco. The joyful, living festivals gave way to solemn marches of solidarity against the war. Again, the poets of the San Francisco Renaissance were conspicuous by their presence. Snyder, Corso, McClure, Ginsberg, and Ferlinghetti had all written antiwar poems. They followed in the pacifist tradition of earlier poets associated with post–W.W. II American poetry.

On December 9, 1967, Ferlinghetti participated in a demonstration at the Oakland Army Induction Center. The protesters arrived at the center at dawn in order to meet three busloads of inductees as a protest against the draft. Their plan was to block the entranceway as the buses tried to pass through.

Ferlinghetti was wearing a brown derby hat and a red plaid scarf. "Kill the hippies!" one of the soldiers shouted. Then the buses moved forward on their way to the parking lot. The demonstrators tightened their ranks. The police informed them that they were engaged in unlawful assembly and told them to disperse. When they refused to move they were told of their constitutional rights and taken away in paddy wagons. A large group of demonstrators followed them to the Alameda County Courthouse in support of those arrested, but the arraignment was put off until the following day.

Ferlinghetti was arrested along with sixty-seven others, among whom were Kay Boyle and Joan Baez, and a large number of students. Ferlinghetti pleaded no contest to the charge of disturbing the peace, and along with his co-demonstrators received a nineteen-day sentence. They were sent to Santa Rita prison, the central jail for the county. In a statement read to the judge Ferlinghetti said:

> The purpose of the demonstration was to stop war. Its purpose was to block the entrance to war. The motives of the demonstrators were pure and the action was totally nonviolent. It was a legitimate expression of political dissent and I believe such dissent must not be suppressed and prosecuted in a society that calls itself free . . . The American people are suffering this season from a mass guilt complex as a direct result of the American military action in Vietnam. They know that they are doing evil, but they are confused and don't know how to stop.

In prison Ferlinghetti worked in the laundry and kept a journal that was eventually published in *Ramparts* magazine, a nationally distributed monthly edited by Warren Hinckle, a San Francisco journalist. Because he was afraid of having his work confiscated in jail, Ferlinghetti smuggled it out in bundled-up laundry with the help of some long-term prisoners whom he had befriended.

On his first day behind bars Ferlinghetti's journal entry reads:

> Rehabilitate us, please . . . first rough impressions of anybody's first time in jail: suddenly realizing what "incarcerated" really means. Paranoid fear of the unknown, fear of not knowing what's going to happen to your body . . . barbed wire fences and watchtowers. Poor man's concentration camp?

And later, in another entry:

> I told them that I had printing experience and they put me to
> work stencilling pants. I put "Santa Rita" on every pair. "Give us
> something to aim at," the deputy told me, laughing . . . very funny.
> Holy prison named for a Spanish saint . . . Goya should have seen
> a place like this. He did. Goya faces in the morning chow line, a
> thousand of them in the morning chow line, a thousand of them
> sticking out of blue denim.

While in Santa Rita, Ferlinghetti wrote "Salute," a poem in which
he directs his antiwar feelings toward "every border guard at no
matter what Check Point Charley on no matter what side of which
Berlin Wall Bamboo or Tortilla Curtain." The problem in Vietnam,
Ferlinghetti realized, was not just a matter of American imperialism,
but was one more example of the insanity of the nation-state.

When Richard Nixon was elected President, Ferlinghetti became
aware that worse oppression from Washington was on the way. He
had followed Nixon's career since the House un-American Activities
Committee days in the early 1950s, and he saw in Nixon the person-
ification of everything he had been fighting against.

Almost immediately after Nixon's election Ferlinghetti wrote
Tyrannus Nix?, a work which he hesitated to call a poem and so he
referred to it as a political-satirical tirade. This was an apt description of the piece, which was published by New Directions in the author's own handwriting. The work was enhanced by long explanatory
notes. Ferlinghetti calls on the memory of the Populist poets, whom
he had studied in the thirties, as he sets the stage for the indictment
of Nixon:

> Nixon Nixon bush league President This is a Populist hymn to you
> and yours And I begin with your face and come back to your face
> For "our history is noble and tragic like the mask of a tyrant" And
> the mask any actor wears is apt to become his face

Ferlinghetti explains in Number one of the notes section, which is an integral part of the work:

> "populist hymn": echoes Vachel Lindsay's "Bryan Bryan Bryan." A Bryan-Nixon parallel is incidentally obnoxious. As far back as populism, America was already seen as an "empire dealing with its own minorities as it deals with its client-states overseas." (Cf. John McDermott reviewing "The Agony of the American Left" in *The Nation*, June 23, 1969.)

Further on in the text Ferlinghetti brings back Colonel Cornpone, making a prophetic point about the Nixon presidency:

> Nixon Nixon I keep cutting back to your face as if it's all we've got to go on Mon General once said in a Kennedy he saw the smiling mask of America but in Colonel Cornpone Johnson he saw the raw face of America itself And I am thinking Old Slick Dick in you we finally see no face at all behind the great seal of the United States
> . . .

In 1969, Ferlinghetti brought out *Green Flag*, volume three of the *Journal for the Protection of All Beings*. *Green Flag* was edited by two participants in the People's Park protests of May 1969 and was a collection of People's Park Poetry. Many of the poems in the anthology, including Ferlinghetti's "Salute," were read at a benefit poetry reading for the People's Park held in San Francisco. Ferlinghetti wrote the blurb for the back cover of *Green Flag*: "This anthology of poetry by a mob of beautiful poets, some famous, some infamous, some unknown, grew like grass out of the People's Park Movement in Berkeley in May and June of 1969, the poetry itself symbolizes Green Power at its nonviolent best."

The People's Park Movement had sprung up in reaction to a fence erected around a small plot of land off Telegraph Avenue in Berkeley. Students had used the land as their community meeting ground, and when the National Guard was called in to keep them off the newly fenced-in land, which was owned by the University of California, a massive protest was organized, which unfortunately led to a great deal of violence.

Planet News, by Allen Ginsberg, appeared in 1968 and contained poems that had become articulations both of the antiwar movement and of the hippie culture. "Wichita Vortex Sutra" cried out against the Johnson war policies, mourned the loss of a sense of comradeship through the brutality of both the war and the American business machine, and expressed Ginsberg's loneliness, made all the more intense by the war. It was a *Leaves of Grass* in reverse—celebrating all that America could be, but was unable to realize because of the military and industrial power structure that ruled the country.

Who Be Kind To begins with the words "Be kind to yourself, it is only one/and perishable/of many on the planet . . . and ends with the pronouncement "that a new kind of man has come to his bliss/ to end the cold war he had borne/against his own kind/since the day of the snake."

Ferlinghetti wrote to Ginsberg: "Have just finished copy reading *Planet News* and have returned in airmail separately for your answers to various copy-questions. Beautiful book . . . constant ontological preoccupation." And in another letter:

> The Wales poem is really beautiful, one of the greatest you have ever written . . . And it's not like any poem you've ever written before. It's like the English Romantic Poets strained thru the Lake Country into Wales and you. The gravity and beauty of old Wordsworth . . . only without W's draggy keening . . . closer to Dylan (Thomas) of course . . . Scooped everyone again, you bum . . . and of course you really sound like nobody but yourself.

The poem "Wales Visitation" was written while Ginsberg was on an LSD trip. Ferlinghetti had his own first LSD experience in 1967 and later wrote "Mock Confessional" as a result of it.

In a 1970 interview with an alternative paper in New Orleans, Ferlinghetti was asked to name the most relevant and important poets of the times. His answer was that Ginsberg, as teacher, guru, and poet, was the most important, and he knew of no one who could match him. In the same interview he talked about Timothy Leary. City Lights published Leary's last written words from prison in a document called *Eagle Brief*, in which he compared his jailing by federal authorities on drug charges with the plight of a caged eagle.

I N 1967, CITY Lights publishers had moved from the basement of the bookstore and into a storefront on Upper Grant Avenue, still in North Beach, but several blocks from the Columbus Avenue address. The new quarters provided more room for editorial work and book distribution. A total of seventeen books came out between 1967 and 1969, and in 1970 nine titles were added to the list. Ferlinghetti spent most of his time in the publishing office when he was in North Beach and less time at the bookstore. There were now two City Lights storefronts in North Beach. While the publishing house was not meant to be opened to the public, a constant stream of people came in—authors with manuscripts, curious tourists, and young writers hoping to meet Ferlinghetti.

Ferlinghetti expanded the book list: *Mount Analogue*, by the French writer René Daumal, *Poems to Fernando*, by Janine Pommy Vega (Pocket Poets), and *Panic Grass*, by Charles Upton, a long poem about the sixties. Ferlinghetti had heard Upton read his poem at a mass reading and was taken with its clear style and energy. In 1966, City Lights issued Carl Solomon's *Mishaps; Perhaps*, and two years later *More Mishaps* was published.

Other new City Lights books included *M'hashish*, by Moroccan Mohammed Mrabet, Colin Wilson's *Poetry and Mysticism*, and a pamphlet by the scientist Dr. Paul Ehrlich, *Eco Catastrophe*, which warned that civilization was headed for ruin unless attention was paid to the basic problems of population explosion.

Nancy Peters, an articulate young woman, originally from the Pacific Northwest, came to work for Ferlinghetti in 1970. She soon became an indispensable part of the daily operations, acting as editor and adviser. Nancy was the longtime friend and companion of

Philip Lamantia. She first met Ferlinghetti in Paris in 1965, where she and Philip were living. Nancy's own poetry was published by the Black Swan Press in 1977.

The City Lights list was amazingly intact; only a few of the Pocket Poets Series were out of print, and new books were being added all the time.

The first City Lights book to come out in the seventies was Robert Bly's *The Teeth Mother Naked at Last*, a long, rather bucolic anti–Vietnam War poem. Bly lived in Minnesota, where he edited a literary magazine and ran his own poetry press. In 1968 he won the National Book Award for poetry with his *A Light Around the Body*. Ferlinghetti admired him for his reading style as much as for his poetry.

After the Bly volume, City Lights published *Revolutionary Letters*, by Diane di Prima.

Pocket Poets Number 28 was *Scattered Poems*, by Jack Kerouac, who had died in 1969. The poems were selected from magazines by Kerouac biographer Ann Charters, and included a selection from *San Francisco Blues*, a collection he wrote in 1954, which Ferlinghetti had once turned down for publication. An excerpt from Kerouac's *The Origin of Joy in Poetry* was used as an introduction:

> The new American poetry typified by the San Francisco Renaissance (which means Ginsberg, me, Rexroth, Ferlinghetti, McClure, Corso, Gary Snyder, Philip Lamantia, Philip Whalen, I guess) is a kind of new-old Zen Lunacy poetry, writing whatever enters into your head as it comes, poetry returned to its origins, in the bardic child, truly ORAL as Ferling said, instead of grey faced academic quibbling . . .

That was written in the fifties. Kerouac, like Ferlinghetti, believed in oral poetry, and though he was thought of primarily as a novelist, he also wrote a voluminous amount of poetry. Ferlinghetti revised his opinion of Kerouac's poetry and of much of his earlier prose-work writings by the mid-sixties, and has been eager to publish more of it.

City Lights also published *The First Third*, a work by Neal Cassady. He was one of the heroes of Kerouac's *On the Road*, and the mythic figure of Kerouac's work and life. By the time *The First Third* was published, Cassady was already a legend. The book title referred to the first third of his life. Ferlinghetti edited the manuscript, pulling in fragments Cassady had written in different periods.

In 1972, Ferlinghetti brought out *Erections, Ejaculations, Exhibitions, and General Tales of Ordinary Madness*, by Charles Bukowski, a collection of short stories edited by Gail Chiarrello. The stories had appeared in various underground magazines and newspapers over the years and had gained for their author a large following. Bukowski first came to Ferlinghetti's attention for his poetry, published widely in the small literary magazines throughout the sixties. He saw immediately that Bukowski's fiction was a natural for City Lights. Bukowski's stories were set mostly in Los Angeles and related the author's crazy exploits in the proletarian world of racetrack, odd jobs, booze, and low life. Ferlinghetti saw Bukowski as the single most important prose writer of the period and accurately predicted his rising popularity with readers and critics alike. Soon *Notes of a Dirty Old Man* was added to the City Lights list, and Ferlinghetti would have liked to have published an endless number of his books; however, Bukowski remained loyal to John Martin of Black Sparrow, who had published his poems and had long been a supporter and friend. Soon foreign rights were sold in Germany, Italy, Spain, and France, and Bukowski's international acclaim grew. He was called by *Die Welt* the greatest American writer since Hemingway, and many more copies of his books were sold in Germany than in his own country. Ferlinghetti believes that the mass-market paperback publishers and the Hollywood film producers will soon wake up to this prodigious figure.

Another poet Ferlinghetti had been aware of was Harold Norse, an American expatriate in the bohemian tradition who had been writing for more than thirty-five years. William Carlos Williams had singled him out as one of the most important voices in American poetry. Norse had had several publishers since 1953 when his first book,

The Undersea Mountain, was published by Alan Swallow. Norse had moved to San Francisco, and after Ferlinghetti heard him read at the poetry reading for the benefit of the Greek Resistance in 1972, he asked to see more of his work. As a result *Hotel Nirvana*, a collection of fifty-seven poems, became Number 32 in the Pocket Poets Series.

Although the books by Bukowski, Norse, Kerouac, Cassady, and di Prima were indicative of Ferlinghetti's energy, some critics faulted him for taking a safer position than in his early publishing days by printing writers of his own generation. Richard Kostelanetz criticized City Lights for not continuing to publish experimental work and writers pioneering new forms. Still, Ferlinghetti had published Pete Winslow's *A Daisy in the Memory of a Shark* in the Pocket Poets Series, another book of poems by Daniel Moore, and in 1974 the *City Lights Anthology*, in the tradition of the *Journals*, was filled with work by people not yet well known.

And then there was always that most vocal of all the voices of the sixties, Ginsberg, who continued to grow and explore poetics. In 1972, City Lights published *The Fall of America, Poems of These States 1965–1971*, Number 30 in the Pocket Poets Series. It won the National Book Award for poetry in 1972.

The Fall of America included some long poems about Bixby Canyon, where Ginsberg often visited Ferlinghetti. On the back cover of the book Ginsberg wrote:

> Beginning with "long poem of these states" *The Fall of America* continues *Planet News* chronicle tape recorded scribed by hand or sung condensed the flux of car, bus, airplane, dream consciousness person during Automatic Electronic War years.

City Lights Books provided Ferlinghetti with security during a trying period in which he was experiencing marital difficulties. The pressure of a deteriorating home situation drove him more to his own poetry and into expanding his publishing list. He needed to get away, once more, from San Francisco, and in 1972 he embarked with Allen Ginsberg on a trip to Australia, taking his son, Lorenzo, along with him. Lorenzo was nearly ten years old, and father and son looked forward to spending this time together, sharing an experience far away from home.

Their first stop was Hawaii, where they stayed with writer Michael Weiner and his family on the island of Oahu. Weiner, whom Ginsberg was acquainted with, was an ethnobotanist who taught at the University of Hawaii. He felt that scientists had so little appreciation of art and literature that they were in danger of becoming exclusively scientifically oriented and thus cut off from the rest of the culture. This view intrigued Ferlinghetti, as did Weiner's practical knowledge of the land around him. They became friends, and a few years later, when the Weiners settled in the community of Fairfax, north of San Francisco in Marin County, they often saw one another. Weiner was attracted to the poet because of his ability to find humor in otherwise commonplace situations, and because of the way in which he was able to live successfully as poet, bookseller, publisher, and public personality.

Once in Australia, Ferlinghetti and Ginsberg were on a busy schedule. They were joined by poet Andrei Voznesensky, and were to participate in the Adelaide Festival of the Arts, one of Australia's biggest gatherings of that kind. The readings were packed, and afterwards a private promoter booked them into the Melbourne and Sydney Town Halls. At the Melbourne reading, demonstrators showed up to protest Voznesensky's presence. Most of them were Hungarian refugees incensed at the fact that a Soviet poet was being allowed to read. The audience responded to the demonstrators by tearing up their placards, and after a time the Hungarians left, and Voznesensky, who had been very upset, calmed down and the reading continued without incident.

Ferlinghetti and Lorenzo then went off on their own, while Ginsberg remained in Melbourne. They set off on a journey along the Murray River, the continent's largest waterway. Father and son spent a week in a houseboat, and Ferlinghetti kept an extensive journal of this idyllic retreat from the outside world. Perhaps he thought of his own childhood and how fulfilling it would have been to have had a father of his own clearing a space in the world for him as he and Lorenzo were doing:

> Last night on river, tie-up across from high white yellow sandstone cliffs—Geologic ages sculpted down, layer by layer, and stratified cliffs—(maybe 1,000 feet high). Murray River is Australia's Mississippi. Tom Sawyer Lorenzo . . . his fishline in the swift flowing waters . . . The great chain of being rattles into its links, the food chain chatters into the dark, cockatoos dive on swallows, hawks above all, their beaks agape for any Lower creation; Only fish-shape clouds make a mockery of it all, huge sky whales drifting over, flipping their tails in the rising night wind, hammerheads diving over high cliffs, tiny eyes pierced with slanting sunlight—huge over-hanging cliffs tower over the small boy in the skiff where he hovers in the lea of a log pulling up some locals fishline from a deep pool—He finds the line is baited with a live foot-long redfin, hooked fore and aft through, its back with two huge hooks so that it swings eternally around and around at the bottom of the Food Chain—helpless, vulnerable victim for any passing underwater predator.

One year later Ferlinghetti and Lorenzo made another trip together. They spent a week with Michael Weiner on the big island of Hawaii, camping and fishing. Ferlinghetti was intrigued by Weiner's description of it—a tropical paradise near sea level and capped by towering mountains on whose slopes grew an incredible variety of flora.

During the same year as his trip to Australia, Ferlinghetti had moved into an apartment above the City Lights publishing office. One of its three rooms became a workroom where he wrote. He spent a considerable amount of time, however, in the publishing office downstairs on Grant Avenue, working on the growing City Lights list with Nancy Peters.

Ferlinghetti's apartment was crammed with some of the books he had carried with him since his days in Paris and before: *Palimpsest*, by H.D.;

Four Quartets, by Eliot; Pound's *Personae*; *Look Homeward, Angel*, by Thomas Wolfe; and books by Rexroth. He slept on a mat and typed on the same Underwood upright he had bought in 1951, when he first came to town.

Ferlinghetti spent a considerable amount of time putting together *Open Eye, Open Heart*, his most extensive collection of poetry, 148 pages long and containing poems written over a considerable period of time, in many different genres. He divided it into four distinct sections: "Open Eye, Open Heart"; "Poems in Transit"; "Public and Political Poems"; and "American Mantra and Songs."

For the first time, in these poems, Ferlinghetti turned away from the outside world and explored his deepest emotions. In addition to the poems quoted earlier that touched on his feelings about his childhood ("True Confessional," etc.) and his deteriorating relationship with Kirby ("Mock Confessional"), he expressed his mourning for Kenneth Patchen, whom he still looked up to as a master. "An Elegy for Kenneth Patchen" begins:

> A poet is born
> A poet dies
> And all that lies between
> is us
> and the world

and:

> Along with all the other strange things
> he said about the world
> which were all too true
> and which made them fear him
> more than they loved him
> though he spoke much love . . .

Ferlinghetti was all too aware of the way in which Patchen was ignored by the American literary establishment, as represented by the academic world of the colleges and universities and by the Eastern reviewers. Patchen spent his last years in the community of Palo Alto, right next to Stanford University, which totally ignored him. Ferlinghetti often spoke out against the dishonor shown Patchen.

"Sueño Real" calls to mind the poems in *Pictures*. The lines "Back at the cabin in the woods by the stream/the white copy of Venus Aphrodite/stands silent on the porch/silk cobwebs on her/glisten and quiver in the wind" create a mystical experience out of the details in an everyday landscape. In the last part of "Sueño Real," Ferlinghetti recalls his *Palimpsest* poems:

> Transliteration of inanimate objects
> into real beings . . .
> a palimpsest
> an illegible
> manuscreed
> Braille
> night-thought spoke
> by a stream impossible
> to decipher . . .

The lyric is strong in the poem "The Real Magic Opera Begins"—the title alone suggestive of *Pictures*. In "Sunrise, Bolinas," the small coastal town where he and Kirby had lived for a while, he writes: "This little heart that remembers/every little thing/begins the day most of the time/by an attempt at singing some sunny rhyme."

In the "Poems in Transit" section the same tone continues. He wrote these poems while on trips abroad. "A Giacometti Summer" is the strongest, a poem about an exhibition by the well-known Italian sculptor: ". . . where are they going/those strange standing figures/metal shadows of themselves/tall as stone trees . . ." This section includes the "Pound at Spoleto" poem, a selection from *Russian Winter Journals*, and a poem on a spider observed by Ferlinghetti: "In Choloula Mexico!/Twice I spied him—all head—size of a BB-gun pellet . . . "

The section of political poems is a carry-over from his earlier political broadsides. "Las Vegas Tilt" is a montage of an experience in an alien world. Voznesensky was visiting San Francisco, and Ferlinghetti had gone south with him to Las Vegas:

> And now at Angel's Peak in morning light
> thirty miles above Vegas
> Andrei Voznesensky asks no quarter
> but takes a coin of his own
> and drops it into the mouth of the daughter
> of the President of Caesar's Palace
> and pulls her right arm down
> and waits for the Virgin coin
> to fall out below
> if he's that lucky.

Not long before *Open Eye, Open Heart* was published, City Lights had begun a Poets' Theater. It was the inspiration of several young friends of Ferlinghetti's. Among the projects were various mass readings for social and political causes. One, the Greek Resistance Benefit, organized in support of pro-Democratic forces fighting the Greek dictatorship, and which included Robert Duncan, Kay Boyle, Nanos Valaoritis, and Harold Norse, promoted Ferlinghetti's poem "Forty Odd Questions for the Greek Regime and One Cry for Freedom." It is in the political gathering, along with "A World Awash with Fascism and Fear." This grouping of poems made it clear that Ferlinghetti still believed in the anarchist philosophy. He began to feel, about the time he was putting *Open Eye, Open Heart* together, that some of the groups that grew out of the revolution of consciousness in the sixties had now become corrupt. He felt that the most genuine teachers were people like J. Krishnamurti, who rejected all attempts to make him an object of reverence or to make absolutes out of his teachings. Ferlinghetti also felt good about the San Francisco Zen Center, founded by Suzuki Roshi, a Zen master from Japan, who did not believe in the canonization of his teachings and resisted attempts at popularizing them. He emphasized each individual's opportunity to learn from one's own experience and taught the value of Zen meditation. He used the term "psychic authoritarianism" to refer to those who pulled further and further away from personal visionary experiences for the sake of rigid and dogmatic systems of thought.

In a short note to "American Mantra and Song," the last section of *Open Eye, Open Heart*, Ferlinghetti writes:

> Interested in developing chants with American English words as opposed to singing Sanskrit or other unknown tongues, I at one time or another sang or spoke or chanted these verses in varying versions, sometimes with much spontaneous repetitions not herein noted, often with autoharp accompaniment.

It was a straightforward reaction to the virtual epidemic of chants from India and other Asian countries that had infected the hippie culture—and of their use by American poets. He wanted to develop his own songs—from his own experience. "Spontaneous Anarchist Pacifist Buddhist Song" was a refreshing change from the rhetorical political poems he often wrote: "War! War! War!/World! World! World!/Life, Light, Men & Women! All one . . ."

THE PAINTER IN *Pictures of the Gone World*, described as having "a great big Hungry Eye," was also the poet in *A Coney Island of the Mind*, capable of startling people with language, but in the end, "a little charleychaplin man." The painter and poet are one and the same, wandering through the world from a central point, making good use of an ever astonished eye and an extraordinary musical ear. Some critics would not think of him as a particularly profound thinker, as his poetry reads so simply, containing few metaphoric intricacies or subtleties of language, but the poems he created are living artifacts of contemporary consciousness, remarkably visual in effect and charged with a sense of bewilderment in the face of life's difficulties and the closeness of death. They record the surface of life, but then lead deeper into experience than each poem might at first suggest. The poems are ordinary in a very unordinary way, deliberately focused on isolated sights, scenes, and ideas with a sharp clarity that creates space for the imagination to exercise free rein, altering reality with an artist's insight. The painter-poet would never abandon that special painterly quality he achieved in his first book of poems, or his commitment to poetry as oral message established in his second collection. More than most of his contemporaries he expressed the alienation brought on by the growth of consumerism and the division of the world into two separate camps, able to destroy one another several times over, as well as to alter the natural state of the planet. He came of age as a poet during an era in American life when a hysterical witch-hunt for imaginary enemies from within was taking place. Further, the cold war made it clear that individual rights meant nothing in the face of national interests.

Because of the lucidity of his work, he achieved a unique position in postwar American letters, becoming an initiatory bridge into contemporary poetry for younger poets, as well as bringing it to people who might otherwise not read it. Intrinsic to his character was an evasiveness about his private life and background, balanced by a need for straightforward communication in his creative work. Even his novel *Her*, which gives an impression of fantasy and the surreal, remains remarkably accessible. He was a master at conveying the surface of life, but his imaginative powers helped him pierce the veil of direct, sensory experience without sounding obscure or difficult. He worked from the perspective of clarity and yet was able to bring widely diverse meanings into his poems.

Ferlinghetti, the painter and poet, recognized a "little charley-chaplin man" in everyone. That is part of his strength as an artist. He was never overwhelmed by the fame he received, remaining shy and easygoing, with empathy for the work of his contemporaries. It is largely due to his interest in bohemianism, developed over the years of contact with Greenwich Village, the artist and writer's life in Paris, and his first years in San Francisco's North Beach, that he remained free of the academic world and kept his distance from the lofty heights of the literary establishment represented by the Eastern publishing houses. This independence was to keep him emphatic in his decision not to accept government grants either for his own writing or for the publishing house.

By 1972, with the publication of *Open Eye, Open Heart*, Ferlinghetti was one of the best-selling poets in the country. Though largely ignored by the community of critics, and scoffed at for being too simplistic or sentimental, he was able to touch upon the lives of mass numbers of people through a medium that rarely had a large audience.

During the seventies, he was politically as active as in the previous decade. Ferlinghetti participated with fervor in the struggle waged by Cesar Chavez and the United Farmworkers of America to bring dignity to farm laborers, appearing at readings on their behalf. As one who spoke out for years against American nuclear policies, he appeared at readings in support of a California initiative to stop the construction of nuclear power plants, and as a result of his long-term support of the battle to stop the destruction of the earth's ecological balance, he actively aided the Greenpeace anti-whaling campaign. While aboard the *James Bay* anti-whaling vessel, in October 1977, when he sailed as a guest of the crew on the last leg of a voyage into the Pacific whaling areas, he wrote: "Dreamt of Moby Dick the Great White Whale/cruising about/with a flag flying/with an inscription on it/"I am what is left of Wild Nature"/And Ahab pursuing a jet boat with a ray gun . . ."

Ferlinghetti published *A Political Pamphlet* in September 1976 under the imprint Anarchist Resistance Press—"issued from time to time, as the situation demands it." The poems included in it do not have the lyricism of those that would be represented in *Who Are We Now?*, which came out in the same year, but they do make their point directly. In "The Trouble with Revolutions Is the People," Ferlinghetti articulates a theme suggested in earlier poems, such as "A World Awash with Fascism and Fear." He is in Chicago's O'Hare Airport and sees "An exuberance of short pig-like men . . . some with dispatch cases and dead pan faces/some with short pig-like friends or wives or brothers . . . some with no hair no brains and worse vices . . . And these very women & men/the very reason/revolutions degenerate/into governments." "A Banquet in the Suburbs of the Empire" gives a clue to the wrath he felt over the taking of government grants by poets and small-press publishers. He wrote of the "poetry directors of the National Endowment of the Arts," who in the poem were, indeed, banqueting at a popular California resort, that "they and co-operating poets and publishers hardly realized that when the literary history of this strange decade is writ it would be seen to be the time of the ostrich."

Ferlinghetti reprinted two letters he had sent to poet Stanley Kunitz, a Pulitzer Prize recipient, who was Consultant in Poetry to the Library of Congress in 1975. In the last paragraph of the second letter, he wrote:

I'm still concerned with the symbolic importance of a poet lend-
ing his talent to any branch of the government, even if he's paid
privately for it. Poets and intellectuals in foreign countries, for in-
stance (and I'm thinking of my friends in France, England, Italy,
Germany—editors, writers & publishers), don't know about the
"private funding" in any case, and all they see is your participation
in the guilty government. Guilt by complicity, as I learned it chez
Camus, is I'm afraid still to be reckoned with

It was only a few years later that he had his FBI file in hand, sent
to him by virtue of his requesting it through the Freedom of Information Act, and one of the documents read, in part:

Beatnik Rabble Rouser
LAWRENCE FERLINGHETTI is reputed, in some circles, to be a
San Francisco poet. Among his "works" is a thing called "Tentative
Description of a Dinner Given to Promote the Impeachment of
President Eisenhower," which is available in pamphlet form here .
. . This type of trash, so readily available in widespread circulation,
must surely be responsible in some measure to demoralization in
America.

In another government document, from the Secret Service to
J. Edgar Hoover, it is said of Ferlinghetti that "he may be a mental
case." This appraisal came in reference to the same poem.

An understanding of Ferlinghetti's *Who Are We Now?* is partially
aided by knowing something of the events of his private life in the
mid-seventies. There are traces of his divorce in *Who Are We Now?*
and poems expressing the readjustments he was making. He and Kirby underwent long and difficult divorce proceedings, and he worried
over the effect of their breakup on Julie and Lorenzo—especially
important to him considering his own childhood. In "Great American Waterfront Poem," a prose poem written during the height of
his divorce difficulties, Ferlinghetti utilized many of the elements
that made up his philosophy of both life and poetics in dealing with

the trauma that had fallen on him. The piece is humorous, nostalgic, illuminated with the spirit of San Francisco, elusive about his private life, and yet touching upon it, and touched with his politics. There is

> the phone booth where I telephoned It's All Over Count Me Out The fog lifting the sun the sun burning through the bright steamers standing out in the end of the first poem I ever wrote in San Francisco twenty years ago just married on a rooftop in North Beach overlooking this place I've come to in this life this waterfront of existence

and:

> The Belt Line Railroad engine stands snorting on a spur next to the Eagle Cafe with a string of flats & boxcars I park on the tracks embedded in asphalt and enter the Eagle Cafe a sign on the wall reading "Save the Eagle—Last of an endangered species"

The nature of Ferlinghetti's earlier phone call to the lawyers is fairly obvious in this passage:

> waiting for my lawyer to call back with the final word on my divorce from civilization will they let Man be free or won't they Will they or won't they let him be a barbarian or a wanderer if he wants to

While still waiting to hear about his divorce he muses:

> and the Bank of America towering over behind me Will Eros or civilization win

Aside from his divorce, which had drained him emotionally, Ferlinghetti experienced another traumatic change in his life. It was the loss of his long friendship with Shig Murao, who had become seriously ill in 1975 and had to be hospitalized. During his absence a temporary manager was placed in charge of the bookstore. He altered the environment, making changes in operating procedures. When Shig returned from the hospital, weakened and yet getting stronger, he planned to recuperate awhile, but had every intention of assuming his old position. Ferlinghetti insisted that he take things easy, and told Shig he liked the new store policies. He asked Shig to work as co-manager at his old salary, assuming a position much like his own, as partner-manager. Shig refused, and said he would not return under that condition. He wanted full control, as he had had for so many years, and would not share responsibilities with anyone. He said, "Lawrence writes his poems with no one standing over him and telling him how to write, and that's how I ran the bookstore, without any outside help." An attempt by Ginsberg to bring the two together was unsuccessful, as were numerous gestures by Ferlinghetti to reach some satisfactory arrangement. No matter what he said, nothing could be done unless he was willing to let things return as they were before Shig's illness. The store was, for Murao, not merely a business, but a way of life. Regretfully, Ferlinghetti bought out Shig's one-fourth interest in the bookstore and a new era began for City Lights, one that would see the expansion of the store into the adjacent storefront that had been occupied for years by an Italian travel agency, an old firm that looked as if it might have come out of a Ferlinghetti poem. The words JAMES FUGAZI, BULOTTI AND CO., FRATELLI FORTE, PROPS., were prominently displayed above the long front window, and the windows were crammed with antique steamship brochures and posters. The place had an aura of the 1940s about it. Ferlinghetti coveted the space for years, and when it was obtained, he hired a carpenter to cut three elegantly designed entranceways into the new area. In the back of the storefront there was a balcony that became the bookstore offices and Ferlinghetti's private working space.

While the trouble between him and Shig was brewing, Ferlinghetti read at a benefit poetry event for Beatitude Press at the Little Fox Theater on Pacific Street on April 12, 1976, not far from the bookstore. The old Beat Generation magazine *Beatitude* had been revitalized by a group of younger poets, and Ferlinghetti was committed to helping them. He waited backstage for his time to appear and made his entrance wearing a derby with a card attached to it on which he had written "Director of Alienation," clearly visible to the crowd of three hundred. He read:

> Looking in the mirrors at Macy's
> and thinking it's a subterranean plot
> to make me feel like Chaplin
> snuck in with his bent shoes & beat bowler
> looking for the fair-haired angel
> Who's this bum
> crept in off the streets
> blinking in the neon
> an anarchist among the floorwalkers
> a strike-breaker even
> right past the pickets
> and the picket line is the people yet?
> I think I'll hook a new derby
> and put a sign on it reading
> Director of Alienation

In 1972, Ferlinghetti had met Paula Lillevand, a woman of Norwegian parentage from Seattle, Washington. He was attracted to Paula by her self-possession and her strength. Paula empathized with Ferlinghetti's affection for North Beach. She intuitively understood his longing for the security of a family life and gave him much of the emotional support he needed during his divorce. The mother of two teenage daughters, she had lived in North Beach, the Haight-Ashbury, and other San Francisco neighborhoods since 1958. Paula lived a bohemian lifestyle, wrote poetry, and had been active in the antiwar movement. Since Ferlinghetti's return from Australia they had gradually become closer. Soon they were discussing the possibility of living together. They rented an apartment, finally, one block from where Ferlinghetti had lived on Chestnut Street in the fifties. They shared more than social and political attitudes—both believing in keeping their living environment simple, with little furniture. Once again Ferlinghetti had a home. Soon after he moved in, Julie and Lorenzo came to live with them.

He and Paula, together with one or another of the four children, spent time in Bixby Canyon, mainly on weekends. It was still the perfect retreat from his daily routine, a place where some of his more quiet nature poems were first written. He commissioned a carpenter to build a small Japanese-style cabin—with tatami rug—partially on stilts and partially on the concrete and stone remains of an older structure. Like his cabin, it was minuscule, but big enough to sleep in comfortably. He and Paula planted a garden and several saplings on the Bixby property, and Ferlinghetti thought of the possibility of living on the land for a while.

Who Are We Now?, written against the perspective of extremes of sorrow and joy, of endings and new beginnings, was almost titled *Visual Beatitudes*, which, considering his pictorial "presence," would not have been inappropriate. The question "Who am I now?" however, was surely timely in 1976. The alterations in Ferlinghetti's life needed to be explored and dealt with through his poetry. Both the "Great American Waterfront Poem" and "Director of Alienation" were in the collection, and as with most of these poems, they have greater condensation of language than do the poems of the sixties and those in *Open Eye, Open Heart*. The range of the work is broader than in Ferlinghetti's previous collection, which was a more studied and self-conscious exploration of the genres of poetry. This journey was less planned and more spontaneous, whereas the format of *Open Eye, Open Heart* was stilted and forced in comparison. *Who Are We Now?* is as cohesive a grouping of poems as *Pictures of the Gone World*. The two sides of Ferlinghetti, the shy and easygoing man on the one hand and the public poet on the other, are revealed in the poems. They range from an intensely personal vision to one that is glaringly public. Reaching both into himself and outward on the world, he struggled with the question "Who am I now?"

"The Jack of Hearts" begins: "Who are we now, who are we ever,/ Skin books parchment bodies libraries of the living." It is a catalogue of all the possible "Jacks" Ferlinghetti could think of:

the one whose day has just begun
the one with the star in his cap
the cat with future feet
looking like a Jack of Hearts
mystic Jack Zen Jack with crazy koans
Vegas Jack who rolls the bones

Again, as in "A Banquet in the Suburbs of the Empire," there is a
criticism of:

the ones with their eyes in the sands
the sand that runs through the glass
the ones who don't want to look
at what's going on around them
the shut-eye ones who wish
that someone else would seize the day

The conjuring up of all the Jacks continues, and Ferlinghetti finally arrives at what is the result of a great deal of introspection leading
toward a definition of his own life:

the one who digs
in the time of the ostrich
and finds the sun-stone
of himself
the woman-man
the whole man
who holds all the world together
when all is said and done
in the wild eye the wide eye
of the Jack of Hearts
who stands in a doorway
clothed in sun

The "great big Hungry Eye" of the poet was still a dominant image for Ferlinghetti. "The Jack of Hearts," a poem of definitions, is followed in *Who Are We Now?* by "Director of Alienation."

"Wild Dreams of a New Beginning" concerns itself with civilization in juxtaposition with the wonders of nature, and because of Ferlinghetti's concern with ecology naturally suggests his horror of "the ledges of concrete" on freeways and Los Angeles, breathing "its last gas." A possible Bixby image, "a cry of seabirds high over/in empty eternity," precedes the last two lines: "as the Hudson retakes its thickets/and Indians reclaim their canoes."

"Lost Parents" and "People Getting Divorced" humorously portray a subject that only a few years earlier had caused Ferlinghetti so much misery. The latter poem ends with two obvious puns:

> and the sole
>> ah the soul
>>> a curious conception
>> hanging on somehow
>>> to walk again
>>>> in the free air
>>> once the heel
>>>> has been replaced

"Dissidents, Big Sur" is an interesting poem dealing with the invasion of "an ordinary monster American fourdoor sedan" in the harmonious wilderness of Bixby Canyon. In "A Vast Confusion," Ferlinghetti hears the "Sound of trains in the surf/in subways of the sea." For an urban poet who also finds comfort and peace in the wilderness, it is not surprising to find him so cognizant of the interplay between city and country. *Who Are We Now?* is full of both urban and country imagery. As in "Great American Waterfront Poem," stamped with the imprint of San Francisco, he can strikingly portray the moods of Bixby: "Dawn/sows its mustard seed/In the steep ravines and gulches/of Big Sur." "Alienation: Two Bees" is a Bixby poem carrying on the theme established in "Director of Alienation."

Ferlinghetti comes upon two bees in his cabin, an angry one and an old one, crippled with age. One is at the window buzzing about, and the aged bee is silent on the counterpane. Ferlinghetti saw that the one at the window wouldn't go out the open door. "Something had alienated him/and he would not go back" to his hive.

Several of the poems in *Who Are We Now?* are centered in North Beach. "Overheard Conversations" is made up of ten separate parts, originally thought of as individual pieces. They record Ferlinghetti's feelings about North Beach in the mid-seventies, as well as his impressions of conversations heard in the community, or, as the subtitle says, in the U.S. Restaurant on Columbus Avenue and the Café Sport on Green Street. They have the mood of lighthearted snapshots, appearing on the page like his more lyrical poems in *Pictures*, but actually having the sound of his oral poetry. "Number 8" is an impression of the changes taking place in the community, as the Chinese expanded out of the Chinatown area and into adjacent areas:

> In the famous U.S. Restaurant
>   in the last Golden Age of North Beach San Francisco
> listening to mafioso conversations
>   interlarded with hardrock wingding jabber
> by Hong Kong longhair streetgang studs
>   with their choppers idling outside

"The Heavy" is an extended portrait of an habitué of the Caffè Trieste. "There was this man who was not myself, this short, squat little man, this hunk of meat, this large toad of a man, sitting in the Trieste café in San Francisco this Saturday noon . . ." The introductory description of the "heavy" is followed by a few lines that give some idea of the mood of the Caffè itself: ". . . in the crowd that comes every Saturday to hcaear the padrone and his son and their friends sing Italian arias, sometimes to jukebox accompaniment and sometimes with a guest guitarist or blind mandolin player . . ." Later in the poem Ferlinghetti says that the "heavy" is "a character in a corner of an Egyptian café in Lawrence Durrell's *Justine*, he was Proust's solitary diner, and he was Dr. Matthew O'Connor in drag in Djuna Barnes's *Nightwood . . .*"

The theme of love is evident in several of the poems, including "Short Story on a Painting by Gustav Klimt." This is a highly lyrical work. The pictorial quality begins in the first line: "They are kneeling upright on a flowered bed/He/has just caught her there/and holds her still/her gown/has slipped down . . ." Concisely he describes: "Her Titian hair/with blue stars in it/And his gold/harlequin robe/checkered with/dark squares . . ." In "The 'Moving Waters' of Gustav Klimt," Ferlinghetti asks: "Who are they then/these women in this painting/seen so deeply long ago/Models he slept with/or lovers or others/he came upon/catching them as they were/back then . . ."

In a much different mood "The Populist Manifesto," the most well-known poem in the collection, written in 1975 and published in leading daily newspapers as well as in dozens of literary magazines, expresses Ferlinghetti's concerns over the state of poets and poetry. After its appearance in the *San Francisco Examiner* on August 10, 1975, the literary community of San Francisco began heated and lively debates about the message of the poem, ranging from total agreement to sheer rage at Ferlinghetti's attitude. It was a call for poets to adopt a "new commonsensual public surface.'" Ferlinghetti felt that an epidemic of inbred literary small talk and irresponsible experimentation—often an excuse for not being capable of finding one's own poetic voice—had caused poetry to become uninteresting. He humorously describes the various "schools" of poetry: "All you Groucho Marxist poets . . . All you Catholic anarchists of poetry, All you Black Mountaineers of poetry . .

Guttersnipe, by Tom Pickard, an English writer, is an autobiographical novel Ferlinghetti published, along with Charles Plymell's *The Last of the Moccasins*, a memoir of the Beat and hippie scenes of the fifties and sixties, beginning with Plymell's youth in Wichita. Both were indicative of Ferlinghetti's interest in new fiction. He was looking for clear and condensed prose—and was impatient with much of the poetry that came to City Lights. Certainly one of the reasons he wrote *The Populist Manifesto* was because of his experiences as an editor, and he was hoping to find poetry expressive of a new American vision written in clear language.

Fast Speaking Woman, by Anne Waldman, whose poetic style moves with an energy that is much looser than the Eastern poets she has generally been associated with, became Pocket Poets book Number 33. The title poem, "Fast Speaking Woman," is an oral poem that helped build Waldman's reputation as a new, independent voice in American poetry. Jack Hirschman, who had edited the *Artaud Anthology* for City Lights, was represented with a book of poems, *Lyripol*, bringing together works he had written in North Beach throughout the seventies. The poems reflect Hirschman's interest in helping to create an indigenous American communism and his belief in the value of the still lively San Francisco literary scene. Ginsberg's sixth Pocket Poets collection, *Mind Breaths: Poems 1972–1977*, breaks new ground, ranging from short and gentle nature reflections to longer works in which he struggles with a desire to escape the pressures of fame. *Mind Breaths* is an interweaving of nature and the poet's escape into it from urban life, and a journey around the planet to places he had been on his travels, including Fiji, where he and Ferlinghetti had stayed en route to Australia in 1972:

> clear winds breathe on Fiji's palm coral shores, by wooden hotels
> in Suva flags flutter, taxis whoosh by Friday night's black prome-
> naders under the rock & roll discotheque windows upstairs—

There is also a series of poems about his father's death, "Don't Grow Old," among the best works in the collection.

Ferlinghetti had moved the publishing offices from Grant Avenue soon after Hirschman's book appeared, taking space in the bookstore. Far from slowing down, the City Lights book list expanded, and in fact plans were made for broadening the scope of the venture. *Thoughts*, a tongue-in-cheek compilation by Nancy Peters of statements by Governor Jerry Brown of California, who Ferlinghetti hoped would bring a radically new perspective to national politics, was published. Even after the Democratic nomination was sewn up, Ferlinghetti believed that Brown was going to capture the presidency. Twenty thousand copies had been sold within two weeks, and more copies were ordered. Then the Jimmy Carter campaign began to show its strength and City Lights was stuck with thousands of copies of the Brown book.

Fortunately, with the publication of some good-selling books, the publishing house had a narrow escape from financial ruin. The list was becoming more diverse: *The Old Ways: Six Essays*, by Gary Snyder, penetrating insights into ecological common sense, stressing the importance of man's dependence on nature and need to see the natural world as a living, breathing entity; *Seeing the Light*, the film criticism of an important San Francisco poet and independent experimental filmmaker James Broughton, whose films Ferlinghetti had admired since the fifties, and *Investigative Poetry*, by Ed Sanders.

Three writers of past epochs added to the diversity Ferlinghetti was developing. There was John Reed's *Adventures of a Young Man*; *The Oblivion Seekers*, by Isabelle Eberhardt, late-nineteenth-century adventurer, traveler through North Africa, and student of Sufism; and *Love Poems*, by Karl Marx. On a back-cover note for the Marx book, Nancy Peters wrote ". . . it is often forgotten that Karl Marx lived and wrote during the final flowering of German Romanticism. These love poems, selected from the five volumes of poetry Marx wrote to the beautiful and witty Jenny von Westphalen, attest to this."

Through the spring and winter of 1978, Ferlinghetti published books by Peter Orlovsky, Ginsberg's longtime companion; James Laughlin, well established as a pioneering avant-garde editor-publisher, but not well known as a poet; Stefan Brecht, the son of German playwright-poet Bertolt Brecht, who had sent his self-published poetry book to City Lights unsolicited; and a full-length play by San Francisco poet Kaye McDonough called *Zelda: Frontier Life in America*.

In May 1978, Ferlinghetti published *City Lights Journal* Number 4, an international anthology. It ranged from prose selections of works in progress by Charles Bukowski, Harold Norse, and young

San Francisco playwright-writer Frank Chin to poetry by Bob Kaufman, Gregory Corso, and a great number of "discoveries" from the San Francisco Bay area and nationwide.

Ferlinghetti kept busy with his own poetry after the publication of *Who Are We Now?* "The Old Italians Dying," which he wrote in 1976, was a definition of his love for North Beach, and the "old ways" as seen from the vantage point of a time of changes. The poem speaks eloquently about the labyrinth of emotions Ferlinghetti felt regarding the old Italians of his neighborhood. It is a gentle, humorous, and lyrical approach to the fact of dying.

THE OLD ITALIANS DYING

For years the old Italians have been dying
all over North Beach San Francisco
For years the old Italians in faded felt hats
have been sunning themselves and dying
You have seen them on the benches
in the park in Washington Square
the old Italians in their black high button shoes
the old men in their old felt fedoras
                          with stained hatbands
have been dying and dying
                    day by day
You have seen them
every day in Washington Square
the slow bell
tolls in the morning
in the Church of Saint Peter & Paul
in the marzipan church on the plaza
toward ten in the morning the slow bell tolls
in the towers of Peter & Paul
and the old men who are still alive
sit sunning themselves in a row
on the wood benches in the park

and watch the processions in and out
funerals in the morning
weddings in the afternoon
slow bell in the morning Fast bell at noon
In one door out the other
the old men sit there in their hats
and watch the coming & going
You have seen them
the ones who feed the pigeons
              cutting the stale bread
                    with their thumbs & penknives
the ones with old pocketwatches
the old ones with gnarled hands
                and wild eyebrows
the ones with the baggy pants
              wearing both belt & suspenders
the grappa drinkers with teeth like corn
the Pie'montesi the Genovesi the Sicilianos
                  smelling of garlic & pepperonis
the ones who loved Mussolini
the old fascists
the ones who loved Garibaldi
the old anarchists reading *L'Umanita Nova*
the ones who loved Sacco & Vanzetti
They are almost all gone now
They are sitting and waiting their turn
and sunning themselves in front of the church
over the doors of which is inscribed
a phrase which would seem to be unfinished
from Dante's *Paradiso*
about the glory of the One
              who moves everything . . .
The old men are waiting
for it to be finished
for their glorious sentence on earth

to be finished
the slow bell tolls & tolls
the pigeons strut about
not even thinking of flying
the air too heavy with heavy tolling
The black hired hearses draw up
the black limousines with black windowshades
shielding the widows
the widows with the long black veils
who will outlive them all
You have seen them
madre di terra, madre di mare
The widows climb out of the limousines
The family mourners step out in stiff suits
The widows walk so slowly
up the steps of the cathedral
fishnet veils drawn down
leaning hard on darkcloth arms
Their faces do not fall apart
They are merely drawn apart
They are still the matriarchs
outliving everyone
the old dagos dying out
in Little Italys all over America
the old dead dagos
hauled out in the morning sun
that does not mourn for anyone
One by one Year by year
they are carried out
The bell
never stops tolling
The old Italians with lapstrake faces
are hauled out of the hearses
by the paid pallbearers
in mafioso mourning coats & dark glasses
The old dead men are hauled out

in their black coffins like small skiffs
They enter the true church
for the first time in many years
in these carved black boats
                    ready to be ferried over
The priests scurry about
                    as if to cast off the lines
The other old men still alive on the benches
watch it all with their hats on
You have seen them sitting there
waiting for the bocci ball to stop rolling
waiting for the bell
                    to stop tolling & tolling
for the slow bell
                    to be finished tolling
telling the unfinished *Paradiso* story
as seen in an unfinished phrase
                    on the face of a church
as seen in a fisherman's face
in a black boat without sails
making his final haul

In 1975 he had begun a second populist manifesto while on a reading tour in Mexico. It would later be called *Adieu à Charlot: Second Populist Manifesto*, appearing in the *Los Angeles Times* and the *City Lights Journal*. Ferlinghetti expounds on his poetics, as well as offering a tribute to Charlie Chaplin, who died soon after the poem was completed. It is "the little man in each of us" that Ferlinghetti had portrayed so strikingly in his poetry . . . "On every corner I see them," he writes, emphasizing the visual. It is a poem celebrating the triumph of the individual, a bringing together of images leading toward the realization that man is alone and yet entwined with all others: "we have always waited with them," Ferlinghetti emphasizes.

ADIEU À CHARLOT:
SECOND POPULIST MANIFESTO

Sons of Whitman sons of Poe
sons of Lorca & Rimbaud
or their dark daughters
poets of another breath
poets of another vision
Who among you still speaks of revolution
Who among you still unscrews
the locks from the doors
in this revisionist decade?
"You are President of your own body, America"
Thus spoke Kush in Tepotzlan
youngblood wildhaired angel poet
one of a spawn of wild poets
in the image of Allen Ginsberg
wandering the wilds of America
"You Rimbauds of another breath"
sang Kush
and wandered off with his own particular paranoias
maddened like most poets
for one mad reason or another
in the unmade bed of the world
Sons of Whitman
in your "public solitude"
bound by blood-duende
"President of your own body America"
Take it back from those who have maddened you
back from those who stole it
and steal it daily
The subjective must take back the world
from the objective gorillas & guerrillas of the world
We must rejoin somehow
the animals in the fields

in their steady-state meditation
"Your life is in your own hands still
Make it flower make it sing"
(so sang mad Kush in Tepotzlan)
"a constitutional congress of the body"
still to be convened to seize control
of the State
the subjective state
from those who have subverted it
The arab telephone of the avant-garde
has broken down
And I speak to you now
from another country
Do not turn away
in your public solitudes
you poets of other visions
of the separate lonesome visions
untamed uncornered visions
fierce recalcitrant visions
you Whitmans of another breath
which is not the too-cool breath of modem poetry
which is not the halitosis of industrial civilization
Listen now Listen again
to the song in the blood the dark duende a dark singing
between the tickings of civilization
between the lines of its headlines
in the silences between cars
driven like weapons
In two hundred years of freedom
we have invented
the permanent alienation of the subjective
almost every truly creative being
alienated & expatriated
in his own country in
Middle America or San Francisco

the death of the dream in your birth
o meltingpot America
I speak to you
from another country
another kind of blood-letting land
from Tepotzlan the poets'lan'
Land of the Lord of the Dawn
                                    Quetzalcoatl
Land of the Plumed Serpent
I signal to you
as Artaud signalled
through the flames
I signal to you
over the heads of the land
the hard heads that stand like menhirs
above the land in every country
the short-haired hyenas
who still rule everything
I signal to you from Poets' Land
you poets of the alienated breath
to take back your land again
and the deep sea of the subjective
Have you heard the sound of the ocean lately
the sound by which daily
the stars still are driven
the sound by which nightly
the stars retake their sky
The sea thunders still to remind you
of the thunder in the blood
to remind you of your selves
Think now of your self
as of a distant ship
Think now of your beloved
of the eyes of your beloved
whoever is most beloved

he who held you hard in the dark
or she who washed her hair by the waterfall
whoever makes the heart pound
the blood pound
Listen says the river
Listen says the sea Within you
you with your private visions
of another reality a separate reality
Listen and study the charts of time
Read the sanskrit of ants in the sand
You Whitmans of another breath
there is no one else to tell
how the alienated generations
have lived out their expatriate visions
here and everywhere
The old generations have lived them out
Lived out the bohemian myth in Greenwich Villages
Lived out the Hemingway myth
in *The Sun Also Rises*
at the Dôme in Paris
or with the bulls at Pamplona
Lived out the Henry Miller myth
in the *Tropics* of Paris
and the great Greek dream
of *The Colossus of Maroussi*
and the tropic dream of Gauguin
Lived out the D. H. Lawrence myth
in *The Plumed Serpent*
in Mexico Lake Chapalla
And the Malcolm Lowry myth
Under the Volcano at Cuernavaca
And then the saga of *On the Road*
and the Bob Dylan myth Blowing in the Wind
How many roads must a man walk down
How many Neal Cassadys on lost railroad tracks

How many replicas of Woody Guthrie with cracked guitars
How many photo-copies of longhaired Joan
How many Ginsberg facsimiles and carbon-copy Keseys
still wandering the streets of America
in old tennis shoes and backpacks
or driving beat-up school buses
with destination-signs reading "Further"
How many Buddhist Catholics how many cantors
chanting the Great Paramita Sutra
on the Lower East Side
How many Whole Earth Catalogs
lost in out-houses on New Mexico communes
How many Punk Rockers waving swastikas
Franco is dead but so is Picasso
Chaplin is dead but I'd wear his bowler
having outlived all our myths but his
the myth of the pure subjective
the collective subjective
the Little Man in each of us
waiting with Charlot or Pozzo
On every corner I see them
hidden inside their tight clean clothes
Their hats are not derbys they have no canes
but we know them
we have always
waited with them
They turn and hitch their pants
and walk away from us
down the darkening road
in the great American night

Tepotzlan '75–San Francisco '78

A collection of poems and journal entries made on several trips to
the Pacific Northwest by Ferlinghetti were published under the City

Lights imprint in the spring of 1978. *Northwest Ecologue* was described by Ferlinghetti as "Brief prose flashes and poems of trips 'up the Coast' last year, including a Greenpeace Voyage, wild river musings, bucolic ecologues and ecological soundings." What he didn't say is that it includes a few of the drawings he had begun doing after this book was written, the most recent of them being his own impressions of work by the Japanese artist Hokusai and the American Ben Shahn. He envisioned a book called *After Hokusai and Ben Shahn*, hoping that an art publisher would become interested in it.

In September 1977, Ferlinghetti was honored by the San Francisco Art Commission and the City of San Francisco as part of the Civic Art Festival activities. It was the first time that a poet was so honored. He was singled out for outstanding contributions to the cultural life of the community as poet, publisher, and bookstore owner. Beginning on September 21 and lasting for a month, an exhibition of historical photographs concerning his life and a selection of his paintings were displayed at the Capricorn Asunder Gallery of the Art Commission.

San Francisco had come a long way since the days of the *Howl* obscenity trial. Ferlinghetti reminded everyone, however, that they were giving an honor to a confirmed rebel, whose principles hadn't changed since he first became nationally known as a result of his defense for an obscenity charge. The reminder came in the form of ten suggestions for civic improvement. One of the proposals was to have an annual awarding of the title "poet laureate" and offer the awardee a free poet's cottage for the year. It was an idea he had discussed with Nancy Peters while they were walking through old Fort Mason, now a part of the Golden Gate Recreation Area and full of former Navy barracks and individual housing units. Another was to lean Coit Tower so that it could become a greater tourist attraction, and more to the point of social criticism, he suggested that the Embarcadero Freeway be torn down along the waterfront.

Ferlinghetti is a survivor. As a living symbol of the bohemian lifestyle that had attracted him as far back as his Navy days, when he spent time in Greenwich Village, he has been uncompromising in his independence as both a writer and publisher. As much as his two populist manifestos speak out for clarity of expression, they are also warnings to the artist and writer that the creative individual in society must not succumb to government pressures that could co-opt them. "Who amongst you still speaks of revolution?" he writes in the *Second Manifesto*.

It is hardly possible to think of City Lights Bookstore as being any larger than it is. That would take away some of its human dimension. Nor is it easy to conceive of the publishing venture as being much larger—that could possibly take it out of the realm of bohemianism. Ferlinghetti thinks on a universal scale—but always with a human perspective. He has never lost an innate ability to capture the mood and tenor of "everyman," and yet, as he had said of Jacques Prévert, he was more of a see-er than a seer. He writes with his eyes first, above all else, then with his ear for language, and then with his intellect.

He had chosen Charlie Chaplin as a metaphor for his poetry because he discerned in the Little Tramp a populist underdog who was charmingly wise and shockingly vulnerable . . . and always cognizant that there were forces of destruction near at hand. In *The Kid* the Little Tramp lives on the fringes of society—a true outsider—trying to remain free from the unfeeling hand of government, and in *City Lights* he is a court jester of the miraculous ordinary life—though down-and-out he is an aristocrat of humanness, capable of unselfish acts of kindness, unrecognized by a cold and cruel social system. The Tramp of *City Lights* is a nation of one unfolding into full self-realization.

When the news of Chaplin's death reached Ferlinghetti, he was profoundly saddened, realizing that the world had lost a great soul who, like himself, had worked well with humor, whimsicality, and clarity of expression. Chaplin's films faced the injustices of society. *Modern Times*; *The Great Dictator*; *City Lights*—they were statements of the importance of individual rights. "Chaplin is dead, but I'd wear his bowler having outlived all our myths but his," Ferlinghetti writes in the *Manifesto*.

For Ferlinghetti, shyness is a profound part of his nature, and yet he has been a public poet for a quarter of a century; a humorous vein runs deeply through his personality and shows itself in his work, yet he is deadly serious about the need for political changes that would put an end to socially, politically, and sexually repressive government; a rebellious nature makes it easy for him to find the energy to create new poetry of his own and to sell and publish the innovative works of others, and yet he has yearned for permanence.

Of the poet he had written in *A Coney Island of the Mind*:

CONSTANTLY RISKING ABSURDITY

Constantly risking absurdity
                              and death
             whenever he performs
                          above the heads
                                    of his audience
          the poet like an acrobat
                    climbs on rime
                              to a high wire of his own making
and balancing on eyebeams
                    above a sea of faces
          paces his way
                    to the other side of day
      performing entrechats
                    and sleight-of-foot tricks
and other high theatrics
                    and all without mistaking
          any thing
                    for what it may not be
      For he's the super realist
                    who must perforce perceive
          taut truth
                    before the taking of each stance or step
    in his supposed advance

toward that still higher perch

where Beauty stands and waits

with gravity

to start her death-defying leap

And he

a little charleychaplin man

who may or may not catch

her fair eternal form

spreadeagled in the empty air

of existence

EPILOGUE

T HE WORD *EPILOGUE* alone signals that the setting sun is soon approaching. For Lawrence Ferlinghetti, that last sunset would be a long time coming: From the time of this biography's original publication, in 1979, more than four decades would pass before his death, a sad day in 2021.

Ferlinghetti's late life found him determined to fulfill the path he had laid out for himself when he first arrived in San Francisco. City Lights became more than just an institution symbolizing San Francisco's vibrant literary culture—it's a catalyst of activism, a meeting place for kindred spirits, and a kind of shrine to creative thinking and imagining. The work that Ferlinghetti and Nancy Peters did to ensure their viability enabled the bookstore and publishing house to sail on even in the midst of the COVID crisis.

As for his poetry and art, Ferlinghetti didn't pause for a moment. His books kept appearing at a clip, and he wrote arguably his finest poem after turning ninety. He spent days on end at his art studio in the old Hunters Point Naval Shipyard, where he found the solitude he craved. His persistence led to exhibitions worldwide.

This epilogue can go only so far in honoring Lawrence Ferlinghetti's busy final forty years—there's only so much paper available, after all. A few facts and a sprinkle of stories will have to suffice.

Picture Ferlinghetti at his cabin at Bixby Canyon in Big Sur in the early 1980s. It's late afternoon in autumn. He is sitting beside the campfire with a young poet friend. They are cooking a chicken over the open flames. The young poet recites some of his favorite passages by Walt Whitman, proud he has them memorized, though he did have to glance at Ferlinghetti's worn copy of *Leaves of Grass* to finish the last poem. When he's done, Ferlinghetti—who has been sitting quietly with his eyes closed—asks for the book. He says he'd like to read one of his favorite Whitman passages.

"I read this when I was in college at Chapel Hill and never forgot it," he says.

Silence.

The sun is sinking lower.

The chicken sizzles.

The air is still.

Silence.

Ferlinghetti tilts the open book toward the campfire's light so he can see the words, then reads: "I think I could turn and live with animals, they are so placid and self-contain'd, / I stand and look at them long and long. / They do not sweat and whine about their condition, / They do not lie awake in the dark and weep for their sins, / They do not make me sick discussing their duty to God, / Not one is dissatisfied . . ."

These words from the Bard of Democracy had become a sort of guiding principle for Ferlinghetti. And sitting by the campfire that day, he still had decades left to live up to the Good Gray Poet's words.

THE 1980S ROLLED in like a bank of fog drifting over Twin Peaks and through the channel into San Francisco Bay. The city was undergoing big changes. One of the few strikingly consistent things was the presence of Lawrence Ferlinghetti's bookstore and publishing house in North Beach. It was still a gathering place for literary people of all kinds, and especially those who appreciated poetry. The reading series held in the poetry room was almost always packed. It was a venue for novels, works in progress, memoir, and nonfiction, too. The mix of people was quite astounding—which was just what Ferlinghetti had envisioned decades earlier.

If San Francisco actually had a "flavor," it was in no small part thanks to the modest but distinct black-and-yellow storefront whose display windows brimmed with books. City Lights had navigated the tricky evolution of becoming both a latter-day shrine for the literature of rebellion and a tourist destination. The days when people could wander in and out without checking their bags at the front counter were long over, but difficult-to-find books remained in abundance.

In the city at large, there had been a move to stop the growing glut of high-rises. This failed. Buildings climbed upward, cluttering the views, and the skyline became evermore the realm of real-estate developers. This was taking place mainly in the Financial District, but gradually the tentacles spread farther, and Ferlinghetti was concerned that San Francisco was being challenged from all directions. He was not surprised to see that the corporate world was determined to make an imitation Manhattan in the middle of town, nor was he impressed. Aside from the business towers, condos were coming into fashion at a rapid pace. Real-estate prices had not yet soared, but they were steadily creeping upward.

The cosmopolitan nature of San Francisco was as vibrant as ever. The gay rights movement had a solid hold: In 1981, some 250,000 people turned out for the tenth-anniversary Pride Parade and in 1982 the city hosted the inaugural Gay Games, an international sports and culture event. San Francisco had become much less a working-class town than when Ferlinghetti first arrived in the city to the aroma of fresh-baked French bread and good red wine. One thing was certain in the 1980s: The labor movement, which had enriched the Port of San Francisco and provided the jobs that kept so many distinct neighborhoods livable for all people, was waning. More and more wealth made its way to the wind-washed peninsula.

For a bohemian like Ferlinghetti, the changes were disheartening. As the city grew, he wished the buildings could remain low, and housing rents, too. The City Lights neighborhood of North Beach remained safe and sane—there were no skyscrapers—but rents were going up. Ferlinghetti loved seeing the residents of Chinatown crowding into the markets for their daily needs and appreciated that many of the restaurants retained enough of a non-tourist atmosphere to keep the environment balanced. One of his great pleasures was being able to walk from his house to the grocery store, or from City Lights to a restaurant. Ferlinghetti always had an automobile, but never wanted to feel dependent on it. He rode his bicycle around town, more often than not cycling along the Embarcadero and stopping in at the few remaining authentic diners.

He was good at finding the few remaining elderly longshoremen and stevedores. Sitting at the counter of Red's Java House, a small dive on the pier in the shadow of the Bay Bridge, he and the owner-cook would swap tales. Red had never been in City Lights; no matter how often Ferlinghetti might have invited him, he just couldn't find a time. Red was likely more comfortable flipping burgers on his grill than flipping through books of poetry. But Ferlinghetti didn't mind. He loved places like Red's as reminders of gone-by days.

Ferlinghetti's poem "The Old Italians Dying" was his love letter of sorts to San Francisco in general and North Beach in particular. He issued it in 1976 as a six-page, photocopied and staple-bound chapbook that sold for fifty cents at City Lights—today, a copy of the small first edition will cost you $50 to $150. Ferlinghetti was close to the poem because it documented the dying off of the elderly immigrants who had brought such an animated life to the streets.

One afternoon in the late 1970s, Ferlinghetti walked into the City Lights publishing office very upset about a response to "The Old Italians Dying." He told Nancy Peters that Allen Ginsberg thought the poem was a humorous piece. Ferlinghetti wanted Ginsberg to see that it was a serious poem and he was distraught. Peters reassured him that there must be a misunderstanding and she would straighten it out. She walked over to the telephone, dialed Ginsberg, mumbled something quietly, and then set the receiver on the desk. She walked back to Ferlinghetti, who was still fuming, and told him that Ginsberg wanted to speak to him. Ferlinghetti took the phone cautiously to his ear. After a few minutes of listening, his expression began to change. When he hung up, he was smiling, his eyes glowing.

"Allen said I misunderstood him," Ferlinghetti proudly reported. "He calls my poem a tragicomic work, and a very important one."

Disingenuous or not, Ginsberg had scored.

There is a calm and whimsical sensibility at work in "The Old Italians Dying," which only enhances its elegiac heart. After all, not only were these individuals passing, but so too was the neighborhood they'd built, and the world itself. As far as Ferlinghetti was concerned, an entire way of life was disappearing. He saw this culture being plowed under by the insatiable, carnivorous culture of commercial enterprise. That's saying a lot, perhaps, but it's how Ferlinghetti felt. And it's not surprising if one knows his poetry, which is full of warnings about the stripping down of humanness.

In the early 1980s, a measure of the old-time grace brought by the Italian community in North Beach remained. There were still restaurants without glossy murals of Florence or Rome, places that served steaming plates of simple food inspired by the old country. At City Lights, things looked pretty much as they had since 1953, when it opened. But the business itself tottered on thin ice financially due to some lackadaisical accounting practices. In 1981, several of the employees, including the store manager, wrote to Ferlinghetti and told him the business was in a nosedive and that something had to be done. He'd spent decades trying to juggle his roles as bookseller, publisher, poet, artist, and public figure—and this last category had at times made massive demands on his time. He said yes to many requests, and only slowly learned the art of saying no, even if it meant forgoing an all-expense-paid trip overseas to give a reading.

Nancy Peters, who'd started at City Lights in 1970, stepped in and took the store's problems in hand. The consensus among the staff was that Ferlinghetti would not have been able to turn things around on his own. Peters double-downed on management during the difficult years and navigated the store safety through a financial minefield. The fact that she rose to the occasion proved to Ferlinghetti that she was essential to the survival of City Lights as a bookstore and as a publishing house, neither of which was a traditional big moneymaker.

Peters's steady hand on the ship's tiller meant Ferlinghetti could place his total trust in her instincts. She found in Ferlinghetti the perfect partner, someone capable of listening, willing to admit his mistake, and, like her, eager to find new voices to publish—and neither shied away from controversy. As a poet associated with the surrealist movement and the wife of the eminent Philip Lamantia,

Peters added an element to the publishing venture that Ferlinghetti eagerly welcomed. The two matched each other in their devotion to crossing borders and, in fact, to tearing them down. They were internationalists who were patriots of the earth, not of an individual country or society.

Paul Yamazaki, who began working at City Lights under the legendary Shig Murao and eventually became the store's main book-buyer, believes that the Ferlinghetti/Peters partnership was based on profound mutual respect. He felt that each of them understood the other's limitations, and because of that were able to work around any difficulties that arose.

Quite simply, the publishing house became a rare thing: a well-run yet bohemian enterprise. This meant Ferlinghetti was able to crisscross the world in his role as a poet, confident that the house was running smoothly and humanely, and that he would return to find his editor's desk undisturbed.

As a famous poet—which is to put the concept of Ferlinghetti's fame by the 1980s mildly—he was constantly pulled away from his desk, invited to give readings at grand events. Yet no matter the demands on him from whatever quarter, he remained loyal to his beloved North Beach. It wasn't just a locale, it was a way of living that he loved. He didn't think of himself as an internationally revered literary figure. He thought of himself as just another North Beach poet standing at the bar, ordering an espresso, chatting with friends. When asked, Ferlinghetti would participate in public readings with young, unpublished poets. He accepted invitations to their Thanksgiving dinners and holiday parties and birthday celebrations. He invited young writers to his cabin at Bixby Canyon. He took them with him to the state capital when he was giving a poetry reading and made sure that they were sitting in the front row, then introduced them to the crowd as "my North Beach friends." Ferlinghetti didn't just love his community; he actively cultivated and supported it.

In 1980, City Lights published *The Unknown Poe: An Anthology of Fugitive Writings*, by Edgar Allan Poe. The book was edited by Raymond Foye, who was not a Poe scholar, but who had to come upon fugitive publications by the great nineteenth-century poet and story writer languishing in the stacks of a university library. When he told Ferlinghetti about his find, they quickly stitched together an idea for a book that included appreciations by other authors, such as the French poets Charles Baudelaire and Paul Valéry. Foye was pleased with the freedom he was given and the trust Ferlinghetti showed. Ferlinghetti was the first to admit that he'd made errors in publishing over the years—mainly, not publishing writers he should've paid attention to—but he also had an uncanny gift for attracting obscure and exciting projects just like the one Foye was asked to take on.

THROUGHOUT THE 1980S, Ferlinghetti went on many trips abroad. His excursions often merged his passions of literature and politics.

In 1983, Ferlinghetti's fascination with the revolutionary upheaval in Central America led City Lights to work with Alejandro Murguía on *Volcán*, a bilingual anthology of Central American writing. Murguía taught at San Francisco State University, but had been a volunteer in the Nicaraguan army; in 2012, he was name San Francisco's poet laureate. The great Salvadorian-born Roque Dalton was featured in the collection, along with Otto René Castillo, of Guatemala, and Ernesto Cardenal, one of Latin America's most admired poets. There were numerous younger writers from throughout the region, too, among them Daisy Zamora, from Nicaragua. Ferlinghetti loved most that the anthology brought together thirty-nine poets from four Central American countries. He saw it as a unique gathering. The politics reflected in the collection resonated with Ferlinghetti's rebellious spirit, as well as his anger with those who ruled Central America as if it were their personal fiefdom.

In 1984, Ferlinghetti decided to visit Nicaragua. He had been talking about making such a trip since the Sandinistas marched into Managua on July 19, 1978, filled with hope for an egalitarian society, and overthrew the dictator Anastasio Somoza. The publication of *Volcán* clinched his decision.

Ferlinghetti was accompanied on the trip by Chris Felver, a young photographer he had met a few years earlier at a bar near City Lights. Felver had many qualities in common with the older poet, such as the ability to listen and an obsession with keeping his eyes open wherever he was so as not to miss a single thing. "You could watch Lawrence sitting in a café and be relatively sure that he heard what people were saying at distant tables," Felver observes. "It was uncanny, but that's the way he was. He really knew where his poems came from."

In his journal of the adventure, during the flight Ferlinghetti was already making notes about his eagerness to land in Managua. Felver could see the anticipation in the poet's eyes. "He's been all over the world, but I think this was really getting to him as he was anticipating a new society with principles close to his own way of thinking," he recalls.

When the two travelers from San Francisco landed in Managua via a flight from Miami, they were greeted on the tarmac by the poet Ernesto Cardenal, who was Nicaragua's minister of culture. Cardenal escorted Ferlinghetti and Felver for their entire seven-day visit, disappearing each afternoon only to pop up later the next day. Like Ferlinghetti, Cardenal was published by New Directions. The two poets had met in the past and had the poet Philip Lamantia as a friend in common. Cardenal was also a priest, closely associated with the Trappist monastery where Thomas Merton lived; he had more than a touch of the mystical and possessed a poetic feeling for the sacred. Ferlinghetti hand-delivered copies of *Volcán* to Cardenal as a symbol of solidarity. Ferlinghetti also brought a seed from a flower at the graveside of Boris Pasternak, which had been given to him by the Russian poet Andrei Voznesensky. This was Ferlinghetti's way of demonstrating his belief in a world without borders.

As he traveled around Nicaragua, Ferlinghetti caused a stir hopping from *mercado* to *mercado* and meeting the people. "There's so much poverty there," Felver remembers, "and it was clear that Lawrence wanted to spread some joy, which he was good at doing through his humor and smile."

The triumphant army of Sandinistas actually consisted of mostly poor and uneducated people; they took their name from Augusto Sandino, the illegitimate son of a wealthy landowner and a servant who became a Robin Hood–like national hero. The Sandinistas' triumphs felt to Ferlinghetti like a sign of hope, not only for their own country, but also that Latin America would end homegrown totalitarianism and throw off the yoke of American imperialism. He was happy with what was happening in Nicaragua, but he maintained a wary attitude and worried that the revolution's ideals would be betrayed. Lurking in the back of Ferlinghetti's mind was Fidel Castro, a revolutionary who had not lived up to the ideals of the revolution. Ferlinghetti was concerned.

"You notice it's a poor country," Felver says, "despite the fact that you could almost touch the energy in the air." Ferlinghetti believed that the euphoria of the moment could easily be wiped away by the reality of the Sandinistas having to run the government. If Cardenal asked his fellow poet for his thoughts, Ferlinghetti very likely advised caution.

One of the more poignant entries in the journal Ferlinghetti kept while in Nicaragua—published in *Writing Across the Landscape: Travel Journals 1950–2010*, edited by Giada Diano and Matthew Gleeson—centers on Cardenal. It is intimate and charming, and a good illustration of his empathy: "Ernesto Cardenal is there on the apron of the field, waiting to greet us, wearing a black beret and a white short sleeve blouse, and blue jeans. The plane door opens and we file down—handshakes and *abrazos*, Ernesto beaming, with that angelic smile of his, his head as always slightly cocked to one side. It is as if I've known him forever, though I've met him only twice . . ."

In another journal entry, Ferlinghetti jots down a kind tone poem, capturing a flash of his fast-paced schedule: "It's late afternoon by the time we get back to Granada, and dark by the time we head up the slope of the big volcano overlooking Managua, for the final stop. By the time we reach the edge of the huge crater it's pitch-dark, and all we can see, peering over into the black, is thick smoke, with a smell of burning sulfur. The huge mountain is like Mount Tamalpais in Marin County on a dark night, but here—someone shouts, laughing—is the smoldering 'maw of revolution!'"

IN 1986, TWO years after his trip to Central America, Ferlinghetti brought out his old friend Ernesto Cardenal's *From Nicaragua with Love* (translated and introduced by Jonathan Cohen) in the City Lights Pocket Poet Series. That same year, the series also released Pier Paolo Pasolini's *Roman Poems*.

Ferlinghetti's admiration for Pasolini was based on the range of the poet's tremendous output of work, which ran from pastoral and lyrical verse and rolling images of the Italian landscape to heated political poetry. He was also a celebrated filmmaker, and political figure whose views earned him worldwide respect from activists. As both an outspoken homosexual and a member of the Communist Party at a time when those two things didn't mix, Pasolini was eventually expelled from the Party. Ferlinghetti honored the Italian in his poem "Poetry as Insurgent Art," writing, "You are Whitman, you are Poe, you are Mark Twain, you are Emily Dickinson and Edna St. Vincent Millay, you are Neruda and Mayakovsky and Pasolini . . ."

Ferlinghetti translated *Roman Poems* with Francesca Valente. The noted Italian novelist Alberto Moravia provided an introduction. The project was dear to Lawrence's heart in many ways. It represented his idea of the best of the great poet's writing, it gave him a chance to translate the poetry from his ancestral language, and it enhanced the cosmopolitan tone of the publishing house.

Ferlinghetti thought Pasolini's poetry had a Whitmanesque view of Italy and its people. The words aimed for the heart of things with directness, like a kind of travelogue of the soul. Ferlinghetti and his co-translator enjoyed bringing Pasolini's open heart of language to American readers, beginning with a poem titled "The Holiday Over . . ."

The holiday over, in a Rome deaf
to all naive expectations,
the night falling like trash on the wind,
returning footsteps, voices,
whistles fading away,
farflung in the streets,
hollow in the hallways.

Ferlinghetti found Pasolini's earthiness enticing and labored to bring
an Italian tone into his translations. Nothing could be clearer than:

I work all day like a monk
And at night wander around like an alleycat
looking for love . . . I'll propose
to the Church that I be made a saint.
In fact I responded to my mystification
with mildness.

"The Search for a Home" was particularly charming to Ferlinghetti. At the time he translated it, he said the first line was such a
startlingly beautiful image that you couldn't help but read the rest of
the poem and bounce off Pasolini's words:

I'm just searching for the house where I'll be buried,
wandering around the city like an inmate
of a poorhouse or a rest home out on a pass,

with a face baked by fever,
dry white skin and beard,
Oh god, yes someone else is responsible

for the choice. But this dull
upsetting day of forbidden life
with a sunset blacker than dawn,

throws me into the street of an enemy city
to look for a house that I no longer want.

Ferlinghetti saw Pasolini as a heroic figure, a man who spoke out in support of Italy's poor and oppressed. As someone who did not shy away from controversy himself, and who never failed to turn his attention toward political outrage, he felt a great affinity with Pasolini. The Italian poet was also something of a tragic figure. Despite being expelled from the Communist Party, Pasolini remained true to the philosophy of Communism until his assassination on a Mediterranean beach in 1975—his body was burned after his killing, his testicles crushed.

IN 1988, FERLINGHETTI's novella *Love in the Days of Rage* appeared, billed by the publisher, Dutton, as "a work of lyricism and commitment, painting and politics, passion and intellect—a work to set beside the great expatriate novels of earlier generations." It was a literary territory Ferlinghetti was proud to claim: He loved so many books in the "American abroad" category, including Hemingway's posthumously published memoir of Paris, *A Movable Feast*. He also admired the lyrical power of André Breton's *Nadja*, which was not quite a novel but more of a surrealist poet's notebook written in lyrical prose to evoke the mysteries of the great French capital; it was that kind of evocation that caught Ferlinghetti's ear. His novella brought together a bit of Hemingway and bit of Breton.

Love in the Days of Rage casts the love affair of Annie, a young American painter, and Julian, a Portuguese banker, against the shadow of the raucous student protests in Paris in the late 1960s that shook the city's universities and spilled over into all aspects of society. It was a time Ferlinghetti had watched carefully, hoping it would bring positive and lasting change to French society by making it a more liberated environment. He felt that the student's ideology was one that avoided the clichés of revolution by being more spontaneous and directly from the heart. Ferlinghetti was well versed in

France's legacy of rebellion by the masses to force social change. The student protests would eventually involve ten million workers. A general strike brought much of the country to a standstill, and engendered some of the worst rioting since the 1930s.

Love in the Days of Rage begins on a whimsical note, immediately announcing itself to the reader as a poetic text, not a traditional novel: "The last time she saw Paris when the last sweet birds sang was from a fast train heading south in 1968 at the time of the student revolution, and it was almost the last train to get out, but that is getting ahead of the story, which began late one evening at La Coupole, in Montparnasse, when someone introduced her to Julian Mendes, and thereby hangs a tale of love in those days of rage." Mood and tone predominate the story of two lovers who play out their affair against the background of social protest and societal turmoil. The slim book, just a little more than one hundred and ten pages, gave the poet a chance to visit Paris without actually being there and to explore the animated streets and those place-names that were written onto his consciousness.

THE 1980S SAW Ferlinghetti embark on a new real-life romance, too.

The journalist, radio producer, and social-justice activist Maria Gilardin hosted a talk show for KPFA community radio in Berkeley, a station Ferlinghetti was both a dedicated listener to and a participant in. One evening he called her show and the pair spoke for some time. Gilardin remembers being quite taken by the exchange and wondering who the caller was. At the end of the conversation, Ferlinghetti told her his name. The call sparked a relationship.

Ferlinghetti and Gilardin bonded over their mutual belief in living simply and in communicating openly and with clarity. Both kept as far from the center of corruption as possible, dedicated themselves to speaking publicly against governmental abuses, and loved the land they lived on.

"Ferlinghetti was a famous man with no attitude, and for that I admired him so much," Gilardin says today. "He was editing a book by Ron Kovic [of *Born on the Fourth of July* fame] at the time we met, and I found his attitude just as wonderful as when we were on the phone. We had a one-year love affair and then one day Lawrence said to me, 'You're too much for me.'"

Through the years, Gilardin stayed in touch with Ferlinghetti by participating in a regular get-together at The Ramp, a Bayside restaurant. Erik Bauersfeld, whom Gilardin knew from KPFA, also attended; he was one of Ferlinghetti's closest friends. The radio dramatist was best known for voicing the squidlike alien Admiral Ackbar in *Star Wars: Return of the Jedi*, he and Ferlinghetti collaborated on various projects.

Many years after their affair ended, Ferlinghetti reached out to Gilardin, who had since relocated from Berkeley to Ukiah, several hours north of San Francisco. He said he missed her very much and wanted to get back together. Gilardin found the elder Ferlinghetti little changed from the man she had come to know decades earlier. He retained a kind of shy and modest nature, at the same time expressing his political views and social commentary directly and sometimes emphatically. Gilardin also loved his sense of humor. She was soon driving down from Ukiah and spending weekends in San Francisco.

As THE 1990s rolled in and Ferlinghetti entered his seventies, his creative energy appeared limitless.

In one of his countless campfire soliloquies at his cabin in Big Sur, Ferlinghetti offered quite a tribute to the Welsh bard Dylan Thomas, whose rise to international fame was quick and his recognition by the literary vanguard firmly in place by his mid-twenties. Thomas was heralded by T. S. Eliot, W. H. Auden, and many others for his innovative poems. Ferlinghetti loved the famous villanelle "Do not go gentle into that good night." The long poem "Fern Hill" also impressed him. He recited from memory, "Now as I was young and easy under the apple boughs about the lilting house and happy as the grass was green . . ."

"I really love the imagery here," he said as the campfire flickered. "This poem had quite an influence on me when I first read it. I was attracted to its bucolic atmosphere."

Ferlinghetti wished he'd known Thomas. In his collection *These Are My Rivers: New and Selected Poems, 1955–1993*, Ferlinghetti included "Belated Palinode for Dylan Thomas." The poem opens with him standing next to Thomas's writing shed in the Welsh town of Laugharne: "where the hawk hangs still / above the cockle-strewn shingle . . ." This is Ferlinghetti at his descriptive best, and the words are as concise as those of the poet he is celebrating. Thomas died young, at only thirty-nine, taking ill and never recovering after a drinking binge at the White Horse Tavern, in New York City. Ferlinghetti would prove to have more staying power.

As City Lights Bookseller began to adjust to publishing in the digital age of the 1990s, the bookstore continued to thrive on not only local buyers but also a great influx of people from around the world who wanted to visit the landmark. It had become a destination. When Paul Yamazaki took over the job of book-buyer years earlier, he pledged he would help run the shop in the spirit of Ferlinghetti and his original partner, Shig Murao—even after he was long gone, Murao's bohemian *esprit* remained central to the shop's atmosphere. Yamazaki remembers talking with Ferlinghetti several times about whether the shop should carry hardback books, Ferlinghetti arguing that it had always been intentionally limited to more inexpensive paperback editions. Over time, a few hardbacks began to appear here and there on the shelves. When Ferlinghetti saw that the change didn't hurt the character of the store, he was satisfied.

In April 1994, an event called Viva Ferlinghetti! was held directly in front of City Lights. It included Juvenal Acosta, Jack and Adele Foley, Alan Kaufman, Michael McClure, Anne Waldman, Philip Whelan, and a number of city officials. Ferlinghetti read a poem with the subtitle "One fine day in North Beach." The occasion was to mark the renaming of Price Row, a street in San Francisco's North Beach, to Via Ferlinghetti. Years earlier, in 1988, Ferlinghetti had suggested to the San Francisco Board of Supervisors that Adler Alley behind City Lights be changed to Jack Kerouac Alley and that it be made into a pedestrian walkway. The move had proved popular in the city and underscored the idea of a City of Poets.

In a statement delivered by Ferlinghetti at his street-naming ceremony, he offered a heartfelt picture of his relationship to San Francisco: "I've spent most of the past forty years walking up and down the streets of little old wooden North Beach, the map of North Beach stamped upon my brainpan. I know the streets and alleys like the palm of my hand... And it's truly unbelievable that a tiny line in that palm should be named for me."

Michael McClure spoke with reverence about his old friend: "I saw Lawrence grow to be the most popular living poet in the English language. Over the decades that have followed, we have seen Lawrence become one of the few living Master Poets in any language. It is an awesome and myriadly inspiring accomplishment that has taken place—both in this city and in the spirit of Lawrence Ferlinghetti."

On a lighter note, but equally as telling of the esteem with which Ferlinghetti is held by his fellow poets, Philip Whalen spoke these words: "Lawrence is probably the only Sorbonne graduate who knows how to split stove wood with a double-bitted ax. He was working outside his little cabin in Bixby Canyon. His weekend guests looked on while drinking their morning coffee. His first book of poems was another wonderful surprise."

After the event, Alan Kaufman released *Viva Ferlinghetti!: Tributes and Poems*, a small chapbook with remarks, poems, and photos of the celebration.

In 1998, Ferlinghetti became San Francisco's first poet laureate. He was honored by the position, which was organized by the San Francisco Public Library, and remarked, "The center of literate culture in cities has always centered in the great libraries."

FERLINGHETTI HAD ALWAYS been proud of his drawings and paintings and had as much ambition as a visual artist as he did as a writer. When John Martin, the founder of Black Sparrow Press, and his wife, Barbara—the artistic force behind the press's iconic cover designs—visited City Lights in the late 1960s, there was a large black-and-white charcoal Ferlinghetti drawing of a nude thumbtacked up on the wall. Barbara said how much she admired it. "When she told him this," Martin recalled decades later, "he immediately took it down and gave it to her."

Martin, who is revered for his publishing prowess, admired City Lights Books. "I told Ferlinghetti that I considered his Pocket Poet series one of the most remarkable publishing successes of the postwar era. He seemed pleased."

Publishing aside, however, in the 1990s, Ferlinghetti's quest to be as famous for his art as he was for his poetry bloomed unabated. His art studio at the old Hunters Point Naval Shipyard in the southeast corner of San Francisco was liberated territory in his mind, and he could work there uninterrupted, pursuing his broad artistic vision. Ferlinghetti was much like Henry Miller and Kenneth Patchen in his equal love for literary art and visual art. He admired Miller's essay "To Paint Is to Love Again" and Patchen's haunting surreal drawings. Ferlinghetti put in more hours at his studio than he ever had in the past and held many exhibitions of paintings and drawings. But his studio was not merely a workplace—like his cabin at Big Sur, it also served as a refuge from his busy life. When the occasional visitors did show up at the studio, they would be shown sketches, drawings, paintings, and other types of art by an excitable older man whose creative force never seemed to wane.

Considering the first poem in *A Coney Island of the Mind*—which famously begins "In Goya's greatest scenes we seem to see / the people of the world / exactly at the moment when / they first attained the title of / 'suffering humanity'"—it is not surprising that Ferlinghetti often mentioned Goya as a primary influence on his painting. The Spanish master's series about the horrors of war haunted Ferlinghetti and appealed to his habit of combining in his writing lyricism and social protest. He wanted a literary sense to his visual work, too, and even added slogans in some of the paintings, though he focused on direct social commentary, like his series on the Statue of Liberty, in which he drives home the point that liberty has been betrayed.

Raymond Foye has pointed out that Ferlinghetti's art is probably best seen in the context of being a writer who paints—like Miller, who spent a lifetime painting watercolors in between writing his books, and Patchen, who made colorful drawings that have since gained recognition. Ferlinghetti told Foye, "I'm a better draftsman than David Hockney or Jasper Johns!" This was during a time when he was asking Foye, then an art dealer in addition to being a young editor, to represent him in the New York galleries.

Although Ferlinghetti had many exhibitions in San Francisco, a few in New York, and some elsewhere, he never gained the level of critical acclaim for his art as he'd achieved with his poetry. Yet he remained passionately interested in all forms of the visual arts, even pursuing lithography when he was well into his seventies. His interest in the medium began in 1992 when he was invited to be part of an authors series sponsored by the Center for Literary Arts at San José State University. The program brought well-known writers to the city and sponsored lectures and readings followed by receptions at which they handed out the authors' latest book. When Ferlinghetti appeared, they also produced a bookplate for the occasion. Patrick Surgalski, a lithographer in the school's art apartment, was invited by Alan Soldofsky, of the creative writing department, to create the artwork for the bookplate. Surgalski and Ferlinghetti took to one another at the event and quickly became friends.

Soon, Surgalski and Ferlinghetti were collaborating on a broadside: the poem "Upon Reflection" accompanied by a color lithograph. When Ferlinghetti expressed curiosity about the lithographic process, his newfound friend suggested that he come to his class at the university and learn how to make one. Surgalski often brought outsiders to work in the print studio with the assistance of some of his more advanced students. Ferlinghetti took to lithography enthusiastically and produced a print of Sigmund Freud, whom he had long admired. He made two images of Freud, one of which was realistic and the other of which was meant to be suggestive of something entirely different. When Ferlinghetti first wrote Freud's name onto the massive limestone, he didn't reverse the letters. The poet didn't realize that the print produced would be a mirror of what's on the stone, so "Freud" would be backwards. Surgalski stepped in and helped get it right.

Ferlinghetti enjoyed the process so much that he and Surgalski decided to work on a portfolio of lithographs together. Because Surgalski had spent time in Paris and Ferlinghetti remained enamored of the French capital, they decided to create a series based on the City of Light, which they called "Paris Transformations." With his classic generosity, Ferlinghetti offered Surgalski use of the Bixby Canyon cabin. The artist accepted immediately. Even without electricity and other modern comforts, Surgalski found the rugged getaway was—just as it had always been for Ferlinghetti—an inspiring place to work.

BY THE END of the 1990s, Ferlinghetti and Nancy Peters saw that outside the windows of City Lights, San Francisco was rapidly changing around them: rents were soaring astronomically throughout the city. The pair knew they had to act quickly and boldly.

For decades, City Lights had paid its monthly rent to a middleman and never knew exactly who actually owned the building it occupied. After a fair amount of sleuthing and many phone calls, Ferlinghetti and Peters tracked down the owner of 261 Columbus Avenue, made an offer, and purchased the distinct, wedge-shaped building. For two people who were very wary of business to pull off the purchase was not only a kind of miracle, but also a prescient move that surely saved the bookstore and publishing house—by securing the building, City Lights was no longer at the mercy of a landlord who might dramatically raise its rent. The purchase also enabled the bookshop to expand.

As City Lights grew and its future felt on firmer ground, Ferlinghetti and Peters strove to ensure that the store was a workplace that treated all the people who worked there as equals. They remained committed to creating a place for critical thinking and creative endeavor. How many businesses in the country hung banners advocating civil liberties and human rights? Or that blasted the government when it took violent action around the world? This dedication drew smart, talented employees to the store. Elaine Katzenberger, who would eventually play a crucial role in the history of City Lights, was one such employee. Katzenberger had been working at the Vesuvio Café, across Adler Alley (later Kerouac Alley), when she decided to take a steep decrease in salary to leave her lucrative bartending job and become a bookseller. Richard Berman, the bookstore's manager at the time—and quite a Blake scholar—would sit at the bar with other City Lights employees before the store opened. He knew Katzenberger was one of them and eventually invited her to come work at City Lights. For the first time in her life, she felt at home—from her bosses to her coworkers, there was a feeling of solidarity based on shared political and social values and mutual respect. Yamazaki said later, "We are a place where people can teach themselves. City Lights has been my university. I've had no other." It was to Ferlinghetti's credit, Yamazaki insists, that "the vessel ran so well."

IN 2001, CITY Lights became a registered landmark. It marked the first time the recognition had been granted to both a cultural institution and a building. It was yet another bulwark against San Francisco's skyrocketing development and costs: Little more than a decade later, Ferlinghetti would talk of tech people pouring into the city "with bags full of money and no manners." Despite entering his eighth and ninth decades in the 2000s, Lawrence Ferlinghetti was still his iconoclastic self and still passionate about North Beach as a creative enclave.

As far back as the late 1990s, Ferlinghetti had the idea for a Poets Plaza in North Beach. He explained that his inspiration was based on the plazas to be found in just about every city or town in Italy. They provided a sense of community and a pride in the environment. He talked up his Poets Plaza vision from time to time, even deciding that it belonged on a block of Vallejo Street with the National Shrine of Saint Francis of Assisi on one side and the Caffè Trieste on the other. It was an ideal location, as it had long been a gathering place for bohemian writers and Beat poets—there was a time when Gregory Corso and Bob Kaufman could often be found holding court either on the steps of the church or on the sidewalk in front of the café. The plaza idea was not surprising coming from an activist poet who had long cherished the idea of San Francisco as the City of Poets.

In 2002, Ferlinghetti helped form a committee of interested North Beach neighbors to explore the idea. He teamed up with nationally known architect Dennis Sullivan, who lived in North Beach. Plans were drawn up for the plaza, which would be called Piazza St. Francis, Poets Plaza. Ferlinghetti wanted to have the words of poets such as Emily Dickinson, Keats, Shakespeare, Edna St. Vincent Millay, and Walt Whitman embedded in concrete around the plaza.

As with all such urban projects, there were those for it and those against it. During this period, one could often find Ferlinghetti in the Caffè Trieste talking up the idea with the locals. One of the complaints from some was that the plaza would attract too many tourists to the neighborhood. Buses carrying sightseers already stopped in front of City Lights Booksellers to explain the Beats. Some of the neighborhood critics were concerned about the traffic inconvenience a plaza would cause: As Ferlinghetti believed that North Beach was overrun with vehicles—describing the situation as "carmaggeddon"—he wanted the plaza to be automobile-free. The idea of closing a section of busy Vallejo Street was controversial, though, even among some of Ferlinghetti's friends.

In the end, those for and against the plaza weren't able to compromise. The plan stalled, then sputtered out altogether.

As THE NEW century began, Ferlinghetti wasn't just willing to embroil himself in community efforts he believed in; he was also an artist still very much in command of his creative powers. In 2002, at age eighty-three, he published *How to Paint Sunlight: Lyric Poems & Others (1997–2000)*. It was handsomely produced by New Directions with a cover illustration by Ferlinghetti himself, who wrote in the collection's introduction, "All I ever wanted to do was to paint light on the walls of life."

The book begins with a poem called "Instructions to Painters & Poets." The poet who'd long had the habit of gently lecturing other poets now had some thoughts for visual artists, too. The poem begins, "I asked a hundred painters and a hundred poets / how to paint sunlight / on the face of life." He then goes on to tell them exactly how it's done in a playful and lyrical manner. He says that you should have your "brush loaded with light."

The poem "Mouth" is not so painterly but displays classic Ferlinghetti humor and is reminiscent of the oral poems he wrote in the 1950s. It begins, "I'm tired of my mouth / It's too small / and it doesn't say enough / doesn't sing enough." Later, "This mouth of mine / always opening and closing / at the wrong time." And, finally, "It just keeps saying / the dumbest things."

IN 2007, AFTER thirty-two years at City Lights—twenty-three of them as executive director—Nancy Peters, Ferlinghetti's trusted collaborator, stepped down. "She held this place together in a way that I couldn't have done," Ferlinghetti said in an interview with the *Los Angeles Times*. "I was flying around the world being a poet with my head up in the . . . oh, I don't know where." Three years after her retirement, Peters was given the Northern California Book Association's Fred Cody Award for Lifetime Achievement.

Elaine Katzenberger, the onetime bartender who became a bookseller because of City Lights, was named publisher and executive director of City Lights Booksellers & Publishers. Over the years, she'd worked her way from bookseller to book buyer to overseeing the shop's finances. Then she moved over to the publishing wing, working closely with Peters as an editor, the marketing director, and vice president and associate director before finally succeeding her mentor.

AT NINETY-SIX, FERLINGHETTI wrote "At Sea" and dedicated it to Pablo Neruda. He offered the poem to Jack Hirschman for his anti-capitalism anthology series, a publication he had appeared in before. Hirschman says, "I thought it was the best poem Lawrence had written. I felt he had finally let Pablo Neruda take him. He wrote a communist poem, not a populist poem. I told him that, and he took it as a compliment but said nothing more than 'Thanks.'"

"At Sea" is a feat of concentration and inspiration that Ferlinghetti sat down in his mid-nineties and wrote a long poem that gathers together so much of the energy he'd put into his work for the past six decades—all those notebooks filled with Paris, San Francisco, New York, Rome, Tuscany, Lombardi, Baja California, Big Sur, "the Boondock heartland of America," and the sea. After so many seasons of his life had rolled by—sometimes quickly and sometimes slowly—Ferlinghetti was still asking questions like *Who are we now?* and *Where are we going?* In "At Sea," he lets his innate lyric gift take full rein and, like Neruda, he takes a wide and wise voyage into the many meanings the sea brings to human consciousness.

Ferlinghetti begins "At Sea" much as he has done with his other poems: directly. So we start with a fine opening: "The sea through the trees / distant / shining / The dark foreground / a stone wall / with lichen . . ." The tone is set. The older poet knows Neruda's fascination with the ocean, its sounds, its odors, and the great myths it embodies; just as Neruda looked at the ocean waves from his home at Isla Negra, in Chile, Ferlinghetti loved and ritualized his walks through Bixby Canyon to the sea. His long poem speaks to the ocean's rhythms: "Far out on the slumbering sea" where "a trawler creeps along / The wind from the south / blows the bait in the fish's mouth . . ." This is not the polemical Ferlinghetti—in "At Sea," he's brought all his lyrical skill to full fruition, and the poem sails along with rich visual lyricism.

FERLINGHETTI'S ENERGY CONTINUED unabated: At the age of ninety-six, he was determined to return one last time to his beloved Paris. When it became obvious that nothing would stop him, long-time City Lights editor Robert Sharrard arranged the trip. Kaye Mc-Donough, an old friend and City Lights author, accompanied him.

"We were there from July 16 to July 30, 2015," McDonough recalls. "His daughter, Julie, was joining him, so we stayed at the same hotel recommended by Sylvia Beach Whitman, proprietor of Shake-speare and Company. Lawrence wanted to show Julie 'his Paris' from when he studied at the Sorbonne on the G.I. Bill, and courted Julie and Lorenzo's mother, Kirby."

McDonough remembers that despite his age and the frailty that came with it, Ferlinghetti was in high spirits about the trip. "I arrived one day ahead of Lawrence so that I could meet his Air France flight at 11:35 a.m. on July 16. He emailed, 'I am getting a wheelchair for free at both ends. I'll meet you wheeling around' and referred to the airport with affection as 'The Charlie de Gaulle.' We arranged to meet at Ground Transportation. I told him I'd have a sign and would stand with all the others waiting. When he made a joke about *Waiting for Godot*, I told him I'd put GODOT on my sign. At that he chuckled and sounded quite happy. He went on to say he couldn't read at all anymore and couldn't walk. I told him it didn't matter. I'd be the old lady holding the GODOT sign and he'd be the old guy in the wheelchair, so we'd be sure to know each other—and he laughed again at that. In the taxi coming into the city, Lawrence said he would actually be Pozzo, not Godot. Pozzo ends up blind with memory loss—more of Lawrence's surprising sense of humor."

Sylvia Whitman was a mainstay of Ferlinghetti's visit, providing him with daily lunches and dinners, as well as companionship at meals and book-signings. McDonough says the old poet was grateful to Whitman. Her father, George Whitman, opened Shakespeare and

Company in 1951 in part at Ferlinghetti's urging. Whitman was not a writer himself, but he valued poets. He was a mainstay of Paris's expatriate scene until his passing, in 2011. His daughter grew up in the bookshop and succeeded her father with aplomb.

Ferlinghetti wanted to show Julie the places that were important to him, like the Luxembourg Gardens, the Sorbonne, where he did his "defense," and a restaurant he and her mother had frequented. Sitting outside Shakespeare and Company in his black beret, a twinkle in his bright eyes, he told anecdotes about his "best friend" George Whitman and enjoyed taking in the Left Bank atmosphere. "His conversations were filled with stories and reminiscences about life in France during the Resistance and his life as a student in Paris" says McDonough. "He'd tease me from time to time by calling me Zelda, because I had a book from City Lights in 1978 called *Zelda: Frontier Life in America* and he told me later when *Little Boy* came out that he'd included me in the final pages as a character named Nadja."

Ferlinghetti's lifelong love affair with Paris hadn't diminished with age, and in fact had grown more intense. It was a nostalgia very much like the one associated with Ernest Hemingway, Henry Miller, and other writers for whom Paris had been important in their youth. The city had served as a playland for them—none had much money, but they didn't have to scramble, as it had not yet become an expensive world capital. Hemingway had various sources of money despite his complaints in *A Movable Feast*, Miller said he was always able to rely on friends, and Ferlinghetti, of course, had the G.I. Bill.

In his poetry, Ferlinghetti played with the idea of Paris as a place of love and sunlight slowly emerging on the boulevards and in the parks. It was reverie and nostalgic sensibility merging. The French capital as evoked by native-born writers such as Louis Aragon, André Breton, Jacques Prévert, and John-Paul Sartre fits into Ferlinghetti's appreciation. So many had painted word canvases celebrating the beauty of the old buildings, the Seine winding through the city, the Luxembourg Gardens, and the façade of medieval cathedrals.

Was Ferlinghetti's French escapade a matter of taking stock and closing down? It seems that while it was a chance to visit the past as he once knew it, his trip to Paris was also a new adventure to gather valuable experience.

IN 2019, FERLINGHETTI published his third novella, *Little Boy*. For a slim book, it made quite a splash, as it was written by a man about to turn a hundred; Ferlinghetti's longtime literary agent Sterling Lord was roughly the same age, only adding to the excitement. *Library Journal* summed up the book concisely: "It's called fiction, but this interweaving of autobiography and history, lightning-flash language and wisdom of the ages by Ferlinghetti . . . is beyond easy definition." The novella is unconventional. But one would not expect a "normal" effort from the poet, publisher, bookseller, and activist known for eschewing the mainstream and embracing the literature of dissent throughout his life. As with much of his other writing, Ferlinghetti borrows from others to embroider his song. Here he tips his hat to Carson McCullers: " . . . so one day it's the song of the sad café all around me with everyone on their portable universes their handheld computers and nobody talking to anyone else . . ." NPR raved about the book: "He's still got it: Ferlinghetti's wits are afire, his wisdom is wide and deep, and this little book is packed with incredible sentences."

The stream of consciousness and the minimal punctuation in *Little Boy* are restlessness. The style might suggest Ferlinghetti's preoccupation with the nearness of death. Perhaps the *New York Times* was more prescient than it realized when a reviewer called the book ". . . a summing-up near the end of a big, wide, productive life." Many reviewers noted the book's autobiographical nature. In fact, Ferlinghetti paraphrases one of his own early poems in the book, a scene in which he refers to his mom and pop and his brother in the other room hearing his first cries. When Ferlinghetti was urged to write a proper memoir years earlier, he said no one would believe it, but here he tells some of the stories that he thought others might find unbelievable, including how he ended up in the arms of his aunt Emily, was taken to France, and then brought back to America to be left with a family in Bronxville, New York, with whom he lived until he went off to college. *Little Boy* takes readers on a ride over the far horizons of the real world into a semi-surreal and dreamlike story.

Mauro Aprile Zanetti, an Italian-born San Franciscan, worked as Ferlinghetti's assistant and personal secretary for many years toward the end of the poet's life. Zanetti helped see *Little Boy* through to its completion, and he remembers how fascinated Ferlinghetti was to be able to tie everything up around the image of a little boy. "It just made everything clear and gave him the energy he needed to complete the task," Zanetti said. He recognized the influence of Breton's *Nadja* on *Little Boy*, which was true for all of Ferlinghetti's fiction.

For a man who often kept introspection at a distance, Ferlinghetti could write "No end no end to the withering of fur and fruit and flesh so passing fair and the neon mermaids singing each to each somewhere . . ." His late prose drifts on rivers of the mind, yet manages to remain anchored in the image of the little boy wandering through life.

And wander he did. But he always wandered home, and home was San Francisco.

A few days after the 1994 ribbon-cutting ceremony for the newly named Via Ferlinghetti, a group of younger poets stopped by the newly renamed alley with Ferlinghetti and read poems aloud to one another and to passersby. Ferlinghetti mused humorously, "What if somebody takes the street sign down? I hope they have a spare one somewhere in city hall . . . otherwise I'd be very disappointed."

After the impromptu reading, Ferlinghetti wandered off in the direction of his home, a few blocks from the Bay, on the outer edge of North Beach. He still cut a fine figure with his bright twinkling eyes, full white beard, and well-worn black Greek sailor's cap atop his head. As he strolled slowly home that night, he must have reflected on his great good luck and his happy life. He must have thought back to his first day in San Francisco, the day he realized he had struck territorial gold.

When he turned one hundred, celebrations took place across the city. On March 24, 2019, throngs gathered at City Lights, filling the store and sidewalks around it. Michael McClure read. Jack Hirschman gave away copies of Ferlinghetti's poem "At Sea." Francis Ford Coppola's Café Zoetrope hosted poetry readings. There was a Ferlinghetti film festival. An a cappella male choir sang. Artists set up easels and painted. All day, one after another, people spoke about what made Ferlinghetti such a singular and influential literary personage. The mayor proclaimed it Lawrence Ferlinghetti Day. It was an event of singular importance in the City of San Francisco and it radiated worldwide, testimony to Ferlinghetti's international reputation.

His eyesight failing and his mobility limited, the birthday boy was unable to attend his centennial celebration.

On February 22, 2021, less than a month shy of his 102nd birthday, Lawrence Ferlinghetti died in his apartment on Francisco Street—a beautiful flat with many windows, it fit the poet well; it was modest and sparsely furnished.

WHITMAN'S WILD CHILD

An Afterword

HIS GENTLE NATURE is missed.

When I first moved to North Beach, Lawrence lived in a small apartment—you'd have to say it was a pocket-sized abode. He was an orderly man who could travel the world with little more than a single satchel, no matter how far or how long he was going. "All you need is one change of pants," he often said; somehow, his Levi's were never wrinkled and his beard was forever well trimmed.

I stayed one night at that small apartment in 1978. It was a memorable evening because it was the twenty-fifth anniversary of City Lights Booksellers. It was also a memorable evening because I arrived at Lawrence's door having a full-blown LSD panic attack.

"Oh, come on in," Lawrence said calmly, seemingly unsurprised to find his disheveled biographer in the throes of a bad trip.

In the kitchen were several of Lawrence's friends, as well as his girlfriend at the time, Paula Lillevand. As Lawrence ushered me through, I recognized Jack Stauffacher, the legendary typographer and master printer of Greenwood Press, and his wife, Josephine. I smiled and nodded hello. The glow of the bookshop's quarter-century anniversary hung in the air. Lawrence's son, Lorenzo, was staying in Bolinas that night, and Lawrence steered me to the boy's bedroom so I could ride out my panic attack in a cozy twin-sized bed.

Even back in those days, the little North Beach bookstore that opened to sell low-priced paperbacks to the masses was already famous worldwide. There was hardly a novelist or poet who didn't make a pilgrimage to City Lights Booksellers when in San Francisco. Back in those days, poets would go straight to the basement, where the poetry books could be found. If they were lucky, they would find Ferlinghetti, tidying the shelves or just looking after things in general.

He was also particularly good at looking after his friends.

LAWRENCE ONCE TOLD me that things just fell into place after he left the East Coast, in 1951, and went west. He said he felt instinctively drawn to San Francisco. From the moment he walked off the ferry at the Embarcadero and began to wander the city, he thought of it as another America, not quite the one most people were condemned to, but a place where even a poet might fulfill his dream of living a life in public.

Soon after he arrived, he met Kenneth Patchen, the ultimate outsider poet, but he also met Kenneth Rexroth, an elder poet who argued for the importance of the arts in American culture and who became about as genuine a father figure as anyone could be. Whereas a writer like Henry Miller could never get truly comfortable living in America after being an expatriate, Lawrence threw himself into his adopted city. And he dove directly into controversy.

In a 1953 *Art Digest* article—still writing under the name Lawrence Ferling—he penned a stirring defense of the WPA-era murals at San Francisco's Rincon Annex Post Office. The twenty-seven murals, by the Russian immigrant Anton Refregier, depicted a history of California brimming with social realism that upset the more conservative elements in the city. Members of the American Legion and of the VFW said the murals were communist propaganda and called for them to be torn down. Lawrence let them have it right between the eyes. The fight to remove the murals sputtered out.

Lawrence's fiercely progressive ideals coupled with his calm, undramatic demeanor made for was a powerful combination. If it weren't for Lawrence Ferlinghetti, I'm not sure there'd be a Beat Generation—I mean the Beats in the big way as we know them today, a cultural phenomenon. During the *Howl* trial, in the mid-1950s, Lawrence stood above the storm and articulated the need for freedom of speech and expression and the importance of the arts.

In the process, he became an international symbol for the free flow of ideas.

But Lawrence was just a man, too.

When I first met him, in the mid-1970s, his biggest concerns weren't literary or cultural; they were domestic: He was having a lot of trouble with his wife. We would go out to dinner in one of the Italian joints he loved and he'd complain nonstop about his home life. I'd respond by essentially ignoring his problems and offering my own litany of complaints about love and my search for it. Bless him, Lawrence would go quiet. He'd sip his wine, eat his pasta, and listen. I have so much admiration for Lawrence's ability to sit back and listen to other people.

Lawrence was often funny, too, even if his humor sometimes got a little biting. He could laugh at himself. He once minimized his accomplishments: "In some ways what I really did was mind the store. When I arrived in San Francisco, in 1951, I was wearing a beret. If anything, I was the last of the bohemians rather than the first of the Beats."

He had a playful attitude toward his fame. I remember one afternoon we were standing on the sidewalk in front of City Lights when a woman came up to Lawrence waving her arms, flushed and excitable.

"Oh, Mr. Ferlinghetti!" she said. "Will you sign a book for me?"

"Sorry," he replied, "but I'm not Lawrence Ferlinghetti—I'm his twin brother. Lawrence is up the street." He pointed up Columbus Avenue. "If you move fast, you can catch him."

The woman frowned, looking hard up the sidewalk full of people. When she began to scurry off, Lawrence chuckled. He called her back and signed her book, still chuckling to himself.

Lawrence had a droll sense of timing. Thirty years after he published a rather long poem of mine called "To the Ferry" in the *City Lights Journal* No. 4, he asked me—out of the blue—"Neeli, what did that poem mean?" After I carefully and thoroughly explained my interpretation of the poem to him, he was silent for moment. Then he said, "Oh, if I had known *that*, I never would've published it."

One of the things that attracted Lawrence to Bob Kaufman's poetry was his sharp sense of humor. After Kaufman passed away, in 1986, a few of us chartered a boat for the purpose of scattering his ashes in San Francisco Bay.

As the boat was putting back to shore, Lawrence stood at the railing and said, "Someday I'll retire and live out on the bay in a little boat!"

"Sorry, Lawrence," I responded, "but poets don't retire."

He laughed.

"And they don't get older," I added. "They *grow ancient*."

He laughed harder.

When I noted that an edition of Lawrence's collected poems would run well over a thousand pages, he replied, "Is it worth cutting trees for!?"

But Lawrence could also be stubborn. He could be argumentative. He could be cheap; he was anti-capitalism, after all. He could brag a bit too much about his abilities as a painter. As I say, he was just a man, imperfect like the rest of us, but his imperfections served to underscore the depth of humanity that people recognized in him.

At the height of his fame, he traveled the world and met famous writers and younger writers, foreign dignitaries and appreciative audiences. They all loved him and his gentle nature. He found it easy to mix with a crowd and put people at ease, as if to say, "I'm not such a big deal. Now, you tell me your story."

Lawrence was adept at sharing the spotlight. He shared the literary spotlight, first with Allen Ginsberg (he campaigned for Allen to receive the Nobel Prize in Literature) and then with every one of the astounding number of authors he published. At City Lights, he surrounded himself with people who served the good name of literature—people such as Shigeyoshi Murao and Nancy Peters, Paul Yamazaki and Elaine Katzenberger—and he shared the spotlight with them. Perhaps one of Lawrence's greatest traits was that he never consciously placed himself above others; he strove for humility.

WHAT MUST A poet do? Write poetry is a good starting point. You can be a poet while president of an insurance company, while practicing medicine in a small city in New Jersey, while running a country or running away from one. Lawrence wrote poetry while being a publisher, bookseller, and activist. Writing poetry is easy if you're possessed by a necessity for it. Lawrence once told an interviewer, "I never wanted to be a poet; it chose me. I didn't choose it; one becomes a poet almost against one's will, certainly against one's better judgment."

What is the rule for poets? If you asked that of Lawrence, he would most likely have told you: *Poets break rules*. And if you wanted to know how a poet sounds, he might have told you to just listen for a moment to waves breaking on the shore or to rain hitting against the windowpane.

All of this, for starters.

Reading Lawrence's poetry in the period since his passing brings a renewed opportunity to view him and his work with a historical perspective. I've found that the long shadow of Walt Whitman continues to imbue his words with greater strength. Like Whitman, Lawrence felt alienated from the American land. He often disagreed with America's actions around the world. He opposed tyrannical governments. He spoke against imperialism. He was an enemy of unbridled capitalism. That said, he continually balanced his anger and sense of righteousness with a profoundly lyrical sensibility. It's why he'd pick up *Leaves of Grass* and actually touch the leaves and walk through the grass and stand by the ocean just as Whitman did in his masterful poem "Out of the Cradle Endlessly Rocking." When Lawrence called for "Whitman's wild children" to come around at last in his "Populist Manifesto," he was reaffirming hope for a miracle in the country, some force for democratic values to bring all people together under one tent. Lawrence credited me for the phrase "Whitman's wild children," but he certainly put it to good use.

As famous as Whitman became, he remained an outsider, and that was important to Lawrence's understanding of where poetry stood in this society and indeed worldwide: Poetry is forever outside of the city gates, even if the city supports it. Poetry is as close as we'll ever get to a sacred dimension; a poet looks within and shares what he witnesses.

Lawrence Ferlinghetti's poetic legacy rests at the place where skilled lyricism and being the bard of what Jack Kerouac called "unspeakable visions" meet. Because Lawrence witnessed vast devastation with his own eyes and found a way to share it, and because he stood boldly against oppression wherever he found it, he became an example of a new way forward. Every young poet should know that the poems in *A Coney Island of the Mind* are both amazingly accessible and serious—there are miracles plucked out of the language and teased from the corners of ordinary consciousness.

To know Lawrence Ferlinghetti was to know a figure celebrated across boundaries—fitting, as he'd always promoted a borderless world. He was a radical thinker, a lyric poet, a painter of light, and an advocate for human decency. The honors that came to him were well deserved. You could honor him as a poet or as a publisher or as a bookseller or as an advocate for human rights and civil liberties—or simply for his whole being. How many times was Lawrence honored during his lifetime? You'd be surprised. They were all richly deserved, though you'd have a hard time convincing him of that.

A few years ago, I was at a literary conference in New Orleans when the poet Agneta Falk—wife of the poet Jack Hirschman—tracked me down and told me Lawrence wanted to speak to me. I was worried, so I found a phone and called him.

"Lawrence," I said when he picked up, "what is it?"

"Oh," he said, "I just wanted to tell you, Neeli . . . you don't know how much you've influenced a lot of people."

His generosity caught me off guard. Flustered, I teased him, "I think you might be talking about yourself, Lawrence."

Silence.

"I love you, Lawrence," I said.

Silence.

"I love you, too, Neeli," he said.

LATE IN LIFE, Lawrence confided in a mutual friend about this biography. "Neeli was too easy on me," he said. "He should have been more critical."

Perhaps he was stung by the review of the book in the *New York Times* in 1979. The reviewer's chief complaint was that I'd been uncritical of my subject and had instead shown him too much "adulation" and "blind loyalty." Maybe this embarrassed Lawrence.

More likely, I think he wanted—at least later in his life—to have his work subjected to the poking, needling approach of literary criticism because he wanted to feel secure in the knowledge that his work could withstand such probing.

But that was never my intent. I wasn't an academic who set out to study a living poet like a lab rat and report back my findings in clinical language. I was a poet who set out to celebrate another poet. In that, I hope I succeeded.

ON THE EVENING of Lawrence Ferlinghetti's one hundredth birthday, we spoke on the phone. He hadn't been able to attend the daylong celebration at City Lights, but he'd heard all about the happenings and told me how grateful he was to the people who had come to speak or just to listen. In the end, the little bohemian bookstore he wanted to remain just so—no matter what happened in the world—brought the world to him. It brought not only poets and writers and artists but people from everywhere and from all manner of professions and ways of life as well. Lawrence was grateful to all of them—his heart was forever open.

"I wish I could've been there," he told me.

Silence.

After a long moment, Lawrence asked, "Do you think people miss me?"

SOURCES

I

The majority of material in the text is the result of more than sixty hours of taped conversations and nontaped conversations with Lawrence Ferlinghetti. The initial interview was recorded on November 18, 1975, in North Beach, and the final interview took place in February 1978. Chapters 1 through 3 are especially indebted to the personal interviews. I also had complete access to Mr. Ferlinghetti's notebooks, none of which is filed, but which he has kept over the years since beginning them in the late thirties.

I did not feel it necessary to put footnotes in the text, but I include here a list of general sources for each chapter, and at the end of this list other sources that helped me in completing the biography.

CHAPTER ONE

"True Confessional," which begins *Open Eye, Open Heart*, accurately describes the situation surrounding Ferlinghetti's first years. Correspondence with his brother Harry Ferling, of Baltimore, Maryland, helped me in reconstructing the circumstances of Ferlinghetti's birth and how he became separated from his family.

Information on the Mendes-Monsanto family was supplied through the library of Hebrew Union College–Jewish Institute of Religion in Cincinnati and Los Angeles, as well as through conversations with Ferlinghetti's great-aunt Jean McGrath, of Bolinas, California. Also, I talked to the late Louis Mendes-Monsanto, of San Bernardino, California, a close relation of the family, and had access to historical documents from the Virgin Islands that helped authenticate some of my information.

In May 1977, I visited Bronxville, New York, and walked through the grounds of Plashbourne, the home of Presley and Anna Lawrence Bisland. There I met Mrs. Grayson Kirk (wife of the former president of Columbia University, current owner of the house), who showed me through the rooms. The small creek Ferlinghetti had described to me was much as it had been years before, and the town of Bronxville had changed little in the past forty-five years. Many people I met remembered the Bislands well, and a few older residents recalled a little boy whom they had taken into their household in the twenties.

Anne Scarborough, the Bislands' granddaughter, now living in San Diego, California, supplied me with a wealth of information about the family, and was an invaluable aide to Ferlinghetti's later years, in his student days at Columbia, and during the death of Mr. Bisland.

"Autobiography," beginning on page 60 of *A Coney Island of the Mind*, recalls Ferlinghetti's Bronxville days, as do several sections of his novel *Her*, some of which I've quoted here. The quotes from his notebooks are indicative of the wealth of invaluable biographical material contained in them. Direct quotes from Ferlinghetti, here and throughout the text, are from the taped interviews I made with him.

CHAPTER TWO

I relied heavily on the interviews with Ferlinghetti for information about the war years. I am indebted to him for the quotations from Presley Bisland's letters, which he keeps among his private papers. He is one of the few poets associated with the San Francisco Renaissance–Beat Generation who served in W.W. II. Ferlinghetti's comments on Cummings are a key to his own work . . . They share much of the same lyricism, whimsicality, and compassion.

He still carries with him a copy of T. S. Eliot's *Four Quartets* dated "1944," which he read, along with other poets, during patrols in the Atlantic.

CHAPTER THREE

Again, the interviews with Ferlinghetti were invaluable in the writing of this chapter.

CHAPTER FOUR

The letters to Mrs. Bisland, copies of which were given me by Anne Scarborough, are the best surviving record of these years. I spoke to Ivan Cousins during a visit he made to Ferlinghetti in North Beach early in 1977. He lives nearby, in Sausalito (on San Francisco Bay), and has a vivid memory of this period, including a sharp recollection of Mr. and Mrs. Bisland.

CHAPTER FIVE

Kirby Ferlinghetti, Ferlinghetti's former wife, spent several hours with me on five separate occasions, and was particularly helpful about both this period and the early years of the Beat Generation/ San Francisco Renaissance.

The poem on Sarolla is Number 8 of *Pictures of the Gone World*.

Ferlinghetti's article on Michaux appeared in the *Art Digest* on October 1, 1954 (Vol. 29, No. 1, p. 15).

The Refregier article was in the *Art Digest* of April 15, 1953 (Vol. 27, No. 14, p. 12).

I received background on the art scene in San Francisco from artist Elmer Bischoff, a prominent figure in the forties and fifties.

CHAPTER SIX

I spoke at some length to Kenneth Rexroth and Miriam Patchen about this period, and also to Philip Lamantia, who attended the gatherings at Rexroth's mentioned in the text.

In May 1977, I interviewed Peter Martin, founder-editor of *City Lights* magazine, both at his New Yorker Bookstore on Manhattan's Upper West Side and at one of his favorite local bars. The results of our meeting aided me in writing this chapter, together with Ferlinghetti's own reminiscences and those of Kirby Ferlinghetti.

I visited James Laughlin in his office at New Directions Publishing Company, in Greenwich Village, and had a valuable conversation with him, as well as receiving permission to quote from the letters I've included here (all of which are in the City Lights archives at the Bancroft Library, University of California at Berkeley).

Kenneth Rexroth's comments on jazz appeared in the Berkeley *Daily Gazette* on Saturday, August 10,1957, page 9.

His poem "Thou Shalt Not Kill" appears on page 267 of *The Collected Shorter Poems of Kenneth Rexroth* (New Directions, 1966).

CHAPTER SEVEN

A tape-recording session with Allen Ginsberg in the spring of 1977 helped get this chapter going, as did my research in the *San Francisco Chronicle* concerning the *Howl* obscenity trial. Ferlinghetti's article, "Horn on Howl," which originally appeared in *Evergreen Review* (Vol. 1, No. 4, pp. 145–58) but is more readily available in *A Casebook on the Beats*, edited by Thomas Parkinson (New York, Thomas Crowell Co., 1961), is a clear, concise overview of the trial. I closely studied and drew from *Howl of the Censors*, edited by Jake Ehrlich, the *Howl* defense attorney (San Carlos, California, Nourse Publishing Company, 1961). It consists of the proceedings from the trial, a brief introductory note by Ehrlich, and the poem "Howl" itself.

CHAPTER EIGHT

For this section of the book I worked many hours at the Bancroft Library, going over correspondence between Ferlinghetti and Ginsberg, looking through critical writings on Ferlinghetti's poetry, and going through various periodicals that kept pace with the tempo of the San Francisco Poetry Renaissance.

The issue of the *Evergreen Review* referred to is of primary importance in the history of the new poetry (Vol. 1, No. 2, 1.957). It is the medium through which many people first read "Howl", by Ginsberg, and poems by Ferlinghetti, Gary Snyder, Michael McClure, Philip Whalen, and Jack Kerouac. This was the first mass-circulation magazine in which these writers appeared at any length.

The *Chicago Review* (Vol. 12, No. 1, Spring 1958), featuring "Ten San Francisco Poets," is another important journal of the period.

"The Origins of the Beat Generation," by Jack Kerouac, appeared in *Playboy* (Vol. 6, No. 6, June 1959).

Growing out of the rising tide of interest in the new poetry and the lifestyle of the artists and writers of the period were several anthologies, all of which contain some work by Ferlinghetti. They are important in tracing the development of interest in the San Francisco Renaissance and the Beat Generation:

The New American Poetry 1945–1960, Donald M. Allen, editor. New York, Grove Press, 1960.

The Beats, Seymour Krim, editor. New York, Fawcett Publications, 1960.

The Beat Scene, Elias Wilentz, editor; Fred McDarrah, photographer. New York, Corinth Books, 1960. A great combination poetry anthology and photograph album on "the scene." Ferlinghetti is represented with "A Tentative Description of a Dinner Given to Promote the Impeachment of President Eisenhower."

Another important book of the period is *The Sullen Art*, interviews by David Ossman (New York, Corinth Books, 1963), which includes interviews with Rexroth, Ginsberg, and others.

Ferlinghetti's own *Beatitude Anthology* (San Francisco, City Lights, 1960) takes its place as a lasting representation of the new poetry.

CHAPTER NINE

Here again I relied very heavily on the taped interviews. Ferlinghetti and I talked about his trip to Latin America at a session in August 1976, and I spent considerable time going through his journals and selecting the entries that appear in the text. I also talked to Kirby Ferlinghetti about this period.

"One Thousand Fearful Words for Fidel Castro" appears in *Starting from San Francisco*. The broadside of the poem, no longer in print, is often available from rare-book dealers.

CHAPTER TEN

It was here that I began seeking assistance from Nancy Peters, Ferlinghetti's co-editor for City Lights Books. Her knowledge and advice, coupled with my continuing reliance on taped interviews and access to Ferlinghetti's private journals, helped me at this point.

The *Russian Winter Journals* comprise one of Ferlinghetti's lengthiest notebooks, and he plans to publish them someday. Excerpts from them appeared in the Los Angeles *Free Press* soon after his return from the Soviet Union.

CHAPTER ELEVEN

Excerpts from Ferlinghetti's *Santa Rita Journal* appeared in *Ramparts* magazine (March 1968).

The quote from Ferlinghetti's letter to Ginsberg is from one on file at the Ginsberg archives at Columbia University.

Ferlinghetti himself supplied me with a graphic description of the Be-In.

CHAPTER TWELVE

Ferlinghetti and I recorded much of the information contained in this chapter in August 1976. My own contact with some of the poets published by City Lights was a help in this chapter. I was at Charles Bukowski's apartment in Los Angeles, for example, when he decided to publish with City Lights and originally encouraged Ferlinghetti to publish Jack Hirschman.

CHAPTER THIRTEEN

By the time I began working on this chapter I had become a very close friend of my subject and had spent many hours with both him and Nancy Peters during the day-by-day operations of City Lights

Books—watching some of the books go through production, often sharing in the excitement of a book selling well, and, as in some cases, participating in the postmortem. Ferlinghetti often gave me early drafts of his poems during this time, such as "The Old Italians Dying" and "Adieu à Charlot: Second Populist Manifesto." We had also shared the platform for poetry readings, and I accompanied him on some of his readings around the state and spent a week with him at Bixby Canyon. We continued doing tapes, and I conferred with Nancy Peters on the history of City Lights Books, checking and rechecking my facts.

II

WORKS BY LAWRENCE FERLINGHETTI AS OF 1979
(Excluding Pamphlets)

POETRY

Pictures of the Gone World (City Lights Books, 1955)
A Coney Island of the Mind (New Directions, 1958)
Starting from San Francisco (New Directions, 1967)
The Secret Meaning of Things (New Directions, 1968)
Back Roads to Far Places (New Directions, 1971)
Open Eye, Open Heart (New Directions, 1973)
Who Are We Now? (New Directions, 1976)
Landscapes of Living and Dying (New Directions, 1979)

TRANSLATIONS

Paroles (City Lights Books, 1958). Translations of the poetry of Jacques Prévert

PROSE

Her (New Directions, 1960)
Tyrannus Nix? (New Directions, 1969)
The Mexican Night (New Directions, 1970)

PLAYS

Unfair Arguments with Existence (New Directions, 1963)
Routines (New Directions, 1964)

FILMS

Have You Sold Your Dozen Roses? (1960)
Tyrannus Nix? (NET, 1969)
Assassination Raga, with Max Crosley (1973)

RECORDINGS

"Poetry Readings in 'The Cellar,'" with Kenneth Rexroth (Fantasy LP, 1958)
'Tentative Description of a Dinner to Impeach President Eisenhower, and Other Poems" (Fantasy LP, 1959)
"The World's Great Poets, Volume 1, with Allen Ginsberg and Gregory Corso, Spoleto Festival, 1965" (CMS LP, 1971)
'Tyrannus Nix?" and "Assassination Rage" (Fantasy LP, 1971)

III

FURTHER BIBLIOGRAPHICAL SOURCES

BOOKS

Carroll, Paul, *The Poem in Its Skin*. Chicago, Big Table/Follett, 1968.
Charters, Samuel, *Some Poems*. Berkeley, Oyez, 1971.
—A detailed critical study of "One Thousand Fearful Words for Fidel Castro" is included.
Everson, William, *Archtype West: The Pacific Coast as a Literary Region*. Berkeley, Oyez, 1976.
—The former Brother Antoninus gives a brilliant exposition on literary history and development in the West, including San Francisco, and something of Ferlinghetti's role in it.

Fiedler, Leslie, *Waiting for the End*. New York, Stein & Day, 1970.

Kherdian, David, *Six Poets of the San Francisco Renaissance*.
Fresno, Calif., Gilgia Press, 1967.

—Includes a chapter on Ferlinghetti at home and at work in the
mid-seventies.

Kostelanetz, Richard, *The End of Intelligent Writing: Literary
Politics in America*. New York, Sheed, Andrews & McNeel, 1977.

—Incisive information on smaller presses in the United States,
including City Lights and its role.

Meltzer, David (editor), *The San Francisco Poets*. New York,
Ballantine, 1971.

—A lengthy interview with Ferlinghetti, covering his first few years
in San Francisco and his political views (interviews with Rexroth,
McClure, and others as well).

Mershmann, James, *Out of the Vietnam Vortex: A Study of Poets
and Poetry Against the War*. Lawrence, Kansas University Press,
1974.

Miller, Richard, *Bohemia: The Protoculture Then and Now*.
Chicago, Nelson-Hall, 1977.

Rexroth, Kenneth, *The Alternative Society*. New York, Herder and
Herder, 1972.

——, *American Poetry in the Twentieth Century*. New York,
Seabury, 1973.

——, *Assays*. New York, New Directions, 1961.

—Rexroth mentions Prévert, Raymond Queneau, and Paul
Eluard as influences on Ferlinghetti.

——, *Bird in the Bush*. New York, New Directions, 1959.

Stepanchev, Stephen, *American Poetry Since 1945*. New York,
Harper & Row, 1965.

—One of the few poet-critics to mention Ferlinghetti, however
briefly.

ACKNOWLEDGMENTS

MY APPRECIATION TO Bill Baker, Elmer Bischoff, Charles Bukowski, Gregory Corso, Ivan Cousins, Harry Ferling, Kirby Ferlinghetti, Lawrence Ferlinghetti, Allen Ginsberg, Jack Hirschman, Jerry Kamstra, Judy Kamstra, Bob Kaufman, Philip Lamantia, James Laughlin, Dudley Lawrence, Jr., Henri Lenoir, Peter Martin, Michael McClure, Jean McGrath, David Meltzer, Louis Mendes-Monsanto, Harold Norse, Nancy Peters, Kenneth Rexroth, Jerry Rubin, Anne Scarborough, Stephen Schwartz, Gary Snyder, Jack Stauffacher, Janet Weiner, Michael Weiner, and Joe Wolberg.

Also thank you to New Directions Publishing Company for the use of Mr. Ferlinghetti's poetry; to City Lights for the same.

The work could not have been completed without access to the City Lights Archives in the Bancroft Library, University of California, Berkeley; and the aid of the Hebrew Union College–Jewish Institute of Religion, Cincinnati.

To my friends Bob Sharrard, Kaye McDonough, Lisa Brinker, and all the other good people of North Beach, my gratitude.

I WOULD ALSO like to thank Elaine Katzenberger and Paul Yamazaki of City Lights, Amy Scholder, Chris Felver, Patrick Surgalski, Mario Zanetti, Agneta Falk, Jack Hirschman, Raymond Foye, Maria Gilardin, Starr Sutherland. and Dennis Sullivan. And thanks to my partner Jesse Cabrera. Also, deep gratitude to my extraordinary editor Joshua Bodwell.

NC

INDEX

(for 1979 biography only)

Neeli Cherkovski is a poet, as well as an editor, memoirist, and biographer. In his early twenties, he and Charles Bukowski launched a short-lived mimeographed literary magazine, *Laugh Literary and Man the Humping Guns*. He is the author of many books of poetry, most recently *Hang On to the Yangtze River* and *ABCs*, and served as the co-editor of *Collected Poems of Bob Kaufman*. He is the subject of the independent documentary feature *It's Nice to Be With You Always*. Cherkovski lives in San Francisco.

Printed January 2022 in Chelsea, Michigan for the Black Sparrow Press by Sheridan. Set in New Caledonia with Lydian for display. Interior design by Tammy Ackerman. This first edition has been bound in paper wrappers.

Black Sparrow Press was founded by John and Barbara Martin in 1966 and continued by them until 2002. The iconic sparrow logo was drawn by Barbara Martin.